The Last of Africa's Cold War Conflicts

The Last of Africa's Cold War Conflicts

Portuguese Guinea and its Guerrilla Insurgency

Al J Venter

Pen & Sword
MILITARY

First published in Great Britain in 2020 by
Pen & Sword Military
An imprint of
Pen & Sword Books Ltd
Yorkshire – Philadelphia

ISBN 978 1 52677 298 5

A CIP catalogue record for this book is
available from the British Library.

Printed and bound in the UK by TJ International Ltd,
Padstow, Cornwall.

MIX
Paper from
responsible sources
FSC® C013056

Pen & Sword Books Limited incorporates the imprints of Atlas,
Archaeology, Aviation, Discovery, Family History, Fiction, History,
Maritime, Military, Military Classics, Politics, Select, Transport,
True Crime, Air World, Frontline Publishing, Leo Cooper, Remember
When, Seaforth Publishing, The Praetorian Press, Wharncliffe
Local History, Wharncliffe Transport, Wharncliffe True Crime
and White Owl.

For a complete list of Pen & Sword titles please contact

PEN & SWORD BOOKS LIMITED
47 Church Street, Barnsley, South Yorkshire, S70 2AS, England
E-mail: enquiries@pen-and-sword.co.uk
Website: www.pen-and-sword.co.uk

Or

PEN AND SWORD BOOKS
1950 Lawrence Rd, Havertown, PA 19083, USA
E-mail: Uspen-and-sword@casematepublishers.com
Website: www.penandswordbooks.com

Contents

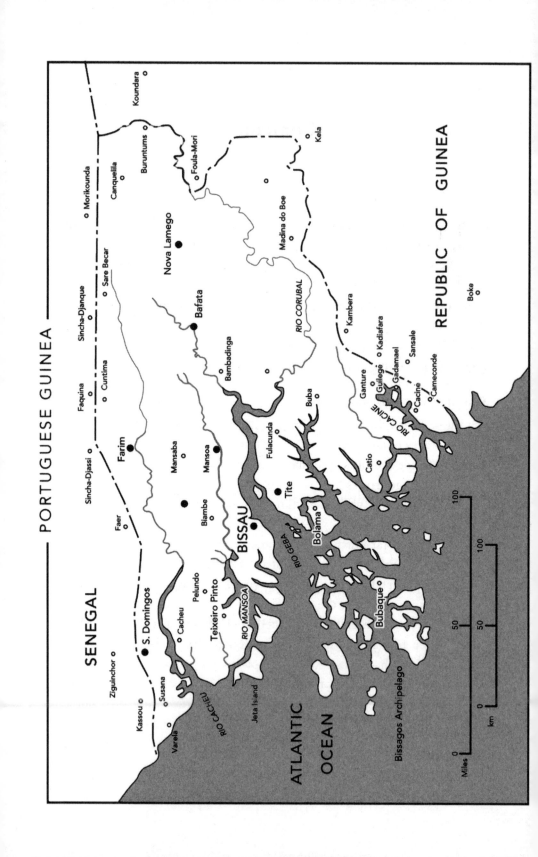

Prologue

Approaching Bissau from the air was always a different kind of experience. I did the trip often, for General António de Spínola was easy on the use of military aircraft by the handful of visiting foreign journalists that could inveigle a visa to cover his war.

Flying in from the Cape Verde Islands, the coast loomed up ahead, stark against a hazy African horizon. A dozen tiny ribbons of rivers snaked through the low-lying swampland approaches, the pattern crazily uneven and broken sporadically by the squares and triangles of hundreds of rice paddies spread out between the mangroves. From where we flew, they looked like angular, heavily lined corduroy sheets. Even thirty kilometres out the sea was a dirty, muddy brown, like the kind of turbulence you see at anchorages outside some industrial harbours, but then Bissau has no industry to speak of. It's the same when approaching the estuaries of the Congo and Niger rivers farther down the West African coast.

Only occasionally was the rhythm broken by the dark-stained sail of a *nhominca*, the Portuguese-type fishing boat which is in everyday use along this seaboard as far north as Mauritania. Centuries ago local fishermen in Senegal, Gambia, Guinea and Sierra Leone adopted the protruding keel design, which tourists today are more likely to associate with Estoril.

Then, quite suddenly, the city lay before us and, viewed from the air, Bissau was a bit larger than expected and semicircular in shape. The resemblance to Banjul, the Gambian capital city – about a hundred miles to the north – was striking, both places lying on a promontory that faced the ocean. This was probably one of the reasons why a Soviet-built Antonov transport plane, bearing the colours of the Guinea Air Force landed at Bissau in 1971. The stocky aircraft had lost its way on a flight between Labe and Conakry in the Republic of Guinea and mistook Bissalanca for Bathurst.

The crew was still being held in Bissau when I was there, though General António de Spínola did try to exchange them for some of his own prisoners of war captured by the PAIGC. President Sékou Touré, the Marxist president of the Republic of Guinea, rejected the offer.

Coming in to land in Portuguese Guinea one couldn't help but notice that all roads leading outward from Bissau's cathedral doubled back again on reaching the outskirts of town, almost as if they had been nudged by the nearby jungle and forced to swing around of their own accord. The uniformity was broken at irregular intervals by rows of barracks and workshops, each distinctive with open ground between twin barbed-wire fences. Machine-gun turrets marked the extremities that in typical military fashion were drab and resembled circular blobs on a more-than-detailed architect's plan. Bissalanca airport, a short drive on the road north out of the capital, was an impressive affair set across an otherwise uninteresting, flat countryside.

Alongside the heavy tarmac fortifications stood rows of squat artillery pieces behind raised gunpits, their muzzles covered in canvas, their role, clearly, to protect about thirty military aircraft, all in various stages of readiness for morning operations. We'd arrived early after an eighteen-hour flight from Lisbon and it had been a long haul.

About a dozen Alouette helicopters and the same number of Fiat G-91 jets were concentrated at the far end of the runway, well away from what one officer referred to as 'the prying eyes of civilians who pass through en route to Europe and beyond'. Still more planes, Harvards and Dorniers, were parked close to the terminal building, their engine cowlings bright dayglo orange paint that reflected in the early morning sun; the gaudiness, I was told, had something to do with identification and spotting in the event of one of the planes being forced down.

On its own pad nearby stood one of Bissau's two Nord Noratlas transports, the same air freighters I'd used often enough to gad about in Angola. These NATO-type planes looked impressive in their wavy green and brown camouflage paint and were tasked for daily supply runs into the interior.

An unusual aircraft, a modern jet fighter, stood on its own in a bunker near the fringe of the airport cluster, its long, low-slung silhouette contrasting with the stocky fighters around it. Incredibly, it was one of

Britain's Second World War Glostor Meteor fighters. On its fuselage, as if someone tried to add a rider to a riddle, was painted, in large black capitals: ENTERPRISE FILMS. Photographs of both this plane and the Antonov were forbidden 'for security reasons' whatever they were. It was perhaps inevitable that I'd snap them eventually as virtually all my movements into the interior were through Bissalanca airport.

The story regarding the Meteor goes like this: during the Biafran War the rebel leader Colonel Odumegwu Ojukwu bought two jet fighters from an international arms salesman, to replace French Vantour bombers that he'd intended to use against Federal lines and which were destroyed on the ground outside Uli airport by Nigerian Air Force MiGs before they were ever put into effective use.

Meantime, both Meteors were flown out of Britain – illegally, it transpired – and once in international air space, the planes headed down the West African coast for Nigeria.

The designers of the Meteor series, a remarkable plane and well ahead of its time – they first flew in 1943 – had never intended them to be used in long-range operations, so it was not altogether surprising that halfway to Africa, one developed engine trouble and had to be ditched into the sea. The other landed at Bissau and like the Antonov, remained neglected, dilapidated and for the rest of the war, little more than an embarrassment to a Portuguese government that only wished to forget that Biafra ever existed.

Tackled on the subject of the jets during my visit, General Spínola refused to be drawn. As far as he was concerned, the planes had made emergency landings and that was that. Their origins did not concern him, he told me, nor where they might have been headed. The Meteor pilot, a Brit, had been repatriated shortly after he'd landed and nobody had ever stepped forward to claim the jet.

What did emerge years later was that Enterprise Films was the cover organization in Britain which handled the sale, ostensibly for use in a long-forgotten film on the Battle for Europe. Legal action had since been taken by the British government against individuals responsible for the sale, all eventually convicted on the grounds that they had not declared the true purpose of the venture. Newspapers concluded at the time that the charge levelled was one of arms smuggling and the offence a military one.

Introduction

The early 1960s were momentous years for the international community. The Cold War had become an uncompromising reality which, in turn, gave rise to much activity within the North Atlantic Treaty Organization (NATO) of which Portugal was a founder member. It was also Elvis-time, the pill had arrived and a swinging hippy society took root in the United States and elsewhere and resulted in an upswing in the sexual revolution. Meanwhile, in London, the Carnaby Street culture sculpted a political landscape that went on to shape an entire generation.

Through it all, France was torn by urban violence and sharp divisions caused by its colonial war in Algeria. That sad chapter ended abruptly in 1962 with the election of Charles de Gaulle as president.

It was little different in Portugal, where the circular peace sign – so often prominently displayed around the necks of American GIs in Vietnam – had already made a tentative showing among some of the more outspoken young officers doing their requisite two-year stints in the African bush.

It struck me as just a little incongruous travelling in thick jungle country with some of the heavily armed convoys, that speakers would often be on full blast and the troops would offer their own renditions of Tom Jones's 'Delilah', followed by some of the most popular Simon and Garfunkel songs. The guerrillas were out there in the bush of course, because they sometimes sniped at us as we passed and must have thought us all crazy. Or possibly they believed the tropical heat had got to some of the young conscripts from Lisbon.

Other parts of Africa also had their moments, with both France and Britain gradually divesting themselves of their colonial possessions, some of which had been under imperial rule for more than a century. Ghana, formerly the Gold Coast, was the first African state to be granted independence in March 1957, followed soon afterward by Nigeria. French colonies also followed the Uhuru path: Senegal, the Ivory Coast, the Cameroons, Gabon, Chad, Mauretania and a dozen or more nations-to-be.

Brussels, tardy in deciphering the writing on the wall, quite abruptly pulled out of its Congo, leaving almost nobody in charge. The departing Belgians left behind the kind of carnage which everybody hoped to avoid: a state of civil war followed and the country is still ungovernable more than half a century later.

Dr António de Oliveira Salazar, in his day an eminent statesman who served as prime minister of Portugal from 1932 to 1968, had his own views on the future of Lisbon's three African provinces. He would often remind his critics that these were not 'colonies' in the traditional sense, but integral to the survival of the metropolitan Portuguese state. Responsible for the *Estado Novo* – the 'New State' or the 'Second Republic' – was the corporatist far-right regime installed in Portugal in 1933 directed by this strict disciplinarian who believed in an authoritarian regime that reflected a strong integrationist orientation. That differed markedly from earlier fanatical European regimes by its lack of expansionism, a staunch but a not-fanatical leader, lack of dogmatic party structure and more moderate use of state force. It did, however, as one pundit commented, incorporate the principles for its military from Benito Mussolini's system in Italy.

More to the point, Salazar was a Catholic traditionalist who believed in the need to control the forces of economic modernization in order to defend the religious and rural values of the country which he perceived as being threatened, and that Portugal's mission in Africa was, as he would phrase it, of a 'civilizing nature'.

There were profound reasons for this approach, the principal one being that Lisbon's roots in Africa went deep. The country had endured on the African continent for almost five centuries and while there had been numerous insurrections in the past in Angola, Mozambique as well as Portuguese Guinea (Guiné-Bissau today), European government authority had always prevailed.

Consequently, when the first ragged bands of revolutionaries started their rampage across the almost-undefined frontier regions that separated

Angola from the former Belgian Congo (only months after that country became independent) the authorities in Lisbon believed they could cope with a threat that they felt, at worst, was transient.

There had been many such uprisings in the past and each had been adequately dealt with. Nobody along the old Tagus River gave serious thought to the probability that this new revolt might have been planned for some time or had foreign backers; least that they were integral to the Soviet pattern of encroachment and encirclement that Moscow's political architects believed would eventually lead to all of Africa falling under the communist banner.

More salient, neither Salazar nor his ministers had any idea that the revolution in Angola would soon be followed by similar uprisings in Mozambique and Portuguese Guinea. That is exactly what was to take place, with the tiny, impoverished European country – then, with a population of about nine million and the second poorest nation in Europe after Albania – having to battle a series of colonial liberation wars that lasted all of thirteen years, or twice as long as the United States military was officially deployed in Vietnam.

It took a while and there were many detractors from within, but with great courage and fortitude the Portuguese army, navy and air force – which had last experienced shots fired in anger against Imperial Germany in the First World War – were able to rise above successive threats backed by half a dozen newly independent African states and supported by the Soviets, Cubans, the communist Chinese as well as a host of other radical groups. While the ground war lasted, Lisbon survived an almost impossible revolutionary situation on several fronts, for which it warrants great credit.

What is also notable is that Salazar's outspoken policy of Portuguese neutrality in the Second World War placed the Portuguese armed forces out of the way of becoming engaged in a global conflict that laid waste to vast parts of the planet and ended with the deaths of something like fifty million people. Right or wrong, he instituted a programme of increased responsibility that kept Portugal's vast overseas territories solidly under the control of the homeland and, in so doing, protected his people, both there and in the *metrópole*.

Lisbon's colonial wars, to start with, were fairly close run, with the guerrillas making many gains in the earlier stages, Angola especially: there the rebels beat a bloody path almost to the gates of Luanda before they were forced back.

Conditions were not nearly as bad when the first group of rebels invaded Mozambique three years later. There Eduardo Mondlane's Frente de Libertação de Moçambique or Front for the Liberation of Mozambique (FRELIMO) was kept on the back foot almost for the duration of hostilities. In fact, the south of that vast east African possession was hardly threatened and Lourenço Marques, the capital (Maputo today), never once came under attack.

Things were very different on the northwest coast of Africa in Portuguese Guinea, a tiny enclave wedged between the Republic of Guinea, headed by a vociferous and passionately anti-French radical and Marxist, Ahmed Sékou Touré, and in the north, by the more moderate Senegal, then led by the eminent poet and philosopher Leopold Senghor, who made secret of his love of the French and their multifaceted culture. Low-lying, fringed by mangrove swamps and inhospitable islands along the coast, Portuguese Guinea was an ungodly place to fight a war. Indeed, of Lisbon's three provinces, it was the most difficult African region in which to come to grips with the enemy. With a population estimated at a little over half a million in the early 1960s, it was a rather unlikely place for the most successful guerrilla movement then active in Portuguese Africa, pursuing what the proponents preferred to call a 'People's War'.

Part of the problem (in fact, the most formidable issue) was its size: it was a tiny enclave, bounded on three sides of four by the enemy. At 36,000 square kilometres – or roughly half as big as Latvia on the Baltic – the issues at stake were distinctly disproportionate when compared to the much more expansive Angola and Mozambique, where the savannah, jungles and bush terrain sometimes go on almost forever. For a start, Angola is twice the size of Texas, while Mozambique, straddling the Indian Ocean littoral 7,000 kilometres to the southeast, is roughly the same shape and size as California.

One result was that Partido Africano para a Independência da Guiné e Cabo Verde (PAIGC) guerrilla bands operating from the Guinea Republic had few problems slipping quietly across the country's ill-defined frontier areas. They would do so increasingly as the war progressed, lay their mines, set their ambushes and then unobtrusively withdraw across the border again when their deeds were done.

In the overall insurgent scenario, Guinean revolutionaries were a cut above other guerrilla groups operating in Africa at the time. Blessed with outstanding leadership, they were headed by Amilcar Lopez da Costa Cabral, a quiet-spoken intellectual with Cape Verde origins who chose his cadres with caution and sent the best of them either behind the Iron Curtain or to Cuba for training. As the distinguished American historian Piero Gleijeses tells us, Cabral was the undisputed commander and tactician of the war and, crucially, he kept an unusual degree of control over its conduct. Also, he maintained constant touch with his military commanders in the interior and was directly responsible for all important decisions concerning the organization of his fighting men, their deployment as well as the coordination of operations being carried out.

It was interesting that I was to observe some of this activity from up close while travelling overland in the Republic of Guinea. After a few days in Conakry in 1965, en route to the Senegalese border just north of Koundara, I was stranded for several days in Labe, a large town in the interior and perhaps three or four hours' drive by Soviet Army Wagon from the nearest Portuguese military outpost in the southeast corner of what was soon to become Guiné-Bissau. With little money to spare, I was offered a corner by a local pair of American Peace Corps workers which I accepted with alacrity. Conditions were sparse but it made the delay interesting because several houses up from where the Americans lived was a fairly large building with numerous antennae protruding from its roof. It was, the two volunteers told me, a PAIGC radio relay station and there was a lot of movement in an out of the structure that clearly had substantial strategic significance for the guerrillas. The house, its exact location and still-undetermined role in the ongoing war in Portuguese Guinea became the subject of much discussion at Portugal's London embassy after I had returned to Britain, at the time headed by a man who was to leave a lasting imprint on his country's war in Angola, the then Colonel, later General, José de Bettencourt Rodrigues.

For much of the war in this tiny embattled Portuguese colony, Amilcar Cabral was not only the brain and moving force behind it, but also its most significant visionary. It was clear to many of those who met this man that he was aware from the start that his was a war he could win and indeed, he almost did. The PAIGC commander-in-chief launched his armed struggle in January 1963, and then only after several years of intense political work in the field. At the end of it, his guerrillas controlled about a third of the country. By 1965, the guerrilla force posed the most significant challenge to some 20,000 Portuguese troops, though once General António de Spínola was placed in command of a deteriorating situation, the war radically changed, even though the Soviets supplied the rebels with all they needed, including SAM-7 Strela surface-to-air missiles which had some effect on limiting air operations.

Throughout, this unconventional insurgent leader was held in high regard both as a military and political organizer and while it took some time – he had started modestly as an agricultural engineer – he was later recognized as the country's leading guerrilla tactician. Like Senghor, Amilcar Cabral was also a poet of note and by all accounts – in spite of radically different political ideologies – the two men became quite fond of one another, having met several times in bids to find a solution to ending ongoing hostilities. It was the Senegalese leader, in fact, who raised the possibility of Lisbon perhaps being amenable to reaching some kind of mutual accommodation with the PAIGC, an issue seminal to the future and dealt with in General Spínola's book *Portugal and the Future*.

Cabral was always multifaceted and in this regard it is interesting that the Cuban ambassador to Ghana in 1963 commented in one of his missives to Havana that he had met the revolutionary leader and found him to be 'a very unusual breed of political exile: everyone respects him'. While the guerrilla commander was influenced by Marxism, he declared, he was certainly not a Marxist and went on to comment that Cabral 'came to view Marxism as a methodology rather than an ideology'.

Yet, for all that, things did not end well. While regarded today as the most successful of all of Africa's sub-Saharan guerrilla commanders, Amilcar Cabral, having achieved nationalist unity throughout his tiny country, at the same time carrying out political mobilization at grassroots level and establishing new political structures in liberated areas, was assassinated by one of his own trusted followers. Sadly, that has so often been the case in Africa. Having begun to form a People's Assembly in preparation for the independence of Guinea-Bissau in 1972, a disgruntled former PAIGC rival, Inocêncio Kani – in a subversive plot with another member of the PAIGC command structure – shot and killed the leader on 20 January 1973 in the Guinean capital. There was talk of course of PIDE, the Portuguese secret police, having possibly been involved, which is not impossible, but is unlikely since American intelligence sources have since disclosed that there were already some serious divisions within the rebel hierarchy. Much more likely, since Cabral had voiced the opinion that there was another way of ending the war – thus his efforts at forming a People's Assembly – the Soviets might have had a hand through their close relations with President Touré. In this regard one must consider the fact that Agostinho Neto, the Angolan leader, inexplicably died while undergoing surgery in Moscow. He too, had grown tired of war in his Angolan homeland and voiced thoughts about ending it

One needs to look back to the history of Portuguese Guinea to understand much that occurred in centuries past. The country came under Portuguese control specifically to provide what earlier mariners would refer to as a 'supply point', where their ships would heave to and replenish their freshwater reserves and acquire fresh produce in order to continue their voyages.

Similar stations were established in the sixteenth century by Portuguese sailors in Angola at Luanda and Benguela (Lobito today) and at Lourenço Marques in Delagoa Bay, Mozambique. These depots – which were more like fortifications – were there to provide succour during lengthy journeys to the Spice Islands of the East, many of which could last two years.

One unidentified source explained it thus: by the beginning of the nineteenth century, Portugal controlled outposts at six locations along or off Africa's Atlantic coast, starting with the Cape Verde Islands, located about 1,200 kilometres west of Dakar, Senegal. Discovered by Alvise da Cadamosta of Venice in 1456 and claimed for Portugal by Diego Gomes in about 1458, this archipelago of eight major islands was devoted in part to sugar cultivation using slaves taken from the African mainland. One of the islands, appropriately named Sal, was also a rich source of salt.

Since they were the first Europeans to explore it systematically starting in the late fifteenth century, the Portuguese had extensive claims along the West African coast. By 1800 however, they were left with only a few ports at the mouth of the Rio Geba in what is now known as Guiné-Bissau. Farther downstream, Lisbon controlled the islands of Sao Tomé and Principe, located south of the mouth of the Niger River and like the Cape Verde Islands, these possessions were devoted to sugarcane production in the early sixteenth century, also using African slaves to harvest crops. By the end of the nineteenth century, Portuguese landowners had successfully introduced cocoa production, again using forced African labour.

In the process of colonial expansion, the Portuguese also claimed land on both sides of the mouth of the Congo River, as well as long stretches of the Atlantic coast as far south as the Rio Cunene. In practical terms, their influence extended some distance beyond, in the form of several ports, such as Cabinda (north of the Congo River mouth), Ambriz, which lay south of that great waterway, Luanda as well as Benguela and including some settlements in the Angolan interior.

Maintaining an effective grip on this centuries-old overseas empire was always a matter of national interest for the Portuguese. And though colonialism became the norm in most African regions subsequently grabbed by Europeans powers, there were rarely charges of racism against those running their fiefs, though obviously, European communities rarely mixed freely with the locals, except when absolutely necessary (as in trading or slave-raiding parties, where Arab slave masters tended to dominate). Indeed, in later years, particularly after Hitler's War, criticism against some kinds of racial discrimination in the Portuguese African territories were refuted on the grounds that all Africans 'enjoying the protection of the Lisbon government' would be Westernized and assimilated in due course through a process called the 'civilizing' mission.

Wars in Africa tend to be somewhat different from those on other continents and with a few exceptions, such as Biafra, they tend to last much longer. There have been hostilities in the Sudan – in both halves of that troubled country, north and south – for more than half a century. The Democratic Republic of the Congo has experienced no peace – not even a single effective ceasefire – ever since it got its mindlessly rushed-through independence in 1960. On a very different level, the Border War that involved South African apartheid forces battling a comparatively sophisticated insurgency, also solidly backed by the Soviet Union, China and Cuba, lasted all of twenty-three years.

Something similar emerged during the course of Lisbon's war in Portuguese Guinea which, in many respects, was more intense than what was going on in Angola and Mozambique at the time. Cabral was aware too, that his enemy, with a few notable exceptions, was reluctant to breach borders to retaliate. On the few occasions that Portuguese troops did cross the frontier on hot-pursuit operations, Cabral or his backers – the Canadians, Scandinavians, the US State Department and others – almost overnight, would refer such 'illegal' incursions to the United Nations.

As a consequence, the colonial war in Portuguese Guinea was very different from those colonial struggles being fought in the 1960s and 1970s in Angola and Mozambique. Because the tiny West African enclave was almost completely surrounded by its enemies, actions by both sides were a lot more regular and were sometimes extremely intense. Also, the casualty count on both sides was consistently higher than in either Angola or Mozambique.

Curiously, hostilities in Guinea were hardly covered by international media and for two reasons. The first was that attention worldwide was focused on what was then going on in Vietnam. That distant conflict was the first time that everyday military events were brought nightly into our living rooms by television, a tradition that has followed ever since.

The other, more salient reason was that Lisbon liked to play a distinctly low-key role with its wars. While the guerrillas only invited known radical journalists and fellow travellers like Basil Davidson and his ilk to accompany their guerrillas on their cross-border forays, the Portuguese were circumspect about whom they were prepared to issue visas to in order cover their wars. Some notables like Jim Hoagland of *The Washington Post* and Peter-Hannes Lehmann of *Der Spiegel* did get clearances and went in with the Portuguese Army (as did I). Now and again we were able to share notes and, generally, the consensus was that this West African guerrilla struggle was the closest to what was going on in Vietnam at the time.

Lehmann made the point when we split a bottle of aguardente at the bar of Bissau's dilapidated old Grande Hotel that the difference between the wars in Angola and Mozambique – and the one on Bissau's doorstep – was that you were much more likely to come under fire in Portuguese Guinea than in the other two provinces. The German could be expansive about his views and was quite explicit about it being essential to be shot at in order to properly do the job.

Another issue we all observed and that came through sharply when visiting Portugal's African conflicts – something continually stressed by our official military 'minders' – was that maintaining Lisbon's almost-five-centuries-old overseas empire was at the pinnacle of the country's national interest. Any kind of criticism against manifest racial discrimination in the Portuguese possessions was, as one correspondent phrased it, 'refuted on the grounds that their African subjects would be eventually Westernized and assimilated.'

That said, there was no question that as hostilities gathered momentum, the war became increasingly unpopular back home. It did not take long for many of those in the European metropolis – including vast numbers of veterans who had already done their military service in Africa – to become increasingly weary, even critical of the ongoing war. People balked at its increasingly obvious futility, which saw Lisbon fighting a war that could only be solved by political means. Its ever-rising cost that affected just about every bank account in the land was just as important.

Yet curiously, Portuguese Guinea aside because it had almost no natural resources, the economies of Angola and Mozambique – the two southern territories, also at war at the time – were booming. Indeed, their cities and towns were expanding and prospering, Angola's at an astonishing rate. But there too, once staunchly pro-communist rebels took over, the utilitarian concept of free markets was rejected and with Marxist dogmas imposed by the revolutionaries who eventually took over from Lisbon, their economies simply collapsed.

One has to look at some of the figures that emerged after the young Portuguese officers' coup d'état to understand the nature and extent of what was going on in the three African colonies at the time.

Though the figures are not definitive – nor will they ever be because of friction between those who were for the African wars and those against – it is estimated that about a million troops served in the three African theatres. Some say it was more, but the ballpark tally makes good sense.

Also, the burden lay mainly with the men, except for small numbers of women in the country's medical services, including airborne-trained nurses who were occasionally dropped into forward combat areas, mostly by helicopter.

In all, almost 10,000 troops were either killed in action or taken out in all three military theatres in the many thousands of accidents that were due to negligence, stupidity or lack of preparation. Roughly four times that number were wounded or injured. Estimates suggest that more than 15,000 Portuguese servicemen returned home with physical disabilities.

The war in Portuguese Guinea started in earnest in January 1963, with a concerted attack on a Portuguese Army base at Tite, south of the capital (not to be confused with Tete, a city which lies on the Zambezi River in Mozambique).

Similar actions soon spread across the colony and required vigorous responses throughout. Fortunately, Lisbon had been made aware of the PAIGC's build-up and was prepared for what was thought would be limited insurgent war, with several squads of experienced counterinsurgency troops having been detached from their units in Angola where the onslaught was already two years old.

For all that, the war in Portuguese Guinea quickly assumed a forceful level of intensity, one of the reasons why some commentators started to refer to that struggle as 'Portugal's Vietnam'. The guerrillas were well-trained, well-led and well-equipped and in the process, as we have seen, received substantial support from safe havens in both neighbouring countries.

It took almost no time at all for Lisbon to accept that they were faced with an insurgency that was very different from what was going on in Angola and Mozambique. For a start, the jungles of Guinea and the proximity of the PAIGC's allies near the border proved to be of significant advantage in providing tactical superiority during cross-border attacks and resupply missions for the insurgents and, as a consequence, conditions for the Portuguese quickly deteriorated.

The success of PAIGC guerrilla operations put government forces almost totally on the defensive, forcing them to limit their response to defending territories and urban areas already held. Unlike the other African territories, successful small-unit Portuguese counterinsurgency tactics took time to evolve in the Guinean sphere of operations. As one source phrased it, 'defensive operations, where soldiers were dispersed in small numbers to guard critical buildings, farms, or infrastructure were particularly devastating to the regular Portuguese infantry, who became vulnerable to guerrilla attacks outside of populated areas by the guerrillas.'

The colonial government was soon demoralized by the steady growth of PAIGC liberation sympathizers and recruits among the rural population. As a consequence, some areas became dominated by insurgent elements who set up what were termed 'liberation' administrative systems. The scale of that success can be gauged from the fact that local people in some areas even stopped paying debts and taxes to government and Portuguese-owned institutions.

The PAIGC meanwhile established its own relatively efficient administrative bureaucracy which organized agricultural production, educated PAIGC farmworkers on how to protect themselves and their crops from Portuguese Air Force attacks. They then went on to establish *armazéns do povo* (people's stores) to supply urgently needed tools and supplies in exchange for agricultural produce. These were all textbook Marxist procedures and worked very effectively in regions where any kind of government presence, civil or military, was marginal.

For Lisbon, conditions deteriorated to the point that two years after the war started, a government commission charged with assessing the security situation in Portuguese Guinea returned to Lisbon to report that the PAIGC was in control of most of the country and there was a real possibility that were a concerted attack to be made on Bissau, the capital could fall.

It was then decided, in 1968, that General António de Spínola, one of Portugal's most experienced military specialists, be sent to Bissau and re-establish control. On arrival, this tough, principled disciplinarian who was appointed governor instituted a series of civil and military reforms designed to weaken PAIGC control and roll back insurgent gains. At the core of it, he put into effect an extremely efficient 'hearts and minds' propaganda campaign that, with proper application, was designed to win the trust of the indigenous population, no easy task because of successes enjoyed by Cabral's cohorts. Spínola succeeded because he quickly eliminated many of the discriminatory practices against native Guineans, followed by a series of significant construction campaigns for public works that included new schools, hospitals and clinics, an improved telecommunications and road network, as well as a large increase in recruitment of local Africans from all tribes into the Portuguese armed forces serving in Guinea as part of an Africanization strategy.

Concurrently, he created two indigenous African counterinsurgency detachments, the first known as *comandos africanos* and with whom I spent time in both Angola and Portuguese Guinea, and the other, a local marine combat contingent. What made the first different from other established regiments in the Portuguese Army was that this fighting force consisted almost entirely of black soldiers, including many of their officers. The African Special Marines (*fuzileiros especiais africanos*) which supplemented other crack Portuguese units, started conducting a number of amphibious operations in the riverine and coastal regions of Guinea that were surprisingly effective. The country's offshore islands – from the start much favoured by the guerrillas and used as launching pads for their raids – were the first to be targeted and the insurgent offensive blunted, but most times the effect was cursory because Spínola did not have the manpower to permanently maintain a presence on captured territory.

In order to make his initial plan work, Spínola initiated an expansive indigenous recruiting programme, culminating in the establishment of all-black military formations such as the Black Militias (*milícias negras*) commanded by Major Carlos Fabião.

Another of the officers, Lieutenant Colonel Marcelino da Mata, a black Portuguese citizen born of Guinean parents, rose from first sergeant in a road engineering unit to an active field commander in the ultra-elite *comandos africanos*.

What was notable about Portugal's wars in all three military theatres, Portuguese Guinea especially, was that government forces were obliged to kick off defensively with the most basic equipment, much of it unsuitable for the kind of primitive conditions in Africa.

Because Lisbon's forces were guarding NATO's western flank in Europe, the African colonies got mostly obsolete equipment: nobody dreamt that their black subjects would be able or even willing to stage an effectively coordinated revolution. As we have seen, they did exactly that in Angola in 1961 – and in Portuguese Guinea not very long afterwards – and it was a tough haul to recover ground lost in the initial impetus launched by nationalist forces.

It says much that the first military counter-offensives were launched using outdated Second World War-era radios, some of which were so heavy that those hauling them could carry little else but their rifle and some ammunition. Squad weapons too, to start with, were totally inadequate, with some, like the German Mauser, dating from the turn of the century. There were some Fabrique Nationale FALs, but certainly not enough to go around.

Give credit where it is due, Lisbon's defence ministry wasted no time at all in calling in the cards of some their NATO allies and were soon manufacturing, under licence, the Heckler & Kock G-3, though these were unpopular with Special Forces units until they came with collapsible stocks. For machine guns, the MG-42 was standard issue until the popular HK-21 arrived and soon supplanted the Uzis, originally acquired from Israel and used mainly by reserve units.

Portugal had nothing to match the Soviet RPG-2 (the ubiquitous RPG-7 was only to appear later), the European force having to settle for American cast-off 3.2-inch bazookas which were heavy and unwieldy in Africa's soporific jungle heat. It is interesting that most of the devices that replaced bazookas in all three African wars – like the locally designed and produced *Instalaza* – had aluminium tubes.

Several armoured cars were deployed fairly early on and almost all were French. These included the Panhard AML, Panhard EBR and the Chaimite, as well as the British Fox which only arrived in-country much later.

Then, of course, there were those who opposed the Portuguese presence in Africa and there were many. During the course of covering Portugal's wars in Africa for a variety of publications and news agencies on several continents – and I did so for decades – I was fated to meet quite a few of the continent's revolutionaries. On a visit to the Tanzanian capital in the mid-1970s, I even had dinner with Janet Mondlane, whose husband Eduardo, head of the Mozambican liberation group FRELIMO was murdered in Dar es Salaam in 1969 by 'persons unknown'. For a long time there was strong support for the sentiment that the man behind his death was Samora Machel, one of Mondlane's more capable field commanders, who was to step into his shoes. An American, Janet Mondlane had befriended her future husband, a quiet, reflective and well-educated individual – and totally unlike the coarse, bellicose individual who succeeded him – when she attended a church camp in Wisconsin. The 31-year-old African academic, then a history and sociology professor at Syracuse University, was giving a speech about the future of Africa. What is also notable is that all three anti-Portuguese guerrilla leaders – which included Cabral as well as Agostinho Neto who headed Angola's Movimento Popular de Libertàcao de Angola (MPLA) – ended up marrying white or near-white women.

One of the sad realities of the war in what was once known as Portuguese Guinea, is that there has been so little published about the events that took place there. Working under the auspices of Professor Ned Munger who founded Pasadena's Munger Africana Library in California, I originally filed a report of my first visit to that war published under the title *Portugal's War in Guiné-Bissau*. From that emerged *Portugal's Guerrilla War: The Campaign for Africa*, published in Cape Town in 1974 and not to be confused with the more recent *Portugal's Guerrilla Wars in Africa* (Helion, 2014) and translated into Portuguese two years later by Clube do Autor under the title *Portugal e as Guerrilhas de A'frica*.

But things are rapidly changing, with many more books on all three African conflicts having been published in Portugal in recent years, the majority by Portuguese army and air force veterans who were involved in these struggles. That all comes after decades in the doldrums when the nation, head in the sand, refused to accept it had been forced to abandon everything it had held precious in Africa for five centuries. In a sense, there almost seemed to be a concerted national move to sweep anything about the colonial wars under the carpet of history, as one wag phrased it 'in a collective act of amnesia'. But all that has changed. There are now scores of books about what went on in Angola, Mozambique and Portuguese Guinea, some with photos galore of 'the good old days in Africa'. A few are outspokenly emotional and tend to paint dark images of what went before in those corners of the African continent that Lisbon's cohorts had administered for many centuries, a lot longer than any of the other erstwhile colonial powers.

Take one example: Nuno Tiago Pinto, a journalist of the Portuguese weekly newsmagazine *Sábado* who published the book *Dias de Coragem e Amizade* (*Days of Courage and Friendship*), and who gathered together the exploits of several dozen eyewitness accounts of former soldiers of his country's colonial wars. This work is both informative and disarmingly honest, a series of no-holds-barred exploits by veterans who explain their actions in blunt, often emotional terms.

One of the exploits that he recounts is that of António Heliodoro, 'a short, strong man who walks with a noble bearing, proud of his military past … he talks with a deep, calm voice, almost in a whisper that evokes the storytellers of ancient times. He lets you know he is not a man of many words, but captures the attention of those who listen to him with a natural authority'. Born on 5 October 1942, he was 21 years old when he was sent to Portuguese Guinea, as a *fuzileiro especial* (special marine) in the Portuguese Navy. From 1963 to 1965, Heliodoro took part in some of the most expansive battles of the conflict in that overseas territory, 'But his voice quivers when he recalls the seventy-two days and nights he spent entrenched in the sludge of Como Island, in what became known as *Operação Tridente* as it brought together, for the first time, the three branches of the armed forces.'

As Heliodoro recalls, 'I fought under the napalm bombs that were dropped from our airplanes to explode and burn in the bush … we were down on the ground and we could feel the large limbs of the trees falling. Everything shook. It was dramatic. I even begged Our Lady of Fátima to make it stop.' But still more came later.

When he returned home he was called a liar, because the Portuguese state never admitted to the use of napalm in Africa, despite several accounts by veteran troops as well as photographs that proved it. Nevertheless, António Heliodoro is an exception. His family know what he went through, and also what he did. Like the time, two weeks before returning home, when he was given the order to kill a local who had been captured in the area of Bigene without firing a shot.

Everything abruptly ended on 15 April 1974 with the 'Carnation Revolution', when a group of young military officers – some of whom, including Major Vitor Alves – one of the arch-plotters I got to know quite well – decided that Portugal's colonial wars in Africa were going nowhere and simply had to end.

Only months later, the new revolutionary leaders of Portugal and the PAIGC signed an accord in Algeria in which it was agreed that all government troops would be removed from the enclave by October that year, the first of Lisbon's three African colonies to achieve that objective. The newly reformed Republic of Guiné-Bissau would then be formally recognized internationally and assume its rightful position at the United Nations and other world bodies.

Also in the agreement were several distinctive clauses which stated that there would be fully supervised democratic elections (monitored by the UN) to elect a national leader as well as sitting members of a new parliament to be built in Bissau. None of this ever happened.

The civil war that followed – and which resulted in the death of tens of thousands of those Guineans who were either involved or suspected of having been involved with Lisbon's colonial epoch – kicked off only days later. Come the handover of power in 1974, hostilities simply changed gears and a horrifically violent civil war followed.

With Portugal's military back in Europe, the shooting in the former colony – now renamed Guiné-Bissau – was supposed to have stopped, but a succession of coups and army mutinies followed with dismaying regularity and had a totally destructive effect not only on the people but also on the economy.

For all of Lisbon's problems in the tiny enclave, at least things worked while the war went on: schools functioned, there were clinics for the sick, roads were repaired and most towns had fresh water and, somehow, the nation managed. That all ended only weeks after the last Portuguese official returned home. Things continued to deteriorate and clearly, by the early 1980s, the country had absolutely nothing to offer prospective international investors. Also, with the collapse of the Soviet Union and Cuba having to tighten its belt as a consequence, all the old friends disappeared.

In the modern period little has changed. The stark reality of Guiné-Bissau's problems today, apart from a succession of coups d'état, is that no one is prepared to invest either cash or resources into a bankrupt state except drug lords. Consequently, that country has emerged as the fulcrum of Africa-based international drug smuggling rings that have targeted Europe and those machinations have been going on for decades. It has become a narco-state.

Henry Kissinger once said, 'The conventional army loses if it does not win. The guerrilla wins if he does not lose.' Put another way, guerrilla warfare has one major advantage in this nuclear age. If employed as an instrument of foreign aggression, it constitutes what might be regarded as an 'ambiguous threat' by confusing the legal, political and even military bases for an effective international response.[1]

We see quite a lot of this sort of thing going on, even today, as this book goes to print with Western and other forces battling insurgency in more than a dozen countries in Africa and the Middle East. The Portuguese Army alone, in 2020, is heavily engaged in counterinsurgency campaigns in at least two of them: the first against al-Qaeda in the Islamic Maghreb (AQIM) in Mali and, farther south, combating a crazed bunch of Islamic jihadists in the Central African Republic. There are some heavy jungle firefights viewable on YouTube and in each case Lisbon's forces emerge on top.

But for all the criticism in the Portuguese Army again being involved in what some call a 'foreign war', at least the nation is doing something positive. There are leaders in Lisbon who are actually prepared to respond to a threat that affects millions of innocents, especially on the African continent.

It was not always so. According to the November 1988 issue of *National Geographic* – barely fifteen years after the army mutiny in Lisbon – three-quarters of American adults could not find the Persian Gulf on a map of the world, in spite of American military activity there during the Iran Iraq war. Twelve million of them did not know their capital city was Washington DC. That, more or less, explains why the Soviets saw rich ideological pickings in places like Angola, Portuguese Guinea and Rhodesia: in truth, very few Americans really cared a hoot about Africa. Certainly, they would not have been able to finger any of those places on a map.

---

1. Peter Paret and John W. Shy, *Guerrillas in the 1960's*, Praeger, underlined and noted edition, 1965.

Portugal's role within NATO has always been seminal to the security of the European mainland. In a beleaguered continental Europe under threat from the Soviet Union, Lisbon was charged by NATO to guard its lower western flank. In Africa, it was generally agreed – within Europe's portals of power – that Portugal would eventually see its overseas territories safely through a series of political and military upheavals that were powerfully backed not only by the Soviet Union but also by most of its allies. That bunch included Cuba, a socialist Algeria, Libya, Ethiopia and Tanzania and, among others, the Republic of Guinea that was thoroughly Marxist. Also within that framework came communist China and the North Vietnamese.

It should be stressed that these were not vague ideological aspirations for power. The Kremlin regarded the entire African continent as ripe for the kind of change that would deliver a majority of countries that would follow decidedly Marxist doctrines. But to get there, some of the obstacles in the way needed to be removed, starting with Portuguese Guinea. Angola, it was argued in the 1960s, would follow and finally, Mozambique. Clearly, there were some commanding forces at work and a lot of willing hands eager to, as some would phrase it, 'do the dirty'.

Pundits familiar with what was going on in Africa at the time offered several reasons for this approach, the first being that in helping the so-called liberation movements actively engaged in Lisbon's three African possessions, the Soviets would eventually acquire a series of strategic bases along the Atlantic and Indian ocean seaboards. From there the Soviet navy and air force could operate, which is what eventually took place from a major military base in Conakry, the Guinean Republic's capital and Russian intelligence-monitoring ships off Cape Town. The Kremlin was already ensconced in Cuba in the west while Sékou Touré's Conakry made for a valuable strategic adjunct on the other side of the Atlantic.

Secondly, with the Portuguese ousted from Portuguese Guinea, the theory running the rounds in Moscow at the time was that Lisbon would soon enough accept the futility of continuing to hold on to Angola and Mozambique and would withdraw its armed forces from Africa. That achieved, it would be much easier to tackle South Africa and ultimately, achieve dominance over the southern sea route around Africa.

NATO, it must be observed, was keenly aware of this menace, the British particularly so. So were the Soviets, for the simple reason that in a world war – which would be the third within a century, but which never happened – shipping lanes around the Cape of Good Hope would become the principal conduit of oil from the Middle East to Europe, all of it big-time Cold War power play at work.

While there are some European radicals who still tend to scoff at this premise, it actually makes very good sense: following the collapse of the Soviet Union that very same scenario emerged as having been part of the Kremlin's Soviet policy all along, with the Soviets regarding much of the continent almost within its grasp.

In the end it was a patent lack of resources, or more bluntly, bankruptcy on the home front that thwarted Soviet planners and brought the Berlin Wall down, coupled to multiple domestic issues that forced the end of the three African wars in which Lisbon was involved.

In the broader picture, Portugal was dealing with a very different kind of problem and one simply cannot ignore the trickle-down effects of the Cold War: Moscow saw the defeat of the Portuguese in her colonies in a strictly strategic context, and to that end spared nothing in giving the revolutionaries all the military hardware they wanted.

One of my first books to appear on Portugal's wars in Africa, titled *The Terror Fighters*, dealt with Angola, where conflict was at its fiercest. It was published in South Africa by a British company, Purnell, in 1969, eight years after hostilities began with a series of attacks when insurgents pushed southward out of the Congo (now Zaire) into northern Angola between 15 and 17 March 1961.[2]

When I visited the country for the second time in 1968, it was said that 17,000 Portuguese whites (the real figure was nearer 500) and between 20,000 and 30,000 black Angolans had been killed, the majority in the first three days of the fighting in a war that was to continue for thirteen years. Yet, for all that, many South Africans still regarded Angola as a holiday resort.

---

2. Al J. Venter, *Portugal's Guerrilla Wars in Africa: Lisbon's Three Wars in Angola, Mozambique and Portuguese Guinea*, Helion, Solihull 2013; in Portugal the book is published as *Portugal e as Guerrilhas de A'frica*, Clube do Autor, Lisboa 2014.

One has a rather distinct sense of déjà vu when reading the blurb on the book's dustjacket, because what I wrote in 1968 raised a titter in semi-informed South African political and academic circles. I was castigated by many of them for projecting an alarmist image about what many said was a minor insurrection that would be over within a year.

I was also taken to task by Parliament in Cape Town, Pik Botha, later the apartheid foreign minister, taking a strong National Party line and referring to me as a 'blithering idiot'. I quote what I wrote:

> The guerrilla war in Angola is not an isolated example of insurgency warfare in Africa. Similar wars are being fought in Guinea on the west coast of Africa and Mozambique to the east. The Rhodesians and South Africans, of late, have also experienced the first thrust of a well-trained, well-armed guerrilla force which is using every trick in the book of unconventional warfare to secure an advantage.
>
> The war in Angola is a harsh campaign. Black guerrillas dictate the way it is fought ... They only engage in battle when they are confident that they have a material advantage. It is for this reason that a Portuguese army of almost 60,000 men is tied down to counter a guerrilla threat of barely a sixth of that number.
>
> But tactics and statistics apart, the Angolan war is also significant historically. It is not generally realized that on its outcome – one way or the other – may depend the future of the whole southern African subcontinent.

In my prologue I added a note to say that the book 'is a chronicle of ... what may be expected in other southern African countries in the foreseeable future.'

There is no question that the 1960s were the great years of liberty, equality and fraternity, and in the eyes of the libertarians Portugal was unequivocally out of step.

That approach was also adopted by the educated classes in Portugal itself. While popular stereotypes tended to depict Portugal as a stagnant backwater for almost three centuries, students, professionals, academics, the military, government officials and politicians in this nation of more than nine million people became increasingly sensitive to the opprobrium resulting from the reactionary policies of Prime Minister António Salazar. He suffered a stroke in 1968 and optimists on both sides of the Atlantic hoped that under Caetano, the man who succeeded him, the country would enter a more liberal phase. It was not to be. Some faces changed, but politics in general did not.

The Brazilian political commentator Marcio Alves wrote scathingly: 'To hold on to the Empire was fundamental for Portuguese fascism. Economically, the African territories – and especially rich Angola – were so important to Portuguese capitalism that Caetano took over from Salazar on the condition that they would be defended.'

Part of the trouble was that in the Portuguese African possessions no political solution to the problem was either sought or found, though to give him his due, General António de Spínola made some effort to seek a compromise with the PAIGC guerrillas with the help of Senegal's President Leopold Senghor.

That said, we all knew that the Lusitanians had hundreds of years of fairly successful African rule behind them, and that in spite of problems, things continued very much as they had in the past. That included rule by force which was not only brutal but also repressive and exploitative. Forced labour continued to be a feature of life within non–white groups until the colonial wars started.

The Portuguese secret police, Polícia Internacional e de Defesa do Estado (PIDE) – later replaced by the Direcção-Geral de Segurança (DGS) – was almost a government in itself. Its methods were most brutal, and in some respects could compare with those of the Gestapo or Sawak in Iran.

Matters were exacerbated during later stages of the African conflict by an almost total breakdown in communications in some areas between the security police and the Portuguese defence forces. There were several cases in Tete and Nampula in Mozambique at about the time of my visits where liberal Portuguese officers informed FRELIMO sympathizers of future movements by PIDE operators in the interior. They knew that such information would be passed on to the revolutionaries and made good use of.

As a consequence of all these factors, there was little social or political development to shout about either in Mozambique or Angola until the final stages of the war. But of course, by then it was too late.

In Portuguese Guinea, General Spínola changed many basics, including recruiting blacks into elite fighting groups, but apart from forming close liaisons with village groups who were shown how to protect themselves and given arms, no substantive advance was possible because of the forbidding nature of the colony's countryside, much of it swamp terrain. There was also little development, economic or otherwise, in Portugal itself, with the result that it was firmly rooted as the second poorest country in Europe after Albania.

The military configuration in Portuguese Guinea offered the observer some striking contrasts. There were the Portuguese, who received matériel though discreet support from much of Europe, their NATO allies, including the United States, and a variety of Western-orientated nations (and even some Arab states like Morocco and Jordan). On the other side, the PAIGC was backed by the Soviets.

The American academic and historian Piero Gleijeses has published widely on this conflict, in particular on the role that Fidel Castro's Cuba played in providing the guerrillas with men and matériel. As he says, and again, I quote:

> I went to Cuba six times between November 1993 and July 1996 for a total of six months to research Cuban policy toward Africa from the early 1960s to 1978. I interviewed 63 Cuban protagonists, and I had access to the archives of the Central Committee (hereafter ACC), the Instituto de Historia de Cuba, the Centro de Informacion de la Defensa de las Fuerzas Armadas Revolucionarias (hereafter CID-FAR), and the Ministerio para la Inversión Extranjera y la Colaboracion Economica, and to documents from private collections. I have photocopies of all Cuban documents cited in this essay.

As a result, he covers several relevant issues, including the fact that there were many countries on the sidelines that quietly and discreetly helped the PAIGC in its struggle. Sékou Touré's Marxist Republic of Guinea provided solid support from the start, as did a number of African states.

In the West, he recalls, Sweden began sending economic aid in October 1969, adding that this was the first time ever that a Western industrialized country gave state support to a liberation movement involved in armed struggle against another Western country. He goes on:

In 1972–73, Norway, Denmark, Finland and the Netherlands followed suit. It was the Soviet bloc, however, whose help was decisive. It provided arms, educational opportunities and other material and political support. The Soviet Union was by far, the major source of weapons. Cuba, too, gave material help, in the form of supplies, military training in Cuba and scholarships. This was a considerable and generous effort for a poor country, but Cuba did much more and its role was unique. Only Cubans fought in Guinea-Bissau side by side with the guerrilla fighters of the PAIGC.

As Nõ Pintcha said, 'In the most difficult moments of our war of liberation, some of the best children of the Cuban nation stood at the side of our freedom-fighters, enduring every sacrifice to win our country's freedom and independence.' This aid was given despite the fact that the PAIGC was not a Marxist movement and its leaders strove to establish a non-aligned Guinea-Bissau.

Chapter One

Build-up to the Conflict

Insurgency warfare in and around this savagely tropical country was
like no other colonial conflict during the epoch that followed much
of Africa achieving independence. It was the only campaign that a
modern European colonial power almost lost.

In contrast, the Algerian War with an Arab society basically trying
to counter European influences was ideologically inflexible, far more
unforgiving and a good deal more brutal. In the end, President de Gaulle
conceded that a political option was the only pragmatic solution both
for France and the Algerians. Independence and a total break from the
colonial motherland that had ruled since 1830 followed soon afterward.

Yet, almost a century and a half later, with hostilities in Portuguese
Guinea in full flow, it was significant that not a single town in this tiny
West African enclave was wholly or even partially overrun by an extremely
versatile insurgent force that was unconditionally backed by the Soviets.
Considering the nature of what was happening in South East Asia at the
time, the largely conscript Portuguese Army was never forced to abandon
any of its strategic positions, although it did at one stage pull back from
some of the offshore islands until fresh attacks put them on the offensive
again.

Also, government casualties by all accounts were manageable and the
Portuguese Army did not flee in disarray after hostilities ended (as the
French did from Algeria).

Indeed, not one of the few settlers who remained after a peace treaty
was signed was driven into the sea following the PAIGC's assumption
of power. In fact, things could have gone much worse had both sides
not had a firm grip on their respective forces. By the time the youthful
officers of the Movimento das Forças Armadas – the Portuguese Armed
Forces Movement – had seized power in April 1974, many of those who
had been militarily active in Africa accepted that had the war continued,

conditions might very easily have gone the other way. One young
conscript with whom I later spent time was of the opinion that when the
news of withdrawal was made public, 'defeat hung heavily in the air' in
the streets of Bissau, Cacine and Bafata farther into the interior.

Moreover, while the fighting cadres of the PAIGC knew they had the
situation in hand, the guerrilla leaders remained tentative about what
lay ahead. Amilcar Cabral had been assassinated more than a year before
in Conakry, ostensibly at the hands of a dissident within the insurgent
ranks. In later years other revelations were to come to light, including
Moscow's fear that this former agricultural engineer, writer and poet –
he used the *nom de guerre* of Abel Djassi in the field – might trade a closer
alliance with Portugal for a more stable homeland after independence
had been achieved. In this, Leopold Senghor, the Senegalese president
who was concerned about the potential negative outcome of hostilities if
a ceasefire were not to hold, offered strong but discreet support. Clearly,
this remarkable African leader who was held in high regard throughout
Europe (he also had a home in France and was always an outspoken
Francophile) had a much better grasp of conditions in West Africa than
many prominent NATO leaders or spokespeople.

Like Agostinho Neto, the always-enigmatic Angolan leader, Amilcar
Cabral – quietly outspoken but not afraid to raise his voice when
something bothered him – might have caused tension within the Kremlin
and there is speculation even today that this might have ultimately got
him killed. It says a lot, we already know, that not long after Neto echoed
those sentiments, he was also dead.

Meantime, Luis, Cabral's half-brother – a sometimes-brutal adherent
of the strict Soviet line – became the leader of the Guiné-Bissau branch
of the party. He was to appoint himself president once Lisbon was out of
the way and ruled the country for seven years. While he initially followed
a cautious line, promising that the rights of all citizens would be respected
– including those who had supported Lisbon and fought against him – it
was never to be.

What set the PAIGC aside from other liberation groups then active
in Africa is that, with rare exceptions, the majority of guerrilla fighters
at senior level were not top drawer when it came to education, intellect
or assessing the 'bigger picture'. In Angola, with the MPLA, there were

a few bright lights, but hardly any who had Neto's almost instinctive gumption: he was a truly visionary leader which might have been his undoing with Moscow.

The same could be said for FRELIMO in Mozambique: nobody could match Dr Eduardo Mondlane in his vivid ability either to be able to think and act 'on the run' or to academically pull out all stops. In Portuguese Guinea, there were several individuals of similar ilk to Cabral, and it is instructive to view their backgrounds and the basic difference there is that the majority were of Cape Verde extraction, which meant they were *mestiço*.

Top of the pile after Cabral, arguably, was Aristides Pereira, the secretary general of the PAIGC at the time of my last visit. A potential successor to the big man, little was known about him apart from the fact that, like Cabral, his parents were from the Cape Verde Islands and that he had been a member of the party from its earliest days in 1959, or even before the movement resorted to guerrilla warfare.

Dr Vitoria (Vitor to his friends) Montejro, originally tipped to head the PAIGC and always a forceful individual within the revolutionary hierarchy, was possibly next in line. Like Pereira, his father also came from the islands and he had an African mother. Very much the academic, Montejro excelled at school and eventually graduated from Lisbon University in economics before taking a job in a Bissau bank. He left Lisbon in August 1971 and went to Conakry by way of Switzerland where he joined Cabral, his wife and children, meanwhile, stayed on in the metropolis. A Portuguese source subsequently suggested that the man was long regarded as the PAIGC's 'man in Lisbon' and had always been a prominent member of the Portuguese underground communist Party.

My last visit to cover the war in Portuguese Guinea was interesting for several reasons, the first being that General de Spínola was still in charge.[1] I spent some quality time with this dynamic, no-nonsense commander and managed to interview him at length, several times, because we enjoyed each other's company. It was then that I got the impression that his views

---

1. I have been to independent Guiné-Bissau several times since, once to make a film of the country which was not much of a success because the place was falling apart.

about the series of African conflicts that faced Lisbon in all three overseas provinces were changing, possibly radically. He gave no indication that he was writing, or had already written, *Portugal and the Future*, the book that prompted a military putsch engineered by a recalcitrant bunch of young officers (including my friend Vitor Alves, who was one of the arch-plotters).

The general's book certainly turned Portuguese politics totally on its head, but all that came later. By the time I reached Bissau in the early 1970s, General Spínola had probably finished writing, but that did not deter him from pursuing PAIGC revolutionaries as and when his forces surprised them. An ascetic and intellectual career officer, yet unusually charismatic and well-informed, there were those who regarded the man as a taciturn conservative because the general was always seen in public immaculately uniformed and, in spite of the enervating West African heat, never without his leather gloves and characteristic riding crop which became his hallmark.

As we now know, the general proved to be way ahead of the game: while unable to achieve direct victory, he quickly stopped the rot after he took up the post of supreme commander in the territory. General António de Spínola had several other traits, among them the fact that professionally, he was certainly 'old school' material and unequivocally regarded as something of a father figure by his men. There were very few soldiers within his command who were not in awe of the man because he was both strong on discipline as well as tradition, without which, he would declare, Portugal would be nothing.

Yet, I sensed that he was not averse to innovation if it made sense and could be applied without disruption. He had other qualities at which he excelled. Few could match his ability as a thinker, tactician, historian and ultimately as a visionary. In this respect, he had a more enlightening effect on the future of Portugal than any other man in the previous century, including the dictator Salazar

Like his contemporary, General Bettencourt Rodrigues – who was to distinguish himself subsequently in eastern Angola – Spínola was remarkably adept at achieving results in what at the time of my visit was a still-undecided conflict, at least until the air force lost the initiative because of Soviet MANPADs.

Among conditions imposed by Spínola on being offered the command in Guinea was that he should have total control of the country without direct supervision from Lisbon. He also insisted that he should be allowed to choose his own staff: both demands were unceremoniously granted by the cabinet in Lisbon, one of the main reasons why the war soon turned in favour of the Portuguese, be it only temporarily.

Other changes followed, some of which displayed Spínola's grasp of guerrilla warfare. Following the example of Sir Gerald Templer in Malaya in 1952, he assumed total responsibility for both civilian and military actions in the enclave and this proved valuable in his attempts to come to terms with the insurgent threat. He also sliced through red tape and interdepartmental hostility which, until then, had become characteristic of the Portuguese war effort in Guinea, and to a lesser degree in Angola, largely because the latter was almost self-governing.

Another result of this general's rule was the execution of long-overdue political and economic reforms. Clearly, changes for the better came too late but, in the final analysis, Spínola stole much of the rebels' thunder, for they too promised changes and were prevented by the war from carrying them out. It actually did not take the PAIGC very long after taking over the country to become even more obstructive to change, obscurantist than even the Portuguese had been before Spínola arrived at his post.

An interesting aside here was an event that took place on my departure back to Europe. I flew out the first time in what was clearly a heavily overloaded four-engine freight plane, a DC-6. With half a dozen critically war wounded on litters toward the rear of the aircraft, attended by a small team of doctors and nurses, we were a couple of hours out over the Atlantic on the way to the Cape Verde Islands when two of the aircraft's engines seized. This was a major problem because of all the incapacitated who would certainly not survive a crash landing at sea, never mind the sharks. Battling with the surviving engines, the pilots turned toward Dakar which, despite officially being at loggerheads with Lisbon, that government gave the plane overfly rights to proceed back to Bissau where we were able to land, but barely.

I was met by Captain de Carvalho, my escort officer, after we had touched down and I explained a predicament that had arisen because of the curtailed flight. I had cut my stay in Portuguese Guinea extremely fine because I had a meeting with the foreign minister of Ghana in Accra two days hence for my newspaper. Unless I could get to a connecting flight in Rome, I would miss it, I told him.

He broached the problem with his general and I was immediately issued a ticket for the next morning's TAP Boeing flight to Lisbon.

Concurrent to my visit, General Spínola appointed two of his officers to assist with my travels throughout the country, which were extensive: unlike most visiting media, they did not accompany me but allowed me to go ahead on my own and advising respective commanders in the field that I was coming. With various operational units I visited the east, south and the north, I was also to go on patrol with a crack bunch of counterinsurgency fighters, the *comandos africanos*.

The first of these characters was Lieutenant Colonel Lemos Pires, a charming and engaging staff officer in the Portuguese Army and a personal aide to his general. His responsibilities involved the Department of Psychological Warfare (as well as press liaison) in Portuguese Guinea. A brief note that I wrote while there adequately characterized him as a 'distinguished and imaginative young officer ... his job is also to implement many of the general's decrees ... thoroughly efficient'. Indeed, Colonel Pires was the fulcrum which centered on the nature and extent of my visit to this tiny West African enclave. It would eventually involve quite a few operational sorties, including a patrol with Lisbon's elite marine (*fuzileiros*) contingent along one of the embattled rivers in the north, near the Senegalese frontier. In his dealings with me, a foreign correspondent (whose bona fides he accepted on the recommendation of Colonel Bettencourt Rodrigues, at the time the military attaché at the embassy in London), the colonel was candid about the difficulties facing the Portuguese Army. Obviously because much of what was going on in the war was classified, I did not get the complete picture, which was to be expected. There was certainly never an inkling that General Spínola was about to resign his post, including the governorship of the country. I suspect Pires was probably aware by then of the book the general was writing – as he should have been, working in such close quarters in Bissau – and the need for his boss to return to the *metrópole* to pursue that side of things, including getting it into print without being arrested for sedition.

The other individual with whom I was constantly in touch whenever I returned to headquarters was an unusual character by the name Otelo Saraiva de Carvalho, then still a lowly captain and who met me on my return. I actually got to know Otelo very well, especially since he was originally from Lourenço Marques and spoke good English. He had enjoyed the company of many of my fellow South African countrymen in the past and we obviously had a lot in common, which meant sharing a few glasses of the hard stuff on several occasions. Like his immediate boss, Colonel Lemos Pires, Otelo was punctilious about his duties. It went further even when he was not in the office because he would often concern himself with the welfare of his African staff and their families. More than once while I travelled about with him, he would load up one of the army Jeeps with a bunch of African kids and drag them along on visits along Bissau's distant shorelines which they loved.

They were clearly fond of their *capitão*. Aware of my South African origins and that things were also going awry there for the ruling National Party – trying to hold fast to its apartheid ideals – Otelo never once asked me to elaborate. Possibly he was already aware that a few years previously I had written a powerful diatribe condemning South Africa's racially inspired politics and thought the better of it.

As we are now also aware, Otelo Saraiva de Carvalho was himself a revolutionary at heart and, as one of the arch-strategists in the so-called Carnation Revolution, which set the army coup in motion, he was to play a significant role in bringing down the Lisbon government in 1974. In fact, he was a lot more radical that many of his colleagues believed and had almost certainly been a card-carrying communist throughout his army career. I know that he greatly admired Lisbon's 'Red Admiral', António Alva *Rosa Coutinho,* which just about says it all.

Otelo's life during that extremely difficult transient period tells us something else about the man. After the revolution, he assumed leadership roles in the first Portuguese provisional governments alongside Vasco Gonçalves and Francisco da Costa Gomes and as the head of military defence force, Comando Operacional do Continente (COPCON). In 1976 de Saraiva ran in the first Portuguese presidential election in which he was placed second, the base of his support coming from the radical ultra-left for which many military veterans have never forgiven him.

In the 1980s Otelo was accused of involvement with the fanatical Forças Populares 25 de Abril and imprisoned. While in jail, he met Maria Filomena Morais and began a bigamous relationship with her and his first wife Maria Dina Afonso Alambre. All that is now history and my old friend, well into his eighties is no longer as active either in politics or with women as he once might have been.

What has puzzled many of us about the man is the fact that though ostensibly a left-wing rabble-rouser, de Saraiva wept unashamedly at Salazar's funeral of in 1970. Possibly he was more of a sentimentalist than we thought.

The civil war that engulfed Guiné-Bissau after independence was absolute, culminating in a series of conflicts that lasted more than a year. It ended with the rout and death of almost all the black troops who had formerly served in the Portuguese Army and though numbers will never be known, some sources maintain that almost 100,000 Guinéan nationals were slaughtered. Those who could fled to neighbouring countries.

It remains a curious anomaly that throughout this extremely violent phase of settling scores, there was barely a whisper of protest from Lisbon's fledgling revolutionary government. More's the shame, because, as we have already seen, I was not only close to some of the more prominent dissidents like Vitor Alves and Otelo Saraiva de Carvalho, but I'd also met quite a few of the others behind their *Revolução dos Cravos*, several in Vitor and Teresa Alves's apartment in Oeiras on the outskirts of Lisbon.

What was notable about this isolated conflict in West Africa was that it bore little similarity to other colonial struggles in Africa, or even France's seven-year campaign against the National Liberation Front (FLN) in Algeria. It also differed markedly from what had been going on just then in Lisbon's other two former African possessions of Angola and Mozambique, and still more liberation struggles that had already emerged along the northern frontiers of Rhodesia and South West Africa (respectively Zimbabwe and Namibia today). There were clearly a number of parallels with what took place in Angola.

The war in Portuguese Guinea, as with so many other colonial conflicts in Africa and the Far East, took a while to develop. Obviously, the Soviets were eager to manipulate an untenable political colonial situation and bring their own interests to the fore and that they did with aplomb. Youthful leaders were sought out among the populace and promised schooling and advancement behind the Iron Curtain, to the extent that the biggest tertiary institution in the Soviet Union that catered predominantly for Third World students – Africans especially – was named Patrice Lumumba University in memory of the Congolese leader who was murdered at the behest of the CIA not long after that country became independent.

Soon afterward, several black leaders on this island-fringed tropical spit of land wedged between the Republic of Guinea and Senegal took the initiative in their bid to force Lisbon out of Africa. A small band of disaffected African intellectuals, mostly educated at Portugal's Coimbra or Lisbon universities and thereafter granted 'most privileged' *assimilado* status, first requested that Portugal withdraw from the territory in the late 1950s. Naturally Prime Minister Salazar scoffed at the idea.

A year or so later those same nationalists – some in self-imposed exile – were issuing decrees from Conakry or from the equally revolutionary Ghana – with the firebrand Kwame Osajeyfo Nkrumah in control – that Portugal should vacate 'Our Guiné-Bissau' immediately.

The demand went along the lines that Lisbon hand over the reins of nationhood to the local African population. Naturally, Salazar's government wanted none of it. And when this stipulation met with no response, the aspiring black leaders tried intimidation: if Portugal were not to immediately withdraw, they warned, arms would be taken up against them.

Concurrently local black workers were urged to embark on various programmes of civil disobedience, which included burning their identity cards and other documents. As might have been expected Lisbon reacted with vigour; it had no intention of letting anybody disrupt the almost-sacrosanct national status quo.

Only after some of dissident Africans had been gunned down by squads of Portuguese police during a violent strike for higher wages at Pidjiguiti docks in downtown Bissau on 3 August 1959 – a date subsequently immortalized by the guerrillas – did the prospect of a military confrontation seriously enter the picture. The guerrilla war followed three years later.

United States Marine aviator Captain John P. Cann had it right when he declared in his book *Brown Waters of Africa: Portuguese Riverine Warfare 1961–1974* that of Lisbon's three African theatres of operations in Angola, Mozambique and Portuguese Guinea, the last proved to be the most complicated and the most difficult war with which to come to terms. As I was to see for myself, it was also the most perilous.

It was certainly the most important for Portugal's miniscule navy, because offshore activities were vital, not only on the tactical but also on the strategic level and the reason was basic. About 80 per cent of all cargo and personnel within the so-called 'zones of conflict' were moved about on boats or pirogues, either by sea or through the river system by the rebels. For the PAIGC, water transport was seminal in keeping its logistic elements alive, and for this reason the policing of river traffic by the Portuguese Navy was as important as its transport role.

In fact, Cann records comments made by junior lieutenant (*primeiro tenente*) Alexandre Carvalho Neto, one of Spínola's military assistants: 'The situation [early on] was absolutely catastrophic … it was on the brink of collapse. Bissau had become practically surrounded,' the lieutenant declared.

Admiral Américo Tomás, President of the Republic, visited Bissau in February 1968 and returned to Lisbon to report to Salazar that 'the war was held by a thread'. Cann continues:

Major General (*brigadeiro*) António de Spínola confirmed this observation with an inspection visit of his own and described the situation as "desperate." He criticized Brigadeiro Arnaldo Schultz, the Governor-General and Commander-in-Chief, for not having an offensive aimed equally at the socio-economic and military problems and further accused the local military commanders of disguising the true state of affairs.

Spínola, who habitually wore the traditional monocle of a cavalry officer, had a broad portfolio of experience on which to base his observations. His resumé included leading a volunteer force in the Spanish Civil War in 1938 and acting as an observer on the German eastern front facing Leningrad in November 1941. In 1955 he was made a member of the Administrative Council of the steel concern

Siderurgia Nacional, in addition to his normal military duties and thus became a beneficiary of Salazar's strategy for managing his military through such appointments.

Normally these were at high levels of government or industry in both the *metrópole* and the *ultramar*, and it was these postings, promotions, and pay that Salazar controlled. Spínola thus had Salazar's ear and confidence.

As Cann explains, Spínola initially focused on this region's rivers, inlets and offshore islands, which he'd already accepted tended to serve as the primary logistical lines of communication for Lisbon's enemies in that part of Africa. All became the immediate focus of attention of Spínola's overall counterinsurgency programmes:

In the south of Portuguese Guinea, four PAIGC supply bases across the frontier played a pivotal role in this encroachment. During this time, the PAIGC had acquired four Soviet P-6 class fast patrol boats, capable 66-ton craft armed with two 25mm anti-aircraft guns as well as two torpedo tubes. The vessels could reach speeds in excess of 40 knots. This was in addition to an assorted collection of locally manufactured motor launches consisting of the *Arouca*, *Bandim*, *Bissau* and *Mirandela*.

Further [Conakry] had similarly received three 75-ton Komar-class fast patrol boats also capable of 40 knots plus. All were armed with two surface-to-surface missiles and a pair of 25mm anti-aircraft guns. This sophisticated capability on the part of both the PAIGC and its host enabled the PAIGC to project power from Conakry to the depot of Kadigné on the island of Tristaõ, and then onto the Portuguese islands of Canefaque and Cambon.

From these bases, a large fleet of canoes and modest numbers of small outboard motor boats consistently penetrated the waterways of southern Portuguese Guinea, largely unchallenged. The situation effectively extended the PAIGC distribution system and consequent combat capability well into the interior. A good proportion of the southern half of Portuguese Guinea as a consequence was thoroughly infiltrated by the PAIGC by 1969, and this dominance posed a most serious threat to Spínola's plans.

Apart from what was going on in Angola, Mozambique and Portuguese Guinea, Portugal faced many other problems, including trained troops avoiding further military service. One figure puts the number of desertions from the military at 25,000, all active serving soldiers. It got so bad that by the time hostilities ended in 1974, there was hardly a bar or restaurant in Paris that was not or had not been employing Portuguese youngsters either in their kitchens or in service roles. There was no stopping them because the frontier with Spain was porous: there were many places where you could just walk across the border.

Many of these men had left their homes clandestinely after receiving their call-up papers and that loss was over and above the 25,000 actual deserters. The real crunch came when fifteen engineering cadets – all regarded by the establishment as the 'Cream of the Military Academy' – who, after completing their four-year course in 1973, one dark night walked across the frontier into Spain.

For many years the strength of the Portuguese armed forces hovered around the 80,000 mark, roughly 60,000 in the army, less than 10,000 in the navy and 12,500 in the air force.

There were two additional problems. Though the country was ruled by a right-wing dictator who abhorred the left, there was no official way of stopping individuals embracing radical political causes: as a consequence the Portuguese Communist Party had a field day. It was actually an open secret that many members of the officer corps were hard-line socialists. There were also communists within the ranks who openly espoused Marxism and were known to sleep with copies of *Das Kapital* under their pillows. While that might sound absurd, it actually happened.

The second problem was convincing the average young Portuguese conscript who had been called up to fight a guerrilla war in Africa that he was doing so for a noble cause, for his country. The argument usually centred on the assertion that he was going to be *protecting* the nation, and while that might have worked on home soil, it simply did not cut it for a youngster who had grown up in Lisbon's suburbs and who was stuck out in some distant jungle outpost thousands of miles from metropolitan Portugal.

Indeed, the distances were vast. Lourenço Marques, the capital of Mozambique, for instance, is 8,400 kilometres from Lisbon and in today's world, a flight of almost eleven hours. In the 1960s it took three weeks or more by ship. Getting to Luanda, though closer to Europe, was also a slog. Consequently, the first question most conscripts asked on arriving in tropical Africa was: 'Why the hell are we here?' When I tackled one young lieutenant in a camp in the north of the country, he retorted with cynical comments such as, 'What's all this bullshit about? This shithole corner of Africa is neither my home nor my country.' Of course, all the majority of these young troops wanted was to go home, with the result that few were prepared to stick out their necks while on active service.

Cabral's PAIGC was not the only political movement eager to see the back of the white community heading back to Europe. Another Guinean political movement trying to do the same was FLING, an acronym for the Frente de Luta pela Independência Nacional de Guiné-Bissau (in French the Front de Lutte de l'Indépendence Nationale de Guinée). Based in francophonic Dakar, the Senegalese capital, FLING was composed of at least four united nationalist movements and was regarded by the Portuguese and the West as somewhat more moderate than the Marxist-orientated PAIGC. Both groups nonetheless had as their common denominator the determination that Portugal should be ousted, by whatever means. Both political movements also underwrote violence as a means of achieving their objectives, which followed in the wake of what they termed 'Lisbon's utter intransigence and violence toward the masses'. The phrase 'People's War' also featured in most communiqués.

However, there were several issues on which the two groups could not agree, the first being the question of leadership, which was invariably a common thing among African liberation groups because everybody wanted to be Number One. Then followed the timing of the takeover and the eventual nature of government they hoped to form.

FLING had indicated fairly early on that it would not be averse to some kind of loose economic and cultural alliance or federation with Portugal, similar to that in operation for instance, between the Ivory Coast or Cameroon and France. In contrast, PAIGC had its own views on this matter. Africa, declared Cabral and several of his lieutenants on numerous occasions, was black, not European and there could be no links with the former colonialists.

Moreover, the PAIGC's standpoint essentially centred on a socialist type of government along Cuban or Algerian lines, with all facets of government – including politics, economics and military affairs – answerable to the party and the party alone. Here Cabral indicated that he had learned a good deal from men like Guinea's Sékou Touré and Fidel Castro, both of whom tended to influence this guerrilla leader's thinking.

Still, in spite of differences, the two organizations, PAIGC and FLING, did cooperate, but only as long as they faced a common enemy, unlike what was going on in Angola at the time with Neto's MPLA trying to slaughter as many of Holden Roberto's FNLA guerrillas as Portuguese troops. That internal dissension eventually got so bad that both revolutionary movements were tipping off the Portuguese secret police about the activities and movements of their opponents

Apart from military activity, both PAIGC and FLING also ventured into a joint propaganda campaign that routinely drew attention to the monopolistic nature of commerce, trade and industry in the territory. Their single-most important targets were the enormous (by African standards) capitalist cartels Banco Nacional Ultramarino and the Companhia Uniao Fabril (CUF), both firms maintaining vast economic holdings in metropolitan Portugal as well as in the overseas provinces. Both also played forceful roles in the course of the wars in all of Lisbon's African possessions, mainly through powerful family connections at the highest governmental levels in Lisbon.

Until matters got out of hand in Portuguese Guinea in the early 1960s, CUF literally dominated trade in the country. Virtually all commercial transactions passed through the books of the company and no foreign or domestic business was tolerated unless it had first been sanctioned by CUF. Thereafter it was invariably conducted through company channels, suitably dressed with the necessary percentage rake-offs. The company also had enough influence to establish market prices as well as buying and selling rates for local commodities. It was usually those who had the least, the peasants, who fared the worst. As a consequence, both companies did well, so well in fact that there are some authorities in Portugal today who maintain that CUF was loathe to suspend military operations in the face of the growing military confrontation. They argue that had it not been for the sway held by the elitist CUF board of directors, Lisbon might have abdicated from that corner of Africa long before it was forced to do so. The question of lives of young soldiers killed in action in Africa seems never to have been allowed to become an issue while the war lasted.

Conflict arrived in Portuguese Guinea when small bands of well-armed and -trained guerrillas crossed over from their exterior bases in Sékou Touré's Marxist Republic of Guinea in 1961. The insurgency gradually intensified until war was formally declared in January 1963 and it was not long before the normally placid Senegal entered the fray by allowing guerrillas to operate from its soil. In effect, the guerrillas now had safe havens in both states, which meant that the enclave was almost completely surrounded.

Chapter Two

Fuel to the Fire

From the start, conflict in Portuguese Guinea was both fierce and uncompromising. Because of its limited size and forbidding terrain, many low-lying areas were impenetrable swamp or rainforest.

Geographically, large parts of the enclave could easily have been mistaken for Vietnam. Also, previous lessons learned in Angola, Malaya, Cuba, Algeria and Indochina were put into effect by both opposing forces.

Things were a lot easier in the rest of the enclave, which rose slowly to a small succession of savannah plains in the interior and which allowed for better roads and regular army patrols. Where Portuguese Guinea also differed from Angola and Mozambique was that there were no friendly neighbours, like Rhodesia, South Africa or what was to become Namibia. On top of which, conditions were not helped by dismal communications; the colony had stultified in virtual isolation for many years. Tourism was never touted nor were casual visits encouraged.

One of the biggest problems facing the military command in Bissau was getting the army to patrol many hundreds of kilometres of waterways that spread-eagled inland from the coast. Numerous small streams were often obscured from the air by heavy jungle growth while others became swamps at low tide and one had to know your way about to avoid being stranded. Quicksand was commonplace, though I personally never saw that side of things because I only got to one of the offshore islands.

But here again the guerrillas had the advantage of help from local Africans who knew these backwaters. Tribal people had been through these waterways for generations so it did not take the PAIGC long to plot many of the more obscure trails.

The single difference of hostilities in Guinea, compared with what was going on down south, was there was little organized terror or mass slaughter of civilians, certainly not on the same scale of the two larger colonies early on. It stayed that way, but only until the colonial war had ended and all Portuguese forces, as the saying goes, had upped sticks and gone home.

There were more reasons for Portugal's colonial demise and they warrant examination. Economic issues feature prominently. For a start, historic development of the overseas provinces had always been slow. It was pitifully, and by today's standards, embarrassingly so, and it was only in the second year of the Angolan war that Salazar started to address some of these issues.

The accent had always been on cheap labour which, in part, meant keeping the populace relatively uneducated. And while the majority of Africans spoke Portuguese – as they still do today more than two generations after the bloody transition – and there was emphasis on what was termed the 'Great Society', there was little real authority vested in the provinces. Anything important was invariably referred to Lisbon, the ultimate authority which, in any event, was a dictatorship.

Moreover, Lisbon's African territories were subject to the bidding of legions of functionaries who, with the military or the law just outside the door, oversaw everything from local government to administration of the civil service and included the departments of education, health, trade, commerce, industry, utilities and the rest.

In theory, with Angola being an immensely wealthy region, there should have been an abundance for all its citizens, whatever their colour. In practice, members of Portugal's African population were relegated to a level of second-class citizenship that would sometimes make conditions in apartheid-ridden South Africa appear almost benevolent by comparison. Beatings, for minor transgressions, for instance, were commonplace. Indeed, government rule was sometimes not only brutal, but also repressive and exploitative. Forced labour was exacted on a substantive scale which would certainly never be tolerated today, with many of the provinces' roads built using either forced or prison labour. It was that bad.

The Portuguese secret police PIDE, later replaced by the DGS, was almost a government in itself. Its methods could be often cruel. There was rarely any quarter afforded to those suspected of colluding with the enemy, with the result that the guerrillas ended up employing equally brutal tactics against anybody linked to the ruling administration, particularly in Angola and Mozambique.

Additionally, while everybody was supposed to be governed by a single, universal set of laws, there were very different criteria for Portuguese nationals and ethnic Africans. Blacks could be arrested at the whim of the local *chefe do posto* – similar to the British district commissioner – for a trivial offence. Not paying the mandatory head tax or perhaps using bad language in the presence of a Portuguese woman could result in a jail term. Similarly, anybody encouraging labour unrest for better wages or improved living conditions was charged with sedition and imprisoned.

Since the entire country was ruled by decree, any kind of political activity – by black as well as white – was ruled illegal. Harsh laws were imposed by equally callous and uncompromising bureaucrats. Often mindlessly brutal, they were rarely made to account for their actions, even when lives were lost. Coupled to that, wages for blacks in Angola, Mozambique and Portuguese Guinea were among the lowest on the continent.

As might have been expected, living conditions throughout this expansive overseas empire were cheerless, for African people especially. Lisbon would always argue that in the long term, it was better for all because nobody starved. Nor did they, but by the end of the Second World War this political scenario was also a clear-cut recipe for revolt.

Yet, in the overall picture, the real downfall of Portuguese interests in Africa ultimately came from within the armed forces. To start with there was great dissatisfaction among members of the Portuguese military over service in Africa. A two-year period of service overseas was usually followed by six months back home and then another two years in the provinces. That practice had a crippling effect on morale in the war zones.

There was also bad feeling between regular soldiers and conscripts, particularly within junior and middle ranks of commissioned officers; in some military areas the air force was almost an entity unto itself, as was the army and they sometimes did not talk to each. Worse, there were many instances where they would not share fresh intelligence about recent developments within the enemy camp, information that would obviously have made things easier for the men on the ground shouldering the bulk of war effort. As one officer joked after he had explained some of these differences to me, using an ancient adage, probably from Roman times: 'Those whom the gods wish to destroy, they first make mad ...'

For all that, the MFA, or the Armed Forces Movement that organized the 1974 coup did recognize fairly early on that no political development was taking place either in the military or in the African territories.

The military line-up in Portuguese Guinea for the duration of the war was a strategist's exercise in contrasts. Mustered militarily in two opposing camps were the Portuguese on one hand, who had the material though discreet support of much of Europe, their NATO allies, including the United States and a variety of Western-oriented nations. On the other hand, there was the PAIGC which remained unequivocally backed by Russia, China, Cuba, Algeria and most East European states for the duration of the war, all channelling their multifarious aid through Sékou Touré's passionately anti-French republic.

There were racial aspects present in this war from the start. In the beginning the conflict took the nature of a largely black–white confrontation. Over the years, however, Lisbon relegated colour to a matter of secondary importance, mainly out of economic considerations and came to rely increasingly on the services of its black African volunteers. The elite *comandos africanos* was one of these.

The only white faces in the ranks of the insurgents were their Cuban and Russian advisers and the very occasional Portuguese defector who was incorporated into PAIGC ranks. But there too, there were problems, because in the eyes of the organization's Central Committee, 'a white Portuguese will always be a white Portuguese'.

Though a deserter's intentions might have been sincere, to the extent of rejecting everything for which that his former motherland stood, his mettle, PAIGC leaders would discreetly maintain, was better tempered outside the fighting zone, preferably behind the Iron Curtain or within the control of the exiled, communist-dominated Frente Patriótica de Libertação Nacional (FPLN), headquartered in Algiers. A perpetual preoccupation with matters relating to security was a trait the PAIGC appears to have inherited from the Portuguese.

For most of the war, the great powers remained very much in the eaves of the fray. Russia, Red China and America covertly backed their respective proxies, except when it came to votes at the United Nations, though they were invariably evasive on the subject internationally. China too had a role on the periphery. There were quite a few reports of Chinese 'specialists' operating subversively with PAIGC cadres in the southern jungles of Portuguese Guinea, but this was always denied by Cabral.

Cuba too was active. This was underscored by the capture of an officer of the regular Cuban Army, Captain Pedro Rodriguez Peralta, who was taken prisoner after being wounded in a battle in the Guilege region. This officer was sentenced to two years' imprisonment by a military court in Lisbon in May 1971.

Piero Gleijeses made some interesting comments on Havana's role in the war in one of his dissertations on Portugal's wars in Africa. As he says, 'The rebels of Guinea-Bissau fought for independence from Portugal, Cuban military instructors stood by their side and Cuban doctors treated their wounds. Joining the rebellion in 1966, and remaining through to the war's end in 1974, this was the longest Cuban intervention in Africa before the despatch of troops to Angola in November 1975 and was also the most successful.'

He was forthright too about Castro's pledge to send doctors, military instructors and mechanics, to which Luis Cabral (Amilcar's brother) added: 'Everything was simple in Amilcar's talks with the top Cuban leader … Fidel told Amilcar, "Come with me, I'll take you to the Escambray."' A car took them from Havana to Trinidad, from there they proceeded in a Jeep and, in some places, on foot. The trip lasted two or three days and during it, Cabral asked Castro to appoint a new ambassador to Conakry who would serve as a liaison with the PAIGC.

Another nation involved in the war was North Vietnam, then fighting its own war against the Americans in the south of that country. What only emerged years later was that there were always discreet and circumspect North Vietnamese cadres who played something of a role with the guerrillas. Notably, there were many rumours of their presence because language-wise they slotted in admirably along this coast where most of the countries had originally been French colonies – but their activity was only highlighted when the British journalist and historian Basil Davidson identified two of them in his book on the war, *No Fist Is Big Enough to Hide the Sky: The Liberation of Guinea-Bissau and Cape Verde, 1963–74*. The men were named as Tran Hoai-nam and Pham Van Than, both having served with the Liberation Front of South Vietnam, aka the Viet Cong. According to Davidson, Hoai-nam was a veteran member of the Central Committee of this organization.

Washington too played its hand. It had granted Portugal the right to buy and use Boeing passenger jets as troop-carriers for her African wars, a concession previously denied Lisbon, even a partner-member of NATO. Portugal bought two Boeing 707s and one Boeing 727 for military use with options on more aircraft if required.

Other countries involved in this grim war of attrition were Algeria, Egypt and Nigeria. The latter entrant surprised us all, considering that Lagos had only recently extricated herself from its own crippling three-year civil war in Biafra.[1] General Gowon was obviously not allowed to forget Portuguese aid to Biafra by his advisers, particularly the use of the offshore West African island of São Tomé which was used as a base by Joint Church Aid for supplying General Odumegwu Ojukwu's starving Biafran millions.

Consequently, it did not come as that much of a surprise to see reports in early 1971 of Nigerian pilots flying sorties across Portuguese Guinea in Russian-supplied MiG-17s stationed in Conakry: the last time I visited Bissau the jets buzzed Bissau twice. The flights, I was told, were for reconnaissance purposes and for that reason the Portuguese Air Force jets based at Bissau were reticent to intercept for fear of escalating the struggle still further.

That the Portuguese were concerned about the possibility of aerial attack on Bissau and other sensitive targets caused Lisbon to institute a number of anti-aircraft measures in and around the capital shortly afterward. Blackout and air-raid rehearsals were held during my visit to the territory.

The weapons used by these two adversaries also reflect extraneous interests. While the guerrillas were armed with the best Soviet and Chinese hardware available – including the ubiquitous AK-47 Kalashnikov and the full range of RPG rockets and heat grenades, landmines were to take a distressing toll of lives and limbs among Portuguese troops active in the

---

1. Until after the Biafran War, Lagos was Nigeria's capital; in a subsequent reshuffle of states, it was removed to Abuja, as it is today.

enclave, the majority similar to those deployed by the Viet Cong against the Americans and her allies in South East Asia.

Portugal retaliated with mainly Western equipment, Lisbon's standard weapon being the German-designed Heckler & Koch G3 carbine which was issued to all her troops in Africa. Some Portuguese Special Forces units took to fielding captured Russian and Chinese equipment in preference to their own, the AK invariably coming out tops.

Other items included stub-nosed Daimler armoured cars and Second World War-vintage Harvard T-6 fighters which, surprisingly, were considered by American specialists to be only second to the helicopter in efficacy in anti-insurgency operations. It stayed that way until Lisbon bought French Puma troop-carrying helicopters.

Also deployed in the war were Italian-designed Fiat G.91 jet strike aircraft, West German Dornier Do 27 spotter and light support planes as well as NATO-type Noratlas transporters, together with enough American drugs and pharmaceuticals to supply three armies the size of Portugal's.

If the make-up and mechanics of this war are interesting, the fortunes of the two opposing factions are even more so. Almost unknown to the rest of the world, apart from a few informed Africanists who made it their business to keep themselves abreast of events, the world was almost oblivious of what was going on in this dirty, distant West African war for most of the decade that it lasted.

One of the reasons for the news blackout was the reticence on the part of the Portuguese to allow newsmen into Lisbon's African possessions to cover the conflicts. As with Mozambique and Angola, the press was only allowed sporadic glimpses of action, mainly because it often took months to organize a journalist's visa to any one of the war zones.

Meanwhile, the fortunes of both sides engaged in the struggle seesawed haphazardly with Portugal's standing on the international front. In the early years – as we are now aware – it all went rather badly for Lisbon. Things deteriorated steadily until about the mid-1960s. At that stage Lisbon's shares were at their lowest when Salazar's often misdirected controls from abroad were most stringent: he tended to distrust the media, often with vehemence.

It was only when he was replaced as prime minister by the more liberal Prime Minister Caetano who promised a relaxed, more open-handed regime, did conditions improve. Once the younger leader took over, the ebb and flow of those reporting on Lisbon's African conflicts still remained relatively marginal, but the propaganda edge, it seemed, always remained with the guerrillas. In retrospect, Cabral and his spirited fighters appeared to take the initiative from the Portuguese on just about every external front.

Chapter Three

Death of a Brave Soldier

Only weeks before, I'd been with him in the jungles of this remote West African country that had been at war for eight years, a colonial struggle that pitted all the forces of a profoundly Western nation like Portugal against what was then being termed in some quarters as Moscow's Evil Empire.

The war had been a long time coming, very much a part of the gathering anti–imperialist struggle that had almost totally enveloped the continent of Africa. From passive or disobedient phases in the tradition of Mohandas Gandhi, the struggle had regressed to a succession of conflicts that stretched from Algeria on the Mediterranean to Mozambique on the Indian Ocean in the extreme southeast.

Kenya's Mau Mau insurrection by then was already history and Rhodesia's war was just about to begin. Nkrumah's dream of independence for black people all over the globe – by violent means if necessary – had already taken root. Ultimately, the Ghanaian leader declared, it would encompass the entire continent, including white-ruled South Africa. In the end, it did, but this was the 1970s and Lisbon was engaged in a grim succession of wars in all three of its African mainland possessions.

An indication of the intensity weathered by Lisbon came from American academic Douglas Porch who wrote a dissertation on Portugal's military role in Africa for Stanford University Press. Titled *The Portuguese Armed Forces and the Revolution*, Porch tells us that with over 150,000 men in Africa by 1970, 'the Portuguese deployment represented a troop level in proportion to the Portuguese population [that was] five times greater than that of the United States in Vietnam in the same year'.

Throughout, Lisbon's leaders – and many of their people too, let it be said – fought a hopeless rearguard action. They had neither the hardware nor the numbers to counter groups of rebels supported and armed by Moscow and the rest of her Warsaw Pact allies.

With her young men dying in increasing but not overly large numbers, the powers that drove Lisbon to continue in Africa seemed to most of those who knew anything about these military struggles, as futile. There were those who regarded these colonial wars as akin to some kind of improvised death wish and unquestionably that, and a lot else besides, had been visited upon the Portuguese nation. My Lusitanian friends have a name for this special kind of madness: *loucura* they call it, an untranslatable fatalism or super-optimism that, while it lasted, was also reflected in the way the Portuguese fought their African campaigns.

João Bacar, a black man and a full captain in the Portuguese Army, was one of those who died. A brilliant tactical fighter and counterinsurgency specialist, he had been immersed in this guerrilla struggle since its start. He had seen it rent his tiny West African nation as no other upheaval had done since the great Malian general Mansa Musa had swept westward, past Timbuktu, to bring the writ of this vast African empire to the verge of the great Atlantic, six centuries before. Short, lean and as tough as Muslim Africa makes them, Captain Bacar was a distant product of this astonishingly wealthy and influential civilization which has left its mark on Africa to this day. He relished and vouchsafed its traditions, handed down through thirty generations, but still intact. He rallied to what he termed was the defence of the principles which had been laid down by his illustrious forefathers and which, in the present era, as far as he was concerned, were being threatened by an alien and ungodly force from beyond. He was vocal about the enemy, telling his men that Amilcar Cabral's followers were nurtured by powers which had only self-interest and quasi-imperialist designs in mind.

Not for a moment did this commando captain – one of whose few gestures to the western society in which he lived was the small moustache he assiduously cultivated, very much like most of his other fellow officers – ever consider that this same self-interest could have been applied to the flag under which he fought. Bacar was born under that splendid green and red banner and considered himself proudly, often arrogantly, as Portuguese. Nothing else would do and he often said as much.

The Europeans from the Iberian headland, 3,500 kilometres to the north, qualified that fealty by treating this black warrior as one of their sons. Their mutual empathy peaked shortly before Bacar was killed, when they rewarded him with the country's highest military honour, the Portuguese equivalent of Britain's Victoria Cross or America's Medal of Honor. The Futa Fula[1] captain had become one of the few.

Death holds no awe for military immortality. So it happened, early one Sunday morning that April that João Bacar made his final gesture to the people, the society in which he so implicitly believed.

A week after I had left him at Tite – while on an extended patrol in a dense jungle area in which we had spent two days scouring for the enemy – he was killed. He died in an early morning skirmish with the black guerrillas of the West African guerrilla movement that called itself Partido Africano para a Independência da Guiné e Cabo Verde. Caught in the crossfire of a heavy enemy ambush along a stretch of jungle south of Bissau, his unit took the brunt of a well-planned and -executed rocket and mortar attack. Aware that they were up against the man himself, the PAIGC guerrillas had laid their trap with great care.

Three 'ballerina' anti-personnel (AP) mines – the same type known to the Americans in Indochina at roughly the same time that all this was taking place in Africa as the 'Bouncing Betty' – were placed in shallow ground across the path along which the Portuguese troops were expected.

None of the vanguard noticed the nine prongs, three to each mine, bulging slightly in the red dirt. The first soldier to cross the area would set off the explosion. The blast would also be the signal for the guerrillas to attack.

Curiously, and in keeping with the quirks of war, five of Bacar's soldiers managed to cross the kill zone without any of them triggering the prongs. The sixth followed confidently, probably satisfied that if there were mines in the path ahead, they would have been spotted or tripped by the usually eagle-eyed scouts who led the way. He'd probably already stopped following in the footsteps of the man ahead of him, for the unit was on its second day of patrol. Number six was wrong.

At the touch of his soft-soled rubber jungle boot, standard issue in the Portuguese Army, the 'ballerina', with a dull thud, leapt upward out of the hollow in the earth where it had been placed the day before. It was still spinning when it hit its shoulder-high apex and exploded downward, killing number six and badly mauling number seven. Numbers eight

---

1. A geographic and ethnic region in the interior.

and nine received superficial wounds in the legs and thighs and for some minutes remained too shocked by the blast to comprehend the battle which raged viciously around them. They lay and grimaced in the dust, barely conscious of further explosions along the line. Perhaps this shocked sprawl saved their lives, because two or three more soldiers were cut down by rocket and rifle fire in the minutes which followed.

One man, João Bacar, was killed by a grenade, his own. Bacar's reflexes were functioning almost before he heard the muffled explosion that triggered the 'ballerina' AP mine into the air about 100 metres ahead of him. He was already firing by the time the mine went off within touching distance of number six.

So were twenty more of his unit, by now crouched low in the long elephant grass on the verge of a stretch of ragged rainforest with its dinosaur-spine of tall palms giving the jungle around them a crazy trunkular effect.

Once the first ammunition clips had been exhausted, fire wavered momentarily on both sides. Bacar didn't have to order his men to reload and keep firing their G3s. They were the best of Portugal's commando force in Guinea and the swarthy captain must have been satisfied with their split-second reaction because he issued no orders throughout the action, the survivors recalled later. For more than two minutes the shooting continued. The black Portuguese troops under Bacar knew the routine: exhaust a clip and hurl a grenade to back up the three bazookas that were retaliating into the adjacent jungle and then back to their G3s again. They had done it many times before, first in training and afterward, for real. Mortars were out of the question at such short range and, in any event, much of the action was random.

The enemy attack slackened briefly and there was uncertain movement in the jungle ahead. Still silent, Bacar palmed his second grenade and pulled out the pin. He rose abruptly to throw it. But a silent, unexpected force knocked his legs out from under him: he had slipped on a patch of wet marsh clay which was not unusual in a region that has more rain in a month than parts of Europe and Africa enjoy in a year. He hit the ground hard, the grenade still in his hand.

The normal detonation time of a Portuguese hand grenade – a long tubular affair that looks more like a khaki can of shaving cream than a deadly instrument of war – is roughly four seconds after the pin has been pulled. When Bacar momentarily came to his senses and found himself lying there on his stomach with the grass above his head and the two nearest men only a metre away, he probably had one of those seconds left. In must have been the longest of his life.

The way his superiors reconstructed the attack afterward, he might theoretically have tried to disentangle himself from his crouched position and, who knows, succeeded in getting rid of the grenade. He must have been aware too, that if he did that, there was a likelihood of killing others around him. The decision was immediate: Captain João Bacar pulled the device in close to his body with both hands and dedicated his life to his beloved Prophet.

None of those around him at the time remember his last words, for they, too, were frozen in horror. One of his men, a young corporal who had joined the unit from the north shortly before, recalls seeing Bacar's lips move and reckoned afterward that it could only have been a final call to Allah.

It was ironic too, that at that critical moment, Bacar was facing the rising sun, looking east, which was the direction of his much-revered Mecca. That was when the explosion flung his body into the air.

Bacar, the warrior, had finally immersed himself physically, mentally and spiritually into what the Portuguese like to refer to as 'this Christian War', even though his own divine beliefs differed radically from the deity of his Holy Roman Catholic patrons.

The news of Bacar's death swept through Portugal and her African empire in a tide of shrouded sorrow and whispered dismay. João Bacar was dead, the people in Portuguese Guinea told one another in quiet tones, almost afraid the next man would hear the news, as if he had not already. By the next morning there wasn't a *tabanca* – a tribal village – in the country that hadn't heard the news. Drums echoing into the interior late into the night played an eerie but pivotal role in passing the message along. Within the hour, the base camp at Tite[2] from which Bacar and his men were operating – and where I spent a lot of my time while in this tiny

2. After Portugal's colonial war, the scene of huge battles between competing liberation groups that left thousands dead.

country – had passed on the word. A few hours later they were setting the event in hot metal in newspapers in Lisbon, Luanda and Lourenço Marques, complete with comment and the eulogies of a dozen men who had lived and served with this remarkable son of Africa.

The news was carried by the BBC shortly afterward. Captain João Bacar, one of the most famous veterans of Portugal's war in Guiné-Bissau had been killed in action by a PAIGC guerrilla unit, the report read. Bacar had been a recent recipient of the coveted Gold Order of the Tower and the Sword, Portugal's highest military award. That he had been killed by his own grenade was inconsequential. The Futa Fula officer was a victim of that war, as surely as if he had been killed by a guerrilla's bullet.

Many of his countrymen only believed the news when his shrapnel-torn body was flown back to Bissau by helicopter the next day. He had often been reported dead before, usually by the enemy, who fanfared his death on Radio Conakry and the smaller guerrilla station just across the frontier, Radio Libertação. In eight years they had only succeeded in wounding him four times and he had reciprocated, always ruthlessly, by killing that many dozen of them.

It was a sombre twenty-minute flight from Tite to Bissau, across swamp and river with probably a few enemy units huddled in the daytime protection of some of the larger clusters of jungle. The helicopter swung low over the jungle to avoid taking enemy fire from the surrounding bush. Not for nothing had a few foreign correspondents, recently in the country, referred to this West African patchwork quilt of jungle and rice paddy as Africa's own Vietnam.

A deep sadness pervaded Bissau's Bissalanca airport, with its rows of snub-nosed Fiat G.91 jet fighters and vintage Harvard T-6s drawn up in echelon on the tarmac. Huge crowds of mourners were gathered on the road beyond the security fence.

The entire civilian and military population had turned out to greet the body of the hero as it was brought into town, his coffin draped ceremoniously with the Portuguese flag, a mantle so large it splayed out over the back of the truck. A train of military and private trucks and cars a mile long followed behind at walking pace. Two outriders led the way. There was no need to clear the route; the crowds stood grim, silent and respectful away from the road. With characteristic full-blooded Iberian emotion, men – black and white – cried like boys when he passed.

There are not many reports of what happened across the border in the Republic of Guinea when the news of the Portuguese captain's death came through that night. It was from this former French colony that the ambush unit had originally set out and it was in that direction that they returned after the mission had been accomplished. Some reports say that many of the younger guerrillas had danced in the streets of Conakry, Boke, Koundara and Ziguinchor to the north, for Bacar's name had become synonymous with all that Portugal's presence in Africa represented. Now the frightening symbol was gone and they rejoiced.

But there was also some hushed talk and a certain undefined reverence for Bacar, particularly among some of the older guerrilla veterans. They remembered him well, for they had often crossed swords with this seasoned fighter. They respected both his guile and his tenacity, even if they despised the man for what he represented. At the same time, he was still one of them: in their native idiom, 'a man of the soil'. More importantly, his courage spoke the language often only understood by adversaries of long standing, especially in a war that had its own code of ethics and where the fighters were merely the pawns of others' ideals.

There is a postscript to these events. In 2007, more than three decades after Bacar was killed, I was sent a message by Manuel Ferreira, a former Special Forces operative and an old friend from several African conflicts. He included an attachment – a photo of the headstone of Bacar's grave in Bissau, still undamaged – and that in spite of half a dozen post-independence revolutions that have rent apart this tiny community like few others on the African continent.

Chapter Four

West African Bush Base

To really understand how Portugal fought its wars in Africa, you needed to get well into the interior of the country where things were happening. It applied especially to Portuguese Guinea, a colony that faced a very different kind of guerrilla-backed insurgency from Lisbon's two larger possessions several thousand miles to the south. It was easy enough if one of the Portuguese Air Force Alouette III helicopter gunships heading out could take a passenger, which they sometimes did, depending on fuel and the ammunition load.

Alternatively, senior commanders would often use one of the air force's Dornier Do 27 single-engine short takeoff and landing (STOL) planes. With a cruise speed of little more than 200kph, these small aircraft – depending on the amount of kit they were hauling – could take between four and six passengers. The planes were constantly deployed in all the military theatres because Lisbon managed to buy more than a hundred from the German Air Force with another forty being built as new in Spain.

But the machines were both slow and cumbersome and while they played a useful surveillance role and getting people about, the Dorniers were never that popular in areas where the insurgents might be armed with SAMs, as was the case in Guinea, where at least two, possibly three, were shot down by the guerrillas using shoulder-launched SAM-7 Grails.

My first excursion into the bush was from Bissau's Bissalanca airport with the same man with whom I was to go on patrol days later, Captain João Bacar. He had headed across the river by chopper gunship to meet me earlier in the day, but we'd return to his base at Tite in one of the Dorniers.

The Fula officer didn't have much to say after we'd lifted off but he kept his eyes keenly focused on the jungle below as we sped south. This was his area, he explained through his interpreter. At one point he thought he'd spotted movement in a thick clump of palms only minutes out from our destination and ordered the pilot to turn around for a closer inspection, this time ordering him down to treetop level.

Bacar was right. On our second pass, tiny figures scattered in all directions as we shot past barely a metre above a ragged row of tall palms which surrounded a rice paddy. We circled a few more times while the pilot gave directions on the radio, Bacar identifying the clump on a large-scale map which the pilot handed to him, passing on a row of digits to base. The first Harvard T-6s could be seen approaching the site before we moved on.

Tite base was hit by enemy mortars on the second night of my visit and since we were all having a merry wine-inspired time in the officers' mess, the attack caught us short. Everybody scarpered for the door and their designated defences. Moments later, the entire camp was suddenly blacked out: somebody had thrown a switch. Bacar meantime, had also rushed out into the night, shouting over his shoulder as he scuttled for the door that he'd be back shortly.

I learned later that it was his job to assess the direction and distance from which the attack was made, the idea possibly being to send out a patrol if he felt contact could be made. Apparently it couldn't, I gathered afterward: the attackers were more than an hour's hard march away and there was swamp country in between. It would have been impossible in the dark and from what I could glean in the confusion the rebels had carefully chosen their positions for the onslaught.

I'd been left almost alone in the mess after most of the men had rushed out to cope with the emergency. Out of curiosity perhaps, or maybe fearful that the Tite officers' mess would take a hit from one of the shells, I waited a few minutes and then followed them outside where I crouched low in the shadow of a huge baobab tree and watched one the 105mm howitzer crews load, fire, reload and fire again.

They loosed perhaps twenty rounds at potential enemy positions, each one of which had been pre-plotted to a predetermined point of the compass. Degrees and elevation were called out by the officer in charge, reading from a board held in one hand and lit by the pencil beam of his pocket flashlight in the other. His specifications were repeated in a gruff, bucolic voice by the gun aimer who hardly seemed to appreciate any need for urgency because his gestures were slow and deliberate.

Three shells were fired at one position, three at another, then back to the original target again; all barrels were aimed south, the direction from which the attack had come. Obviously, the rebels had come in from Sékou Touré's Guinea and the men worked to precision. The only sounds above the roar of the big guns and exploding shells were readings given by the officers and the responses of their men, navy fashion. They knew what they were after for they'd started firing before the third or fourth enemy salvo had hit the base.

In five minutes it was over. A cloud of white and orange smoke hung in the air and cordite burned our nostrils. Although the camp was blacked out, the scene was lit by a diffused light from an almost-full moon which had started moving toward its apogee late in the afternoon. Only later would an inky blackness descend, but by then the moon would have disappeared over the horizon.

After exchanging a few words, the officers ambled back to the mess in small groups, about twenty of them in all, their conversation animated. Others were elated because there hadn't been any casualties in the camp.

'The big guns that hit us were Russian,' the commandant told me after he'd assessed the damage. Then the mood dampened when word came from the gate that two civilians in a nearby *tabanca* – a native village alongside the camp – had been killed: their wooden shack had taken an oblique hit. There were seven wounded, including a woman who'd lost a leg and who was brought to the base to be airlifted the following morning. She died before dawn.

More serious, the commander commented as we settled back at our tables again, was that the guns were 122mm long-range Russian artillery and it wasn't the first time they'd struck so deep into the enclave. They'd originally been landed at Conakry, the strategic Guinean port city farther to the south then being used by Soviet vessels.

Nor was that the end of the story. The following morning two Soviet-supplied MiG-17 fighters flew low over Tite on their way to Bissau. The jets circled once, their pilots probably intent on seeing the extent of damage. The airmen, it was ascertained later, were Nigerian, though the planes were sometimes flown by Algerians based in Touré's Guinea and, as we were to discover years later, also by Soviet aviators.

PAIGC guerrillas did not strike at Tite again while I was there and it pleased everybody that the attack had borne indifferent results. Altogether twenty-four shells fell either on the camp or in the immediate vicinity, but most landed beyond the defence perimeter.

The garrison at Tite, I was told by the commanding officer, Lieutenant Colonel Baptista Lopes – another Mozambican veteran – worked to a routine that was invariably predetermined whenever an attack was launched, on average once a month: 'The first shells we fire from each of the large guns are geared to go when the gunner is given the signal by his officer. They're already in the breach and aimed at a specific target ... we just have to pull the trigger. When they've fired their first three shots we realign the sights and fire three more at a new target and so on.

'We go on until we think we've covered the full gambit. It's all quite simple, but the guerrillas never talk about casualties on their radios, so we don't know what effect we have.'

There were not many places in the surrounding jungle from which the insurgents might have been able launched their shells, the colonel affirmed. Each of the sites needed to be close to an access route so that the larger weapons could be manhandled into position. These locations had been pinpointed many times in the past and were designated responding targets on a chart in the operations room. 'They always seem to go back to the same positions ... in the morning we'll go and see.'

I queried how effective his howitzers were. Colonel Lopes reckoned that under the kind of circumstances he and his men faced, he couldn't think of anything better for countering this kind of irregular warfare: neither too large nor too small. In any event, the insurgents rarely attacked up close: they'd usually stalk up to within a few kilometres and let rip, and for this reason his calibres had proved adequate.

'Problem is, they still have to make their escape and the guns are bulky, so nothing is easy,' he added.

Seated around the mess table at lunch the following day, the colonel spoke about Bacar's role in the war. Captain João Bacar, he declared, indicating with a nod toward the Fula officer that was clearly deferential 'is part of what I like to call my First Team'. He explained that the black fighter was just then outlining a counter-attack plan to another officer, almost oblivious of the fact that he was the subject of discussion.

This African officer, explained Colonel Lopes, headed a recently established fighting unit known as the *comandos africanos*, an elite group of hand-picked black soldiers who, in the short time they'd operated as a team had distinguished themselves. In almost no time, their fighting and tactical prowess was almost as renowned throughout the colony as it had become in the Guinea Republic and Senegal. Its officers and men, the colonel continued, enjoyed an *élan* of their own which was not matched by any of the white or mixed-race metropolitan units active in the colony, 'and let's face it, that says a lot,' suggested the colonel who spoke excellent English because he'd been to school at Marist Brothers College in Johannesburg, South Africa.

Five other black commando officers were attached to the same mess. One of them, Lieutenant Jimenez, a Futa Fula like Bacar, sat opposite me and didn't have much to say. But he was a friendly soul, smiling and nodding each time our eyes met.

'A good fighter, that young Jimenez,' another of the officers acknowledged when he heard I was to go out with him on patrol in the morning.

'He is as unconventional in his tactics as he is in his dress. He prefers a light-collared woollen astrakhan to a cap and you'll never see him without his AK. That gun is his Excalibur; he took it from a man in the jungle after he had killed him with his knife.'

The other black officer present in the group was a huge friendly hulk of a man, *alferes* Tomaz, who though only recently commissioned as a second lieutenant, had come through a number of scrapes. Tomaz had been recommended for a decoration after a particularly weird attack in which one of his men was wounded and dazed by an enemy RPG-2 rocket. Instead of lying low and waiting for a medic or for the enemy to withdraw, the injured soldier staggered, shell-shocked and disoriented, through the trees with bullets popping all around him. Unbidden, Tomaz left the safety of his own position, sprinted through the jungle, picked the man up like a bag of string beans and returned him to his own group.

Tomaz was of Sierra Leonean stock and he was proud of it, he told me. Also, he spoke good English and ended up as something of an interlocutor between his commander and me while we were out on patrol. That said, he had no idea how or why his parents had come to Portuguese Guinea.

'It certainly wasn't for money,' was his comment. Tomaz also knew some Freetown Creole which his father had taught him, but for all that, this hulking black officer was proudly Portuguese and, like Bacar, willing to fight to uphold that identity which he considered sacred for reasons of his own.

It was an unrealistic and, some would say, unwise dedication which few Europeans or independent Africans understood. But, as I was to discover for myself, his approach reflected the same irrefutable quality that caused so many black men to fight valiantly for the British in Malaya and before that, for the French against General Vo Nguyen Giap in French Indochina and, more recently, with white South Africans in their own border wars. Also notable was the fact that at that time there were many more black soldiers in the Rhodesian security forces than whites, all actively combating African insurgents in the Zambezi Valley.

With his sheer size and physical strength, young Tomaz was probably bigger than Jimenez and Bacar together. He had the power, they'd joke, to lift them both – and perhaps another like them – and carry all three to the edge of the base. They hadn't tried it yet, Jimenez quipped in good English, because he reckoned it would have been too darned uncomfortable. Tomaz was known among his friends as the 'Gentle Giant', though he was considered frivolous by some of the more senior men.

Although a Muslim – 'but not a good son of the Prophet,' he'd argue – he did not hide the fact that he enjoyed his liquor. In contrast to Bacar and Jimenez, both of whom abstained, *alferes* Tomaz drank just about anything handed to him.

In the words of some of the men who shared the mess, Tomaz was 'quite a guy'. Those who served under him, even some troops who were considerably older, held him in deep respect, for in the brief period he'd been commissioned, he'd already proved himself a leader.

*   *   *

I'd arrived at Tite in the long-disputed Quinara region after returning to Bissau with an officer who'd introduced himself as Captain Alcada. I was offered another aide, but refused his services, at least for the time being.

I thought I had an adequate grip on the way was going war, I told Lieutenant Colonel Lemos Pires, my liaison officer in Bissau because in many respects it was similar to what was going on in Angola, a conflict I'd already visited several times. So, if he had no objections I'd prefer to make my own way about the country, I suggested. All I asked for was transport and, surprisingly, he agreed, though obviously I'd be passed from one military unit to another and radio messages would take care of the details. The units I'd be visiting obviously needed to know about a hack by the time I arrived.

In part, my gesture was self-serving. With another man as part of my retinue, I couldn't cadge lifts on the occasional chopper as easily as if I were alone. The same with small fixed-winged planes like the Dorniers. I had to constantly be on the move and on my own, I felt, was the obvious way of doing it. There would always be somebody waiting for me at whatever destination I chose and, clearly, I'd have to tell headquarters where I was heading each time.

At Tite, the regional headquarters, it was business from the start. Two Daimler armoured cars had greeted us on the runway when we arrived and our little party was taken past some pretty formidable defences to the mess.

Colonel Lopes had about 500 men under his command and his was an important zone in the middle of Balanta country; they were often in contact with 'hostile forces'. The Balantas – there were about 20,000 of them – were a cautious lot, neither *for* the enemy nor *against*. The position was best summed up by the officer who spoke to Jim Hoagland of *The Washington Post* who covered the war shortly before I'd arrived; he was speaking about Balanta country: 'There are villages where we go in the day and receive a very good welcome. At night, the terrorists receive a very good welcome, too.'

According to the Portuguese, the men of the Balanta tribe were a gregarious, generous lot. They were good workers, good drinkers and daring fighters with whichever side they chose to embrace. It was not surprising therefore that many PAIGC members were from this tribe, which was also scattered north of the Geba River. Obviously, there were a good many Balantas in the Portuguese Army.

As a people they enjoyed life and it showed. When they threw a party it went on hard, sometimes for more than a day. The Balantas also had some peculiar customs because just about every man, woman and child in the community was animist: they worshiped Ira, their god of fate. Essentially, the nucleus of their belief was that worn old maxim 'what will be, will be' and it was Ira that decided which way the cookie crumbled. It was up to the individual to appease his god in his or her own way in all day-to-day considerations and this was done by making regular offerings of rice or palm wine at a succession of tiny shrines in every Balanta *tabanca*.

It was interesting to observe that the authorities – the majority Roman Catholic – rarely attempted to tamper with these tenets which some regarded as idiosyncratic. Since most indigenous rituals fringed on voodoo or black magic – called juju throughout much of West Africa, with rites conducted by the local Balanta witchdoctor who charged a small fee for his services – it had long been evident that there were Balantas among the slaves who were shipped westward from Africa two or three centuries before.

Full-scale Balanta ceremonies are held at all stages, from birth, early childhood up to puberty and the circumcision stage. Boys as well as girls are circumcised at a certain age, usually about seven or eight and that tradition continues, even in today's world, much to the consternation of many world bodies, particularly where it affects females. The operation (to remove the foreskin) on boys is simple enough and usually performed by the resident medicine man with the help of a piece of broken glass, a razor blade or a jagged jam tin lid. It becomes far more complicated – and unsafe – with girls. The procedure – today the subject of a United Nations campaign to eradicate practices that are universally regarded as both inhuman and nefarious (except in much of primitive Africa) – is to 'surgically' remove the clitoris, almost always without an anaesthetic. In later life, adherents maintain, this is supposed to preclude coitus during intercourse which, Balanta men believe, results in their women remaining more faithful to them than would otherwise be the case, a spurious argument but then this is Africa.

It would all be nonsense if it were not so tragic because of the number of young girls who die as a result of post-clitoral excisions and many suffer in later life from a variety of psychological issues as a result of this trauma. It was also peculiar that at the time, most Portuguese were divided as to its purpose, especially since this was not an issue often raised in public. Since then, there have been a multitude of debates about the debilitating effects such abuse would have in later life, as the long-term effects, as we now know, are grave. In Nigeria's Calabar region, the suicide rate among those who have been subjected to a clitoridectomy are the highest in the nation and have been for a while now.

For the rest of it, the Balanta community appeared to live and work willingly enough under government control. At Tite they were administered by a rather obese, self-important district commissioner who ran local affairs from his office in the base. He struck me as distinctly pachydermic, in both senses. He, in turn, was aided by tribal leaders, most of whom were based on the nearby *aldeamentos* or *tabancas*, the former being the bringing together of rural communities into a protected village under one command, very much as the British had instituted during the Malayan Emergency. The idea was to avoid the guerrillas enjoying the support of unprotected communities in the bush. Tite had formerly been a regional capital and was still an important agricultural centre with rice paddies stretching away in all directions. Coming in from Bissau by air, we spotted paddies just about everywhere.

I should have arrived the week before, I was told. The previous weekend had been the annual crop festival known locally as the *Quesunde*, the most important of all Balanta feasts. Because of the war there had been no *Quesunde* for seven years and the colonel was proud that he'd been able to create a small chink in the enemy's grip.

It hadn't been all one-sided. PAIGC command in the area had served notice on tribal elders that they would sanction no festivities while the Portuguese ruled. Countering this move, General Spínola took the initiative and ordered Tite and other encampments to go ahead anyway. As a result, the first *Quesunde* festival for a long time went off like a charm. A lot of it had to do with the annual crop that had been the best for some years and also that things seemed to be improving all round, even the outcome of the war. Consequently, the message came through that there was no time like the present for a little frivolity. The guerrillas retaliated by warning that anyone taking part in the festival would be killed.

Threats notwithstanding, the feast went ahead anyway during the full-moon phase and about 15,000 Balanta men and women kicked up their heels for three days and nights. Significantly, the colonel commented afterward, there were no insurgent antics; the insurgents waited a week before they hit Tite, the attack I'd experienced.

The onslaught graphically illustrated a remark made to me by one of the officers at Tite, Major Art Valente. He spoke excellent English and served on and off as an interpreter for much of my stay in a region which stretched from the Atlantic to Fulacunda and Buba farther east. For every action made by the Portuguese, he said, the enemy reacted. If Spínola endorsed a fiesta, PAIGC demonstrated its disapproval by hurling shells. If Spínola happened to visit a region outside the capital, the guerrillas would retaliate, if only to make it known that they disapproved and were still active militarily.

Spínola did, visit Tite while I was in the country, the last event I covered before returning to Lisbon. In the presence of thousands of local tribesmen, the general handed out certificates and medals to local civic dignitaries who had stood fast with Portugal during difficult times. The guerrilla ambush in which Bacar was killed followed shortly afterward.

'It's really a point of honour as far as those bastards are concerned; they counter our every move,' Major Valente explained. 'And if they haven't the manpower available just then, they'll send for reinforcements and do it later.'

PAIGC attempts to stymie events at Tite reflected only one aspect of the kind of clandestine operations conducted by insurgent forces in this Portuguese colony. At the same time, it barely concealed the more salient characteristics of guerrilla strategy: that, apart from the military effort, there were also economic and political considerations that involved a huge measure of intimidation of the locals.

If someone was believed to be colluding with the government, at whatever level – attending a government clinic, visiting a relative in a military camp or perhaps paying a government tax – a brief Comintern-type show trial would be held in the village and that person would be executed. Kafka would have immediately recognized the pattern had he been able to visit the place. Unarmed civilians had long been a focus of PAIGC attrition. So had public services, lines of communication, transport, commerce, industry and agriculture – the warp and woof of everyday life in Portuguese Guinea and, to a lesser extent, in Angola and Mozambique.

Such operations as the rebels conducted against the hated colonials were directed – it was repeatedly claimed in their communiqués – to attain greater freedom of action with regard to the real objective: the destruction of the fabric of the nation. By then these same arguments were being bandied about in other guerrilla struggles in South East Asia, Indonesia, Tanzania, and later in southern Africa.

The bottom line about this always unconventional war was that, broadly speaking, guerrilla strategy in Portuguese Guinea was neither offensive nor defensive: it was principally evasive. For example, in areas where government control was relatively weak, the insurgents would go onto the offensive, but that rarely happened. It was more a case of seeking out a soft underbelly, which wasn't difficult in a country so grossly undeveloped. Elsewhere, evasion remained the keynote of PAIGC military strategy.

Chapter Five

Jungle Patrol

Going into battle, or the prospect of a contact with a bunch of trigger-happy, half-smashed, badly trained African soldiers, is not everybody's idea of fun. During the civil war in Sierra Leone, while attached to Neall Ellis's Air Wing, we shared Cotterill Barracks out Aberdeen way on the flank of Freetown's eastern suburbs with a ragtag bunch of government troops. Most were either drunk or drugged from breakfast on: that was when they got their first of three daily quarter-pint shots of local gin, a nauseating brew that we suspected included wood alcohol. It was seriously unwise to go into the bush with those lunatics: ADs (accidental discharges) involving their AKs happened with the kind of regularity that any professional soldier would find alarming.

Prior to that, when the mercenary group Executive Outcomes (EO) took the national army in hand, they would keep this ragtag local militia well away from any contact during skirmishes in the bush or in urban areas. Frankly, the rebels were not much better.

'It was healthy tactic keeping those buggers well back,' a former South African colonel explained. 'Bring them forward and there's a good chance some our guys will take a hit in the back.' Or, somebody else confided, the colonel might get fragged.

While some events during the course of the Sierra Leone war were extreme, these were not isolated events in the African context. After Mike Hoare's and Bob Denard's mercenaries left the Congo, the national army thrived on banditry, and then only when they were sober enough to achieve results.

Even today, the Nigerian Army in its war against the Boko Haram terror group is largely ineffective, though corruption within the ranks and at command level remains the dominant shortcoming. This was underscored by the Abuja regime hiring 75 mercenaries from South Africa in 2015 (the force included a modest air wing), their brief being to do what they could against the jihadists who seemed to most Nigerians to be almost fearless. Certainly, Boko Haram cadres were extremely well organized and not only put government units to flight several times but captured enormous supplies of weapons and armour, which sometimes included tanks and APCs. They actually overran Nigerian Army arms depots several times.

With the arrival of the South African mercenaries, all mostly ex-Special Forces – about a third of the group was white, the rest was black – it did not take this miniscule force very long to change everything. One of the operators explained the role of the South African mercenary role in Nigeria's regional war in the arid northeast of the country: 'We took to dominating the night ... when the sun set we went to war.' That tiny group of mercenaries was in Nigeria for barely six months, which was about how long it took for government paymasters to start fudging payments.

The freelance fighters headed home shortly afterward but in those few months these 'guns for hire' achieved more than the Nigerian Army had managed to do in the previous six years. As my former EO contact explained, 'We were a thoroughly integrated unit, black and white troops working together ... could never have done it without our African brothers.' Notably, the South African private military force went back to Nigeria for another stint against Boko Haram in 2018.

It was much the same in Portugal's wars in Africa in the late 1960s until the war ended in 1974.

Though it took a year or two for Lisbon to appreciate that well-disciplined black troops had a significant role to play in combating the guerrillas, the multiracial floodgates had opened a while back and though the formal transition took time, the Portuguese Army became a much more effective force, in Guinea especially, since the all-black *comandos africanos* were among the most aggressive combatants on the continent. No question: João Bacar's men were at the forefront of many daring escapades launched against the PAIGC.

The all-African patrol that I was embedded with – headed by one of the best black operational commanders – would take us fairly close to a proposed Portuguese Army camp site at Bissassema (not to be confused with Bissau's Bissalanca airport), an extension of Tite's operational area.

I was warned beforehand that the guerrillas were as committed to that corner of the country as were Spínola's men, so we would circle the zone and hope to make contact, which was basically what counterinsurgency was about in that theatre. We were told in our final briefing that ambushes would be set as and when necessary and that Bacar would be guided by local trackers or scouts who accompanied every patrol, mostly Balanta natives from the area.

Earlier, Lieutenant Jimenez had warned that we'd be out for two days, possibly three. His men were fit and this was what they did; consequently, they would be moving fast. He'd actually quizzed me about my ability to keep up because he'd warned that the schedule planned was unrelenting. I was also cautioned that this was a serious business: our adversaries were equally tough and fit, perhaps even more so because they didn't have the comfort of a local base to return to once they'd 'walked the beat'. We'd rest possibly once every four hours, he reckoned, but once on the track it was all systems go and would stay that way for as long as it took … we'd sleep in the wild and haul our food along with us.

'If things start to happen and it looks promising, we're going to go for it, even if it takes an extra day or two,' he quietly stated, and then posed the obvious: Did I still want to go?

I nodded, well aware that he didn't need a 'passenger', which was when he said something about bringing in a chopper to haul me out of the bush if things got really bad. 'Or possibly if you are wounded.'

I told him not to worry: I was more than eager and had been doing my 400 metres in the pool each day in recent months. Still, he was concerned and, as a concession, I'd be allowed two additional litre cans of water as opposed to the single water bottle issued to the rest of the squad and he'd carry them for me. They'd be refilled from streams along the way, which, for me, meant taking along a supply of water-purifying tablets. The rest of the group had been drinking unfiltered water all their lives and each time I filled my bottles and popped the pills, the procedure was viewed with quiet amusement by the rest of the team. Give them their dues: they never said a word.

It was clear that I faced a stiff challenge. Because of the heat, I was going through two pints of water before breakfast. It was worse in the jungle where conditions were stifling. I'd sometimes find myself dehydrated after an hour's march. More to the point, this operation would be more testing than anything I'd tackled so far – including a Kilimanjaro climb. Still, I was young – in my mid-thirties – and possibly a little overenthusiastic. And while everything pointed toward the impossible, I wasn't going to let up, especially since I might never get the opportunity again.

Much of the country we'd be passing through would be heavily overgrown terrain, some of it triple-canopied and interspersed by swampland or rice paddies. While there were paths galore, we'd avoid them if possible because of mines. Since I'd managed under similar conditions in some of the other African wars that included Biafra. Rhodesia, Angola and Mozambique, I felt confident.

Each member of the thirty-man patrol was handed his rations the evening before we left. This so-called 'rat-pack' consisted of a box that weighed perhaps two kilos and contained a tin of sardines, two small cans of sausages, chocolate milk in a carton together with a number of tubes containing a fruit concentrate, marmalade and butter. Bread was issued separately, just before we pulled out, with each man getting two loaves. According to the camp doctor that was 'more than enough for the time you'll be out'. The rations were expected to last a soldier two days. The package was standard issue and used throughout Portugal's African wars.

Saturday morning – the day we were scheduled to depart – came and went without the unit pulling out. It felt a bit of a bind, but we'd have to hold over for another twenty-four hours, the colonel explained. A patrol already out in the bush had made tenuous contact 'with something' and was in the process of deploying in a broad-phased encircling move. Since there was the possibility of an ambush later, some of the squad were made ready for a heli-airlift and they'd be deployed in a stop-gap role.

Later that morning, I gathered that the unit already out there was having a particularly tough time. They'd been moving at the double for many hours at a stretch and their food had run out, but the colonel responded with a comment about the men being accustomed to hardship: 'This is how we normally operate, the good with the bad.'

We left the camp in a long file before dawn the next morning. Tite lay somnolent and unprovoked against a dark jungle screen that crept up on all sides. Occasionally a figure moved about in the darkness as we passed and once or twice we could hear the guards as they shuffled at their posts. Nothing was clearly visible because the moon had long since faded.

Bacar took point and said little, except that I should stay near Lieutenant Jimenez who, for the first leg, would be my guide, or more appropriately, my mentor. In the end, young Jimenez was with me for the duration; I was manifestly his responsibility.

The two of us pulled aside to let the column pass and took up a position toward the rear. Tough, disciplined men shuffled past, their austere faces unsmiling, more because they were still heavy with sleep than because of what lay ahead.

Only Tomaz, the jaunty junior officer barely out of his teens could manage any humour at this ungodly hour; the hulking youngster loped past as if he were off to Sunday school. 'Hi,' he croaked cheerfully with a flash of white teeth. I don't know how he did it because he'd led the liquor stakes in the mess the night before. Tomaz patted his kit bag before hurrying forward with the rest: 'I'll have something for you here later,' he grinned, 'a small carafe of wine for our supper.' It was the last time he spoke normally: for the rest of the time we were on patrol we communicated in whispers.

The early morning was cool, but because of the humidity it started to become uncomfortable within an hour of leaving base. The men in the column hauled a strange assortment of weapons and quite a few carried something that I'd not previously spotted in any of Portugal's wars in Africa: a rifle grenade about twenty-five centimetres long that protruded from the tip of the rifle barrel. Its business end was oblong and distended around the middle, like a badly swollen finger that had been jammed in a door. It was deadly, I was assured by Jimenez. Known as the Instalaza, the weapon was of Spanish manufacture and design and had an effective range of about 400 metres. The anti-tank version could knock out an APC or an armoured car, but in Portuguese Guinea it was used mainly in an anti-personnel role. The colonel had explained earlier that the Instalaza was a small weapon which gave the infantryman a solid bit of muscle. Under attack, a dozen men using this kind of retaliation would be enough 'to send the enemy scurrying', he reckoned. Not only was it handier than the bulkier Chinese-supplied RPG-2 rocket in everyday use by the insurgents, it was a lot lighter and more portable.

Another piece of hardware in our ranks was a recoilless rifle adaptation which had been designed and built by Portuguese engineers around the 37mm French Matra aircraft rocket. Special firing tubes with dozens of ventilation holes it distantly resembled an improvised bazooka; its firing pin was activated by a small portable battery fixed to the barrel. Like the Instalaza, it packed an even more destructive AP punch. Each operator in the squad who carried the device had about a dozen rockets that he hauled around in special sleeves slung about his body. Two men on either side of him shared the load and carried some of the warheads. The downside was that if any of these projectiles took a hit, there would be quite a few more hurt among those nearest the initial casualty.

Three mortars tubes were included in our section, one each fore and aft and another toward the middle of the column where I eventually marched. Again, the two soldiers on either side of the tube had still more of these bombs strapped to their belts. The tubes were covered in swabs of sacking that prevented the mortars from chafing against anything metal.

All the men had two or three grenades suspended from their lapels or protruding from their top pockets. While grenade belts were provided, the men preferred it this way; it made for easier access in an emergency, they reckoned.

It took about an hour for the dawn to clear and by then we were well away from the camp, moving west at a steady pace. We would reach a position to the south of Bissassema and then swing north, Bacar had reckoned before we departed. After that, he'd told his troops at the pre-departure briefing, we'd double back on our tracks again.

The squad kept hard at it while still in open country, moving from one rice paddy to another. Then, as the first stretch of jungle loomed, everything went eerily still. Jimenez whispered that this was PAIGC country and from herein on we were on our own – as if we hadn't been since setting out.

It did not take long to appreciate that as an old hand at the game, Bacar tended to base a lot of what went on in the bush on past experience. Whenever our patrol approached a potential ambush site, he would detach a couple of men and send them forward, independent of the rest of us. Some of the heavier stuff would be brought ahead to offer fire support while others would deploy round our flanks.

Several times before, he'd explained during his briefing, he'd found that an enemy ambush group had withdrawn in the face of this encircling action.

At other times he would move his men carefully a kilometre or two down a jungle grove and then quickly double back. Once he deliberately flanked a huge patch of palms and bush, working us through an open paddy field, but out of any effective close-quarter contact range.

'We're waiting for them to present themselves,' he told me later when we stopped for a break. 'The PAIGC uses the Maoist principle of tactical retreat, kind of cat-and-mouse. They strike only when they're certain of being able to knock us hard, then they pull back ... this way we hope to draw them into making contact or perhaps making a mistake.'

Part of the problem facing Bacar and other Portuguese officers was that the enemy rarely stood and fought. They'd hit and run, or strike at a camp and melt away to avoid retaliation. It was a well-orchestrated and coordinated system: feint, strike, retreat or play possum in the tall grass or possibly come in from behind.

Earlier at the base, I'd been shown a set of PAIGC directives that had been captured. These warned that under normal circumstances any kind of serious contact with government forces was to be avoided. As one of the Portuguese officers explained, Cabral and deputies had been trained in the tradition of Mao and Giap: guile, stealth and better to live and fight another day.

We made our first long stop at noon for a meal. Some of the men ate in small groups between the trees while others stood guard out of sight in the jungle beyond. The procedure was reversed later in the day

When everyone was done we left, but I noticed immediately that our patrol had noticeably thinned. Following pre-arranged instructions, about a third of the group had disappeared into the jungle to set up an ambush position along the track along which we'd arrived.

'We're under no misconceptions that the enemy doesn't know we're here ... they've been conscious of that from the start ... they have their own intelligence system and it works well,' was Bacar's comment, laconic and to the point when I asked him. Though he spoke no English, his translator was an educated man and managed easily with the sometimes-difficult diction.

It was Bacar's system to always maintain momentum, to move from one area to another, sometimes across open country and paddies, the idea of not giving the enemy time to plan ahead. More often than not the guerrillas were able to observe the column as it moved and, as he told me, 'once we're spotted, they'll try to keep tabs on everything we do, day, night, every minute ... but only if we are lax and allow them to do it ... When they're about, you can be pretty certain that they're likely to do something. Then we act. That's why I have left some of the men behind. If they head on in – then slam! we'd have them, and of course we can follow up because we're in radio contact. Or we call in air support, which they don't have. That's it, in theory, anyway.'

We'd taken a short break about mid-morning and Bacar sent off some of his men to check a booby-trap position. As always, we'd been moving at a steady pace and must have covered at least fifteen kilometres by then over some fairly difficult terrain that included last-season's paddy fields half-filled with water. There had been a few aircraft passing across our line of vision for some of the time, followed by concentrated strafing and rocketing toward the southeast. The targets, toward Buba and Fulacunda, were visual, Bacar reckoned ... another patrol must have had a contact ... or have been ambushed.

Though our column would have been clearly visible to Portuguese Air Force pilots operating in the area, we were reasonably secure: our position was constantly relayed to base and, in turn, passed along to Bissau. Prior to emerging from any area that was foliaged, he'd call in.

During several trips across the country while in Portuguese Guinea, I often spotted patrols out in the bush and at first it amazed me that the operations centre could keep track of so many fragmentary groups in the field. But tracking systems employed by headquarters were pretty old hat by then, even if the Portuguese Army and PAIGC guerrillas wore a similar kind of camouflage. Still, accidents happened. More than once there had been men in the field who came under 'friendly fire'. Usually the air force was responsible and then only because procedures weren't properly followed. That, too, happens all too often in modern-day warfare.

In Bacar's words, the column's radio was the next best thing after his rat-pack. He liked to make contact with Tite every few hours, his radio operator always hugging his heels. The man lugged a bulky American-built Manpack transmitter which, he said, could reach Bissau.

There had never been a patrol in the past where he had not called for air strikes, especially if he saw a guerrilla group slipping away before his unit was able to make contact. But it did require a reasonable amount of precision on the part of the aviators because his men were never far behind.

The fact that a Bacar patrol had yet to be hit by the air force spoke volumes for this commando officer's control and direction, especially since his men could sometimes be as little as a couple of hundred metres behind the guerrillas while on the chase.

Bacar also liked to keep in ready radio contact with the extremities of his patrol. This could be difficult because the column was sometimes spread out over more than a kilometre. The officers used handsets, something that I hadn't seen Lisbon's fighters doing in Mozambique.

'They're handy when the other people are about,' Bacar said, stating the obvious.

Thanks to the radio equipment, orders were given quietly and competently, for sound travels far in this humid climate. Instructions were first relayed on the sets and then passed on down the line from man to man in whispers. There was rarely need for more.

It was noon before we made contact with the patrol waiting to be relieved. We met up with them as planned along an overgrown ridge of high ground that I'd observed from a distance earlier in the day. The feature was notable, because Portuguese Guinea must be one of the flattest countries in Africa without a single mountain, or anything even resembling one. Bacar had deliberately avoided taking the shortest route on the off chance that guerrillas lurking nearby might have been aware of the other group and possibly have set an ambush.

The patrol which preceded us into the jungle was led by two native Guineans, a Lieutenant Alphonse and a young *alferes*, like Tomaz, who called himself Manuel. Both men were dressed as we were, with one curious difference: both leaders wore gleaming black monkey skins over their heads, like large shiny bouffants that made them look more animal than man when glimpsed from a distance.

The troops with whom we made contact were exhausted. They had been out on their own for days and were tired, hungry and eager to get back to base. Through it all, they'd not had a single contact, though it had been close and Lieutenant Alphonse didn't elaborate. Because their stay had been longer than expected, Bacar had brought along a few supplies which were handed over with little ceremony. Like our own unit there were no white faces among them and they were surprised to see mine.

Words of parting were cursory: a hand raised and hardly a salute and then they were gone, very much as we'd arrived, melting silently away into the jungle. They were keen to get back to their families, Bacar said.

We passed several villages during the course of our trek. A few were abandoned, though there were those that thrived and were typical of *tabancas* throughout this part of West Africa, the majority comprising a medley of children, goats, chickens and a few skeletal hounds. Occasionally there would be a monkey at the end of a rope or a lonely parrot tied to a stalk. There'd always be women pounding corn or millet somewhere near the verge, usually within sight of a roadway or track and if something promised trouble, they'd be the first to sound a warning. Overall though, these villages were domestic and fairly secure, reflecting a deceptive, laid-back approach which had settled on this land wracked by almost a decade of war.

Jimenez and Tomaz took few chances in some of the more remote areas where loyalties followed traditional jungle law of not having to take chances if you didn't have to. Whenever we approached a *tabanca* that might not be familiar to the men, they'd go on ahead after leaving a detachment on the fringe for cover. It was the same pattern as before, since there had been quite a few PAIGC 'reception committees' in the past.

Only after friendly contact was made did we pass through. It was no secret that the enemy covered this ground as often as the Portuguese did – sometimes many times more – because their secure bases lay across the border. The civilians we encountered had long ago accepted the philosophy of extending a hand of friendship to all-comers, which was fundamental if you were going to survive in a region where political differences could be terminal.

Once we stopped at a village not far from Bissassema. It was late afternoon and we would have to grab a bite there before going on for the night. The place was evidently used by both forces as the locals welcomed us with a courtesy that was both friendly and guarded and Bacar accepted the gesture in good faith. It was an uneasy but pragmatic symbiosis in the fluctuating fortunes of war.

These people, Bacar felt, would eventually choose for themselves on which side their allegiance lay. If things continued as they were, he explained later, it wouldn't be with the PAIGC.

Our patrol mixed easily with the many of the local tribesmen and their families. They were accepted with amity; some even shared their food, as they probably would with the next PAIGC patrol that might arrive out of the murk. Our intrusion lasted barely an hour; Bacar handed over some money for the effort and we went on our way.

On how the enemy operated, the black commando officer was specific. The PAIGC, he said, followed classic communist insurgency doctrine on how relations with civilians were to be conducted. It was actually something that had been decided early on in the war when a rebel directorate declared that PAIGC forces were to be concerned with establishing and maintaining good relations with all the country people, whatever their political affiliations. PAIGC policy was based solely upon the identity of their aims, or so it was declared.

The people, said Amilcar Cabral, the rebel leader who had a penchant for echoing the words of his hero, the great Chinese leader, 'were to the army what water is to fish'. He'd included that maxim in the PAIGC code of honour which, like the Viet Cong, took the form of an oath. It declared that 'in contact with the people, each comrade would follow three fundamental recommendations: help the people, respect the people and defend the people'.

The village stop was perhaps the second or third time I'd been able to refill my water bottle that day. The locals provided fresh water from a pump set in the ground; take as much as we liked, they said. The troops could drink it as it came out of the ground but I filtered mine, an agonizing thirty-minute wait since I'd finished my original two cans some time before. I polished off those two and refilled them again.

We set our ambush for the night shortly after leaving the last *tabanca*. Bacar marched us due south just off to the side of a well-used track and we went on like this for about an hour. Abruptly, he left the route and doubled back toward the village, keeping close to bush cover. If the enemy was to follow us to the settlement that night, we'd have them.

African village noises – beautifully melodious and echoing across the terrain sometimes from far away – followed us into the night and then we turned again as the locals were preparing to settle in for the night. There was music, laughter, conversation and in the distance someone banged a gong. Another called on a bugle-like instrument which I had spotted earlier, fashioned from the horn of an antelope; it sounded a single discordant note which carried deep into the dark. I was to hear it afterward in Bissau; it boasted a resonance that couldn't be mistaken once you'd heard it the first time.

There were more noises somewhere toward the east. In the far distance the women of another *tabanca* were singing. This was Africa talking: melodious and harmonious in some regards, but guttural and bizarre in others, though not displeasing: simple, human sounds that signified age-old settlements in the bush.

Bacar carefully spread his men out a short distance off the track. We were about a kilometre from the village, with the troops on a small rise and roughly equidistant from each other. Riflemen were spaced between some of the others handling heavier weapons. Behind them were the rocket carriers and Instalazas. At the two extremes the light machine gunners were positioned, their muzzles trained in a wide arc to cover just about all points of the compass. Behind us he stationed his mortars. They were positioned in a clearing just beyond some low trees over which they would fire should it become necessary. The men worked on the elevation while Bacar directed elsewhere, but they also needed their backs covered and several pairs of men were detached from the main group.

It was indeed an ideal site for a contact. Once the deployment had been completed, he sent two of his troops into the jungle behind us in a bid to command the distant rear. They quickly disappeared into the bush where they would lie up, secreted for the rest of the night with only a small hand-held radio to make contact if things started to happen.

Bacar never had to explain the need for quiet. There were no half measures where security of the unit was concerned, he told me earlier and that applied as much to me as to them. No talking and certainly no smoking either.

The men settled down silently in groups, first one lot then another, leaving about a third of the patrol awake at any one time while some of the officers moved silently between their charges. Only Allah could help the man who snored, never mind caught sleeping on his watch. Bacar had his own brand of punishment and it was ruthless.

Then, with our heads low, it was an interminably long wait till dawn. Ants and mosquitoes – some as big as houseflies – as well as other jungle insects were resolute, with the crawlies particularly fierce, especially since we lay on bare ground with no netting. There was no question of using lotions or cream: the enemy would get a whiff of it long before the mosquitoes did.

Nobody thought of spiders or snakes, or even scorpions – of which I'd been told there were a lot – or if they did, they kept it to themselves. They were there, to be sure, but it's different when you're with a large group of men: it's usually the other guy who will get bitten or stung.

Earlier in the evening, before everybody had properly settled in, Tomaz had approached and produced his promised elixir: it was like magic. We each drank a little wine that night and had a couple more sips after it got light in the morning. I'd never handled liquor for breakfast before and it made a change, especially since I'd hardly slept. I suppose it was a good substitute for coffee under the circumstances, but I'd have preferred water. Mine was long gone.

The night was uneventful and I found it difficult to remain alert, even though we had the moon as company for many hours. Occasionally there'd be a rustle in the dark and one of the men would start, but there were few other distractions. All weapons were cocked and it stayed that way because any metallic click in open bush country can be heard over hundreds of metres by a trained ear. Bacar had imparted his basics well.

Shortly before midnight we heard a muffled explosion somewhere to the south. It came as a dull thump in the dark and Jimenez, who was dozing alongside me, raised his head but said nothing. I knew what was going through his mind. Someone had probably detonated a mine somewhere.

One of ours? Theirs?

Capitão Bacar's circuitous jungle safari followed a set pattern. The entire route had been detailed between him and the colonel before we left camp and they'd taken a while to settle the route, Bacar's boss wanting the men to go in one direction and Bacar in another. The black officer must have made good tactical sense because he'd won the day. The route had to be established beforehand for two reasons. The first was to advise air force command at Bissalanca so the men wouldn't be rocketed while out in the open. Second was the eternal threat of mines: Portuguese landmines that had been set along some of the routes we would traverse and quite a few tracks had been mined or booby-trapped by government forces.

But as we were all aware, two could play at that game, Bacar explained. To avoid injury to the civilian population, tribal leaders were ordered to keep their people within the bounds of the territory they normally frequented. They were familiar with the paths that led to the watering points or to the next village and so were his people; however, beyond those limits their safety could not be guaranteed, was the warning. Obviously, the Portuguese Army also had to observe these strictures because shortly before I arrived at Tite a soldier had his leg blown off trying to return to camp along a route which had been mined by Colonel Lopes's men. It was a vicious cycle.

We left our positions in the jungle at the first hint of a false dawn. Like an effulgent curtain, the glow crept slowly over our position, diffused and evocatively transient. One moment Africa is jet black and then, within minutes, trees suddenly begin to appear perhaps a hundred metres away, as if through a 1950s London smog. The men were up and on the move even before many of the birds had stirred, and like phantoms we slipped silently onto the track and were on our way again.

It came as a surprise to us all to learn later that morning that a PAIGC unit had set up an ambush only a short march from where we had lain, and on the very same track. But Bacar said nothing, nor did Jimenez; not then, anyway. Apparently, shortly after we'd left our ambush site, our trackers found the evidence. The unit had been large – two sub-groups – about sixty men in all, the scouts had estimated. Had contact been made it would have been tough. Like Bacar, they'd laid out an L-shaped position from which to attack and it might have been the luck of the draw that we stopped where we did in the dark. Or perhaps it was the PAIGC on whom the lady smiled that night, for this was the same bunch of guerrillas that ambushed Bacar seven days later.

*   *   *

I was to return to that country several times in the decades that followed. Twice I went in to make television documentaries of the nation, whose representatives now sit at the United Nations, with the nametag Guiné-Bissau before them on their desks. It had been an extremely difficult transition because the country has teetered from one violent insurrection to the next with tens of thousands of people killed.

They even murdered one of the presidents, former General Niño who was much respected during the bush war, but emerged as a brutal and sadistic tyrant when he came to power. They cut him into pieces and threw the detritus into the bush for predators to scavenge.

The lovely old town of Bissau is today a shadow of what it was when Lisbon prevailed. Disjointed and destitute beyond compare, even by contemporary African standards, I found its buildings battered or imploded as factions battled one another for control with heavy weapons in downtown areas. Many of the old historical buildings, some centuries old, had been defaced.

I wandered about the interior with my film crew for weeks, though not to Tite. That small community, some of the locals told me, had become one of the biggest 'killing fields' in all of Africa, with the rebels initially ranged against the same black troops who had once fought loyally for the Portuguese. Hostilities went on until they were all wiped out. One source said that in the end, anybody even vaguely linked to the *comandos africanos* had been cut down, some tortured. Not a single member of their families was spared, infants or otherwise. There was no word of young officers like Tomaz or Jimenez or even the monkey skin-clad Lieutenant Alphonse or the rest.

During the course of our peregrinations I also went north to Bigene, where the early Portuguese navigators landed on this stretch of coast five or so centuries before. The squat old fort still stands, quite tiny by today's standards and one can only speculate how the early visitors to Africa from

Europe survived. After independence it became a repository of some of the colonial relics that couldn't find a home elsewhere, including many of the bronze statues, everything stashed behind two-metre-thick granite walls, including one of Vasco da Gama, the first man to round the Cape on the sea route to India. With metal prices hitting the rafters, they have all probably been melted down and sold as scrap.

Half a kilometre away, along the narrow estuary that leads into the sparse interior, was one of the original gunboats used by the Portuguese Navy in the closing stages of this colonial war. Lying high and dry on the beach, the craft had been stripped, its aluminium plates long ago oxidized, in places right through. These were proud little fighting craft in their day and had been handed over intact to the new regime. Within a year, they'd been beached and left for scrap. Word had it that their powerful diesel engines were sold to a passing Chinese fishing boat and nobody knew who pocketed the money.

Chapter Six

The Country and the War

Portugal's African colonies have often been referred to as 'The Last Empire in Africa'. So it was, because Lisbon followed Germany, Italy, France, Britain, Belgium and Spain, all of whom had divested themselves of their colonial possessions in which some still like to refer to as 'The Dark Continent'.

Dark it certainly remains in places like the Congo, Central African Republic, Equatorial Guinea and Somalia. But for the majority of African states, despite malfunctioning administrations and corruption that can best be described as crippling, there are those who try to make a go of things in the tempestuous world in which the rest survive. Indeed, a few African states are even succeeding.

In the Portuguese epoch that ended with an army mutiny in 1974 not many critics made mention of Lisbon's troubled history in Africa which lasted almost five centuries. Nor, as imperial history went, that the Portuguese were first to enter the Africa milieu in any strength in the late 1400s and were the last to abandon these fiefs in 1974.

Lisbon's mariners – the intrepid few who originally discovered the trade route to spice-rich Asia by rounding the Cape of Good Hope to reach India and the East Indies – set the ball rolling. They established several stopping points along the African coast which were used to replenish their caravels on their inordinately long ocean hauls that could sometimes last two years. Some of these points on the map eventually became permanent settlements and the focal points of the colonies of Angola, Mozambique and Portuguese Guinea.[1]

---

1. Portugal's remarkable early maritime expeditions under the auspices of King Henry the Navigator were exceptional for the period and what was eventually achieved. There are several chapters detailing these adventures in my books *Portugal's Guerrilla Wars in Africa* (Helion) and *Shipwreck Stories by Al Venter and Friends* (Protea).

Obviously, the interior of these countries held great promise for both the foolish and the brave in search of fortune, especially since parts of West Africa were long known to be rich in gold, which was one of reasons why present-day Ghana was called the Gold Coast by early British explorers. So it was too, with much of this treasure being funnelled northward toward the great Islamic city of Timbuktu on the fringes of the great Sahara Desert. From there this bullion was sent in camel caravans – with thousands of these even-toed ungulates sometimes spread out over a distance of ten kilometres or more – to Egypt, Morocco and present-day Libya (once the domain of the great warrior Hannibal who taught the Roman legions a few lessons during the course of the Second Punic War).

But early arrivals in Angola and Portuguese Guinea, though quite enthusiastic in searching their own interiors for the source of this legendary wealth, found little of value except hardwoods and ivory and, of course, local African inhabitants. So it was that the slave trade became the basis of their economies and with time, horrific excesses – which resulted in the shipment of millions of Africans in bondage to the so-called New World on the far side of the Atlantic. That nefarious trade spread farther afield to territories where other European nations had gained footholds. Business was obviously good because the trade flourished and by the beginning of the nineteenth century, Portugal controlled outposts at six locations in Africa. One was the Cape Verde Islands, located about 1,200 kilometres west of Dakar, Senegal. The other was Bissau, at the very same little fort at Bigene that we visited.

In the modern period, no two conflicts, uprisings, insurgencies or revolutions are the same. There might be a lot of the same where violence is concerned, but each conflict has a specific identity of its own and what went on militarily in Portuguese Guinea was unique. Peculiarly, there are a few parallels of what took place in Portuguese Africa to what had happened before in British Malaya. London never referred to the communist uprising on that distant Asian peninsula as a war, but rather as an 'emergency'. To have declared a full-scale war (and it sometimes fringed on exactly that) would have had serious trade and insurance ramifications for both Lloyds of London, the insurers, as well as the colony. So like the Kikuyu-backed Mau Mau rebellion in Kenya, it was all distinctly downplayed. Yet the Malayan insurrection is worth looking at in relation to what took place later in Africa. The communists in Malaya (later Malaysia) declared war in June 1948 and from then on terrorism became part of daily life for the entire nation. Chinese and European estate-owners were murdered, rubber workers terrorized into cooperation, estates, mines and factories burned and rubber trees slashed. Something similar took place in Angola in 1961.

With arms caches stored by mainly Malayan Chinese dissidents during the war with Japan, coupled to wallops of experience of jungle life under adverse conditions, the communists aimed to set up 'liberated areas' as demanded by traditional Maoist strategy. The 'terrorists' as they were referred to by London and the country's media, hoped to create so much chaos that Britain would be forced to concede defeat and leave the field clear for the establishment of what the dissidents were already referring to as a 'people's democracy'.

Initially – as with Angola and Portuguese Guinea – everything seemed on their side. The Chinese-led insurgent force organized hit-and-run raids from camps hidden deep inside the jungle, always competently screened from the air with sentries routinely posted out to a kilometre or more and escape routes worked out in advance. Those leading the struggle controlled a corps of underground sympathizers – including ethnic Malayans – in the countryside who numbered tens of thousands. For its part, the Min Yuen, as the revolutionary structure was called, guaranteed the supply of money, food, intelligence and medicine.

In response to this assault, rubber estates, tin mines, police stations and isolated homes became armed camps surrounded by high wire fences and lit at night by searchlights. Planters and miners slept with revolvers under their pillows, with grenades on their bedside tables. They moved about in heavy vehicles converted into armoured trucks, complete with escorts. No stretch of road could be guaranteed safe from ambush, and railway travellers had to contend with derailment as a permanent hazard along isolated sections of track.

It is remarkable how similar the situation was to Angola after the first attacks took place in the northeast of the country adjacent to the Congo in 1961. Initial communist successes in Malaya did not give a true indication of their position. These were largely a result of the slow response by the British, caused by the death of the High Commissioner,

Sir Edward Gent, in an air crash over London soon after he had declared the Emergency. His successor, Sir Henry Gurney, was not appointed until September, and the real military response hardly got under way until General Sir Harold Briggs, a veteran of the Western Desert and Burma, arrived to direct operations in March 1950. It was only then – incorporating shades of General Spínola's personal experiences in Guinea – that the severe disadvantages under which the communists were operating began to emerge. There was no rush among local folk to suddenly join the Malayan Races' Liberation Army. Even the two and a half million Chinese in the country showed little interest in embracing the tough discipline and harsh life of the mainly Chinese guerrillas.

Insurgent strength in Malaya never much exceeded 10,000 and the Malayan guerrillas had little significant help from either the Soviet Union or China, something that was quite different when compared to the African wars. Throughout the 1950s these weaknesses became more and more obvious until the insurgency threat dissolved. There were reasons for their ultimate failure. The first was that there was no initial realization that to terrorize those British who remained behind – coupled to their economic organizations – was to bring untold hardship to the workers and peasants, in other words the 'masses' that the terrorists were trying to draw to their fold. According to the teachings of Mao, these were the same people whose hearts and minds they should have won.

Instead of ensuring overall sympathy, the most the rebels got from towns and villages was a grudging and often fearful level of cooperation. Their plans of establishing 'liberated areas' went by the board when estate owners failed to flee. In fact, the expatriates running Malaya's rubber estates and plantations, having survived a Japanese conflict, were hardly likely to succumb to pressure from a bunch of locals with guns. Instead, they rapidly set about building up their own defence forces and their workers remained remarkably loyal unless terrorized.

At the same time the war that evolved was a painfully slow progress. This can be judged by one of the operations launched by the British and detailed in one of the most illuminating publications on insurgency warfare during that period. It was written by T. N. Greene, an American officer serving with the US Marines and titled *The Guerrilla And How to Fight Him*.

Much of that work deals with Operation Nassau, which began in December 1954 and ended nine months later. It took place largely in the South Swamp of Kuala Langat, an area covering roughly 200 square kilometres and comprising dense jungle with trees reaching up to fifty metres where visibility on the ground was limited to perhaps thirty metres or less. After several assassinations, a British battalion was assigned to the area. Food control was achieved through a system of rationing, convoys, gate checks and searches. By the time full operations had been launched, all available British assets were brought to bear and included artillery and mortars. Royal Air Force planes began harassing attacks in South Swamp.

Originally, the plan was to bomb and shell the swamp day and night, the idea being that the insurgents would be driven out into ambushes. Instead, the rebels were well prepared to stay in hiding indefinitely. Food parties would occasionally emerge, but the civil population was too terrified to identify or report them. Consequently, plans were modified and harassing attacks were limited to the hours of darkness. Meantime, ambushes continued and patrolling inside the swamp was intensified. Operations of this nature continued for three months without results. Finally in late March, after almost two days of waiting, an ambush party succeeded in killing two in a group of eight terrorists. Thus it was that the first two red pins that signified confirmed kills appeared on the operations map and local morale was given a minor boost.

Another month passed before it was learned that terrorists were making a contact inside the swamp. One platoon established an ambush; a single rebel appeared and was killed. May passed without a contact, but in June, a chance meeting by a patrol accounted for one killed and one captured. A few days later, after four fruitless days, a platoon en route to camp accounted for two more. The third most important guerrilla leader in the area promptly surrendered. Under interrogation he disclosed that British food control was so effective that one of his men had been murdered in a quarrel over food.

By early July, two additional companies were assigned to the area and patrols and aerial attacks were intensified. Three terrorists surrendered, one of whom led a patrol to his leader's camp. As a consequence four insurgents, including their leader were killed. Other patrols accounted for four more and by the end of July, only twenty-three terrorists remained in the swamp with no food or communications with the outside world.

This essentially, was the nature of operations: 60,000 artillery shells, 30,000 rounds of mortar ammunition as well as 2,000 aircraft bombs for only thirty-five terrorists killed or captured. Each enemy represented 1,500 man-days of patrolling or in ambush, a hardly impressive tally for all that effort and expenditure. It seems absurd at the time that so much effort should have been expended to eliminate only thirty-five insurgents. Yet, as in Mozambique, the tally – though measured in terms of a couple here, one there and perhaps five somewhere else – grew steadily over the years, for such is the nature of the modern guerrilla struggle, even today.

In Portuguese Guinea, as we have already seen, hostilities were far more intense. It is worth noting that at the start of the Malayan Emergency, the rebels had less than 5,000 men under arms. Three years later this figure doubled and they were actively supported in the field by nearly 50,000 civilians, mostly locally resident Chinese. In contrast, government forces at the outset totalled about 21,000, an approximate ratio of five to one.

It is interesting that in later years the trend in Vietnam was exactly the reverse. Initially, according to Sir Robert Thompson, one of the foremost authorities on unconventional warfare in the twentieth century, the ratio in favour of the Saigon government was fifty to one. By 1963, in spite of some expansion of the government force and the formation of a full-time hamlet militia, the ratio had fallen to under twenty-five to one as a result of the Viet Cong having increased their strength to nearly 25,000. The ratio continued to drop in favour of the Viet Cong until the beginning of 1965 when it settled at around ten to one. It fell still further until American combat troops arrived but, even then, the tally never regained its original numerical advantage. Thus, says Sir Robert, the morale of the civilian population is of vital importance to the success of any counterinsurgency venture. He remarks:

A loss of morale in the civilian population is likely to occur quicker than in the government forces, where there is greater discipline. This particularly applies to the regular troops, who though they may become discouraged and less aggressive, will still remain capable of putting up a stiff fight if attacked or if attacking under favourable conditions.

The many abortive operations, however, in which they will have taken part begin to take their toll, and the confidence of the troops in those directing the war effort is not improved by information blurbs issued by the government claiming victories which in many instances the troops themselves know to be false.

A more dangerous loss of morale will occur in the police and other local territorial forces of a para-military nature which will have borne the brunt of the insurgents' advance into the populated areas. They will have suffered heavy casualties and a loss of weapons on an increasingly large scale; recruiting difficulties will have caused units to be greatly under strength; officer material will almost certainly be poor and inexperienced.

In Malaya, one of the vital aspects of the emergency was the ability of government forces to recover weapons from the Min Yuen. According to Sir Robert, successes in this regard contributed greatly to the eventual defeat of the insurgents.

When I first visited Portuguese Guinea in the early 1970s, about 40,000 people – of whom only a fraction were continental Portuguese – regarded Bissau as home. That was about double the number at the start of colonial hostilities in 1963. Even so, this island city – it is separated from the mainland by a shallow canal – remained a modest, listless place. In its heyday, Bissau could be regarded as typical of some of the Portuguese conurbations found a generation or two ago in some of the more remote regions of Lisbon's African empire.

With its central cathedral dominating the scene for miles around, pavement cafés, plump, dark-haired Iberian wives waving at one another and the ever-smiling bootblacks who pestered you long after you'd paid your single escudo and had your shoes polished with much ceremony and banter to a mirror-like glaze, it could easily be compared with Luso in eastern Angola or the city of Tete on the great Zambezi River in Mozambique.

As a freelance military correspondent, almost all these conurbations were integral to my assignments and while these were difficult times and I went down with malaria and half a dozen other tropical diseases including typhus, I enjoyed going there: it was better than working.

But Portuguese Guinea was different: it was always a tough call, even getting in and out of the country. As mentioned, I once tried to leave in a Portuguese Air Force DC-6 loaded with war wounded. In covering the war there – and it meant staying a while – I was never able to become acclimatized to the environment where the humidity was as intense as it might have been within the jungle walls that surrounded the city.

In its day, Bissau might have been an appealing kind of place if you had nothing else, though like Freetown, Libreville, Nigeria's Calabar and Lagos, Abidjan in the Ivory Coast and Accra farther down the coast, the early settlers suffering appalling losses from 'the fever'. Heaven knows why the early navigators settled on making Bissau – in its formative days little more than some houses adjoining a swamp – one of their major settlements along the African coast.

Even with its quaint, rambling waterfront and a setting that was quite attractive but different to anything in either Angola or Mozambique, nothing could have compensated for that oppressive, soporific climate where mosquitoes ruled. As someone was heard to comment while I was there, Bissau, while not colonial Portugal at its best, was nevertheless home to thousands of émigrés from the metropolis.

On the West Coast of Africa, the city that Bissau then most closely resembled might have been Bathurst – Banjul today – somnolent capital of the former British colony of Gambia, a couple of hundred miles up the coast. The same brand of enervating heat pervades the sticky atmosphere, which greets you like a steaming, clammy face-wrap the moment you step off the plane. The same lethargy seems to affect the townspeople. They amble about their business, dragging one foot reluctantly after the other, often preferring to rest a few moments in the shade before again crossing the street. Or they spend hours talking aimlessly about yesterday's weather, which is the same as today's and almost certainly tomorrow's. Only then might they get down to the grit of business, such as it is in these parts.

Graham Greene admirably captured that ambience in his novel *The Honorary Consul*, even though that plot was set in the French-speaking colony of Dahomey, or what we refer to today as Benin.

Greene got it right because he spent part of the Second World War in Freetown, the capital of Sierra Leone, working for British intelligence. There are other similarities with Greene's African milieu. Here and there among Bissau's multicoloured crowds, one could pick out traces of the same Creole and pidgin English spoken in Freetown and Banjul and sometimes echoed in the towns and countryside of Liberia. Also, there was movement between Gambia and Portuguese Guinea, limited to about one boat a week outside the rainy season.

Even within the context of architectural layout, the two were similar. Bissau's waterfront is spread-eagled across the lower or 'downtown' region. Strange picturesque hotels, looking more like mysterious mansions out of a novel set in the Carolinas, are tucked away behind clusters of mangrove and bougainvillea on what little higher ground there is on this rehabilitated marsh. The roads, too, all lead to one central square somewhere near the docks, a layout which appears to be the norm in West Africa. They call it the 'colonial touch' and, as some say, it is regarded as a legacy of some long-forgotten regiment of town planners in Paris and London, few of whom had ever seen Africa, much less lived there.

As far as Bissau's African community was concerned, it was in the vicinity of Pidjiguiti docks where most things happened. They still do today. Here, near the always-bustling, raucous market the town was once a rush of movement and activity from first to last light with black and white faces outnumbered by the tawny complexions of mulatto traders and fishermen that crowded ashore through a succession of well-guarded harbour gates. Photography in this area, the scene of a brutal 1959 massacre, was forbidden then and still is.

Though I'd been warned about the restriction beforehand I thought it a pity because the area was one of the most colourful anywhere along that stretch of coast. Here the mammies could be seen trading in thousands of items of everyday use: corn, cloth, flour, stinking dried fish which turns brown in the sun and is regarded as a West African gourmet's delight, birds' eggs, rusty tins of canned milk, vegetables and fuel and cooking oils in battered old paraffin tins. Inevitably, there was also palm wine, the universal beverage of choice among the natives of West Africa. In Bissau in the old days it came in a variety of bottles, flasks and casks, some of which looked as if they'd survived a century of use. Palm wine is a potent drink which starts to get lethal the longer it is left in the sun. Add some real hooch and it'll knock the unsuspecting imbiber flat after the second round, even though locals drink it by the pint, usually starting with the first meal of the day.

Bissau's other market area, closer to town, combined a succession of tiny kiosks with the local fresh meat, fish and vegetable store. Because of the heat and the lack of refrigeration, the wise like to shop early. Here too Fula and Hausa traders from the north matched wits with townsfolk selling everything from a pair of shoes to a witchdoctor's potion which would exorcize a wandering spirit in a *tabanca*.

What was not generally known – even to some of the Portuguese living there – was that this place had a few secrets of its own. In this large shaded building with half a dozen exits and entrances, one could buy genuine Ashanti gold dust and nuggets as well as diamonds brought across overland from Ghana and Sierra Leone. All were smuggled into the country, only who-knows-how if you consider that this land was totally surrounded by its enemies.

The gold and silver filigree work some of the craftspeople displayed behind glass-covered cabinets and trays was intricate and sometimes reflected superb craftsmanship. A lot of it was reminiscent of similar items which were once on sale in Zanzibar, but that was before Beijing helped drive out many of the traditional Arab gold- and silversmiths.

And for those who wanted them, there were ebony carvings such as one today finds at every airport along the West Coast of Africa. The bulk of it was meretricious and stereotyped, but the wood had been well worked and sometimes it was possible to find a good piece at a reasonable price. So too was the odd chunk of carved ivory, though Bissau then boasted nothing as outstanding as the works of art one sees today in Abidjan, or farther east in the markets of Douala and Yaoundé in the Cameroon Republic.

The bartering that went on for all these goods was a constant jumble of noise and dialects, interspersed here and there by the colloquial Portuguese of young metropolitan housewives – mostly espoused to local traders – who arrived to do the morning shopping. Military wives, in contrast, rarely went to the market themselves; few of the women who came out to Africa to be with their men in uniform had fewer than two servants.

Another resonance, sometimes an echo, which one picked up clearly when walking through the downtown area was the unmistakeable cry of the Quran being chanted in Arabic by some faraway imam. The high-pitched, ascetic voice always came over in fits and starts as one of Cairo's broadcasting stations or Radio Algiers faded and then picked up again. The lips of the devout hardly missed a verse as they followed the chants in silent, abstract mimes, the presence of Islam as distinct as in the great cities of the Middle East.

It is even more so today, now that Lisbon's influence has been whittled away to perhaps the use of a common language and some of the dishes that will always remain popular. One felt at the time that the Muslim presence was perhaps a little incongruous in this staunchly Catholic land, but then the Portuguese have almost always been more tolerant of others' beliefs than their European neighbours. In truth, Lisbon's hierarchy was trying to learn to live with other people's creeds once Spain's Inquisition was over its worst.

A stone's throw from the harbour still lies the original old fort built centuries ago by the descendants of the legendary globe-trotting navigators. The building, dilapidated today and scarred by half a dozen coups and attempted army mutinies, remains a legacy of that period when Lisbon's kings finally decided to 'pacify' this coast in a bid to capture a portion of the meandering Sahara trade from the north ... and the slave trade. Granite-walled, low-lying and speckled with cannon running the gamut of almost five centuries of Portuguese ordnance, this was General António de Spínola's military headquarters while the war raged in the interior. He rarely used it, preferring to work at his desk in the front room of the far more stately governor's residence. I recall being told that the general would regularly join his staff officers shortly after seven each evening for a run-through of the day's events in the castle's map-lined conference room.

Chapter Seven

A Luta Continua!

The rewards of guerrilla warfare are devious. For two days I trundled about the southern jungles of Portuguese Guinea looking for insurgents with the *comandos africanos* and found nothing. A week later I was taken on a brief waterborne patrol in a convoy of high-speed rubber boats by a party of marines based at Bigene, a few kilometres from Farim in the north where the war was at its worst. We had been on the water barely ten minutes when a fusillade of shots staccatoed across the water in our direction from a nearby jungle thicket.

The soldiers on the boat – three of them, armed with a variety of weapons including two light machine guns – had been kind of expecting this; in fact they had warned me beforehand that the area was hot – so they retaliated, as did those in the two other boats following close behind us. For a couple of minutes the riverside bush was scoured by a steady stream of tracer bullets and for good measure the centre boat peppered the jungle with a heavy American bazooka. We chose the easy option and did not stick around to see whether any of this had had an effect.

The three rubber boats had been moving fast when the first shots sounded, but instead of slowing down and allowing for better accuracy, all three craft gunned their engines toward the opposite bank while the men on board let go with everything they had. We shot across the water at a dizzy pace, leaving a foaming three-foot crest of churned-up water in our wake. The young officer in charge of the patrol, marine *Tenente* Tony Verela, reckoned later that speed was his best defence, adding that he could not afford to give the enemy an easy target by further exposing the boats on the open water. Having a grandstand view of the goings-on, it was obvious that it took a considerable amount of skill for the man with the bazooka in the boat nearest us to fire accurately. Not only did he have to counter the movement of his fast-moving rubber duck but he also had to counter the boat's violent surging as it crossed our wake.

Certainly these youthful *fuzileiros* had offered the enemy a choice target but had they been better trained, they might have caused damage. But they did not, and though there were about ten of us exposed to enemy fire, nobody was wounded. It was interesting I discovered later, that while the revolutionaries seemed ready to tackle smaller patrol boats, they rarely fired on the larger navy gunboats which patrolled the upper reaches of the Cacheu River, probably because the naval craft were armed with batteries of 40mm rockets which could demolish a village in minutes if necessary.

Talking about the events of the morning with Verela in the mess later, he was sceptical about the ability of the PAIGC to conduct an effective insurgency. For a start, he declared, their accuracy was rarely what it should have been, especially since they were firing at us from the shore, a stable platform. He had operated on the river for almost two years and although he made contact with the enemy fairly regularly – serious contact in which shots were exchanged – only two of the 200 men at the marine base had been killed on the river in that time, though he conceded that there had been more wounded, some seriously.

Land operations, he elaborated, were different. There were more Portuguese soldiers killed in occasional ambushes laid by the enemy and by landmines. But still, he averred, Cabral's men had been given many opportunities of inflicting major damage and they rarely took the initiative.

'The first shots are usually accurate ... that's when most of the damage is done because they have the advantage of time to aim their initial bursts,' he told me, but after that their fire was invariably erratic, almost as if the guerrillas closed their eyes and fired at random. 'Of course we are very happy that this is so because then we are able to retaliate more effectively; but remember too, that this is a war and things happen.'

Lieutenant Verela was of the opinion that had his assailants been of the calibre of the Viet Cong, Portuguese losses would have been much more severe. He elaborated by stating that some of the insurgents were very well-trained and would distinguish themselves in any man's army, but they were in the minority. The majority seemed to lack that little something extra which it took to turn a successful attack into a rout when the opportunity presented itself.

Verela was also the first to admit that Portuguese troops – but not his own *fuzileiros* who were all trained as Special Forces – could sometimes be as lackadaisical as the enemy. 'Trouble is,' he conceded, 'with the majority of conscripts, their hearts are not into what is going on here in this African hell-hole ... and it gets worse the longer you are stuck here.' He continued: 'If you consider that this war has been on the go for almost ten years and during that time the enemy has never succeeded in overrunning one of our camps, you will understand what I mean. Often some of the outlying positions are manned by only eight or a dozen men at a time. Yet, the PAIGC have never once succeeded in dislodging any of our units from a fortified or static position.'

Yes, he added, the Portuguese Army had abandoned camps of their own volition: Beli, in the east as well as Cacocoa, and Sanchonha, military strongpoints that Bissau considered either too remote or impractical to maintain effectively, and also some of the offshore islands. 'But when our people moved,' he declared, 'it was organized and not at all disruptive. We were never driven out or forced to abandon any one of our positions.'

There were four marine bases in Portuguese Guinea like the one at Bigene. Another was at Buba on the river of the same name toward the east of Tite, with two more along the coast.

Most of the operations were undertaken at night with priority given to intercepting enemy pirogues which tried to cross the waterways with supplies and men while they were heading, always without lights, for the war zones. Of the 200 men under his command, Verela said, about sixty were operational at any one time, some on the river and still more on land patrols in adjacent areas. His men – all professional career-orientated troops – were highly trained and skilled in the art of anti-insurgency warfare. He considered them the metropolitan versions of Bacar's black commandos. Certainly, he commented optimistically, his unit had been every bit as successful as the *comandos africanos*.

Over the previous four months, prior to my arrival only a couple of his men had been wounded, compared with ten terrorists killed in confirmed body counts. There may have been more, he said, because it was one of the enemy's priorities that their wounded and dead be removed from the scene of a battle to avoid giving the Portuguese people any kind of psychological advantage.

'Obviously, due to circumstances this is not always possible. During the period under review that we're talking about a couple of rebels had been captured, as well as a handful of their civilian helpers, all taken from canoes with war supplies on them.'

This bunch had apparently come through from enemy bases in Senegal.

Other details provided by Lieutenant Verela were that he and his men operated a series of basic search-and-destroy systems on their daily river patrols and sometimes into open water at the estuary. His boats customarily went out in pairs during the late afternoon, though never at fixed times and sometimes, to confuse those watching, after dark.

Once night had blanketed the jungle, the engines were cut and the boats were either rowed upstream or floated downstream on the current. The region is tidal for about eighty kilometres inland and the men made liberal use of ebb and flow.

'Obviously, we all prefer to work in the dark because we are not as easily spotted. But then they have that advantage too, but on the water, where boats are easily picked up.' Asked whether his unit had been issued with night vision equipment, he was evasive, but was adamant that the PAIGC did not yet have that kind of advantage.

'If they had, our losses would have been much more severe, so we can discount that theory,' he stated, though he did subsequently confide that in training back home he had been able to handle something similar to the Soviet 1PNxx, which were labelled 'night sights'.

'It is always after dark that most of the enemy matériel is taken across the water by insurgent units, though they have operated in the day in the past. They lie in wait in their shallow boats until our patrols have passed and when they think the coast is clear they shoot across and hope like hell they're not spotted from the air.'

Life at the marine base at Bigene was not unpleasant. The river regions were cooler than the dry interior of the north and east. The broad river waters and surrounding jungles tended to provide their own diversions, including fishing for marlin and shark and even duck hunting during off-hour periods. The record marlin taken at the base, a day's river journey inland from the Atlantic, was landed a month before I arrived by a young medical orderly who had spent most of his savings at the only sports shop in Bissau. It tipped the scales at over 300 kilos and took him two hours of hard fighting to land. Only once had his line snarled among some mangroves and he was helped by a rubber boat to untangle it. When he brought the huge fish ashore hundreds of his own men as well as army troops and locals were there to witness the occasion: justifiably, he was a proud man.

Barely a day went by, I was able to observe, without one of the boats bringing back something for the pot. The day after our little fracas, I went out once more and three ducks were shot a kilometre from the base, picked off on the wing with army service rifles; clearly, these marines were crack shots.

Occasionally they would bag a crocodile for no other purpose than to rid the region of these pests which had claimed many lives in the past, particularly among the children who swam daily in the murky waters. The Portuguese officer reckoned he was certain some were taken by sharks which were fairly common so far upstream, and that those deaths were attributed to crocs. As a consequence, his men were not encouraged to swim in the river. Instead, the lieutenant had had a hand in excavating a large pool near the water's edge which was regularly filled by a pump.

The officers' mess at the marine base was an old administrative building, probably belonging to the original *chefe do posto*, situated about halfway between the river and the airstrip. About a dozen officers were billeted there and the atmosphere was casual and uncomplicated by the rigours of living among their men, as was the case in other camps in the country.

The walls, as might have been expected, were decorated by the latest full-colour *Playboy* foldouts and similar objects of interest. On the door of the officers' mess was something I had not seen elsewhere in Portugal's African wars: a large poster laying out point-for- point in Portuguese, the United Nations Declaration of Human Rights. A photo of the manacled legs of a black man adorned the top of the poster, providing sombre reality to the scene as we sipped our beers on the open, colonial-style verandah that one still finds in many former Portuguese possessions in Africa. Asked about it, Verela responded by saying it helped to keep things in perspective 'in this often terrible struggle.'

I went by air from Bigene to Teixeiro Pinto, one of the large new so-called 'liberated zones' north of Bissau: by implication, there was no longer an overt enemy presence in the region. On my way to the marine base a few days before, I had passed over the region and had spotted dozens of trucks on the road linking the two centres. The vehicles travelled independently of one another and not in convoy as was the case in other areas, indicating a marked degree of licence in a part of Portuguese Guinea that only three years before had been a guerrilla rallying point.

Waiting at the airstrip was Major Luis Inocentes, a jovial, friendly-faced career officer who had spent three years as Portuguese military attaché in Salisbury, Rhodesia, during the frantic post-UDI period after 1965. His English was fluent, his forte golf, though he had been unable to play for a year as there was no course in Bissau and was certain that lack of practice would adversely affect his handicap of 10. Major Inocentes had spent 28 years of his life in Africa; first in Angola, then Mozambique and followed by Rhodesia.

'Now I'm in this 'hell-hole.'

His parents were still in Lourenço Marques, while his wife and three children waited for him in Lisbon. His only contact with his southern African period of service was a huge Rhodesian ridgeback which followed him around the camp. Its name was Big Boy – in its original English – and had been presented to the major by the South African military attaché in Salisbury.

Part of the major's schooling had been completed in the Mozambican capital. After that he had attended the University of Lisbon at roughly the same time that Cabral and the other African guerrilla leaders were either studying or incarcerated there. The major had learned one trait from the Africans among whom he had lived and worked while living in southern Africa and that was the many advantages of keeping himself in good physical trim. He did not smoke and drank frugally, if only to be sociable. Although well into his forties, he would don a pair of running shorts each day and jog for an hour along what passed for roads around Teixeiro Pinto, always with Big Boy in attendance. Did he not fear being attacked by guerrillas who might have infiltrated that far south? His answer was direct. 'I'm in charge of the military side of things in this area and if any of them have got through, I would be the first to know. Anyway,' he joked, 'I can run pretty damn fast and they've first got to catch me.' We laughed.

Teixeiro Pinto, the main base in the region and home to Major Inocentes, is the headquarters centre of the Cacheu Zone, a region with about 11,000 inhabitants, mainly of the Manjaco tribe. These are a people who are traditionally orderly and passive and who, by the time I arrived had not thrown in their lot with either the Portuguese or the PAIGC.

There was also a fair sprinkling of expatriate Gambians who came from Bathurst to trade in the region. Many of the locals consequently understood the Gambian lingua franca, pidgin English as well as native Creole.

The senior commander of the region, a stocky bald-headed veteran of the Lisbon Artillery School, Colonel Freitas Doamarel, had roughly 2,000 men deployed in three battalions throughout the region, which included a commando and a marine unit.

A priority project during the preceding year had been the tarring of all roads in the area. The target set was about 150 kilometres by the end of 1972, which included all roads linking important centres as well as the main highway to Bissau. Of that almost two-thirds had been metalled by the time I visited the headquarters.

Notably, the road surfacing programme had cut down fatalities to a minimum and mine casualties were limited to very occasional anti-personnel bombs placed in some of the more remote regions and which claimed almost as many civilians as they did Portuguese troops.

Two other important settlements dotted the region, Bula and Pelundo, both to the east of Teixeiro Pinto. Apart from these, General de Spínola had embarked on an ambitious programme of establishing more than twenty other settlements or civilian *reordamentos* where houses were being built by the army, all to be completely independent of army control.

Notably, the civilian population was not armed because the Manjaco inhabitants preferred not to tempt the fate of their jungle gods, which included the sun, the soil and the river.

Major Inocentes later gave me a run-down on military conditions in the zone. In the two years since January 1969 that the colonel had been in command, there had been a number of actions with Cabral's forces. During those twenty-four months altogether forty Portuguese soldiers had been killed in the Teixeiro Pinto zone and 330 had received non-fatal wounds. Most of these incidents resulted in contact, one way or another with the enemy, including ambushes and mines. He estimated that about 50 per cent of the total casualties in his region were as result of accidents and roughly 10 per cent caused by mines, though that threat had diminished now that the road-tarring project was nearing completion.

'Also, we leave it to the people to compare what they are getting from us to what they might expect the PAIGC to offer should they come to power,' he commented briefly.

What started to emerge after the first week or two in Portuguese Guinea was that while there was a good deal of contact between opposing forces, the war had ground into a slow, dreary struggle for control of the populace. There were enough short, sharp encounters, but little of the kind of activity then being experienced by the Americans in Vietnam. To some, it had become a phoney war that bored, which was one of the reasons why so many of the men on the ground volunteered for service in Special Forces like the commandos and *fuzileiros*: both units always went where there was action.

The men at Sare Bacar for instance, thought highly of the *comandos africanos* whose combatants were regarded as exemplary and dedicated fighters, though not everybody was certain of their motivation. They had seen Bacar's men in action a few months previously when he had been stationed at Farim, to the south, where the authorities were building the road north.

Speaking about the black fighters, the bald-headed officer, Captain Matos, maintained that Portugal should be thankful that they were there. 'We have seen them in action,' he said, 'and they can smell a man's tobacco breath at a hundred metres. If they spot a footprint in the sand they can tell us whether it is one of ours or that of the enemy, and how long since the person who made it has passed along that way.'

He reckoned that they would follow a group for two days, whistle like birds when there was an alarm and make the bush sounds of a dozen animals to keep track of developments between the two extremities of the patrol. 'They actually read the language of the jungle like you and I read a newspaper,' were his words.

I had seen some of this for myself while on patrol with Bacar, in a region where every shadow that moves and every rustle of wind in a nearby thicket betrays the thoughts of yourself and those about you, but the region in which this white officer operated was very different: it was almost semi-desert in the dry season.

Captain Matos was responsible for an area of roughly 300 square kilometres stretching for some distance along the Senegalese frontier. Apart from his 165-man garrison, he had two civilian militia groups – all black – under his command. His troops were divided into four combat groups, of which two were on patrol outside the main Sare Bacar base camp at any given time. The remaining patrols either rested or carried out guard duties.

Enemy attacks, while not rare, were sporadic, composed largely of mortar or rocket fire and usually centred on the camp itself. Most of the munitions fired from Senegal were Chinese (as opposed to Soviet hardware in the Republic of Guinea). The former were predominantly 120mm Chinese rockets and mortars that were rarely fired from beyond six or eight kilometres away, well inside Senegalese territory.

Matos commented: 'Their aim is putrid. You can see the tops of the buildings here from five kilometres away in this flat country and they haven't hit them yet, in ten years of war.'

He reckoned the calibre of the guerrillas in the north compared unfavourably with General Niño's forces on the Guinea-Conakry frontier. 'They're not as disciplined as the southern rebels and hardly ever take the initiative. A close-up attack with bazookas and AKs is unknown, at least while I've held this command. In fact, these northern guerrillas rarely actually cross the unmarked frontier and seem to prefer to fire at our camps from a distance or possibly lay booby traps along bush paths in the hope that someone will step on them.'

Still, he had to keep his men on their toes for any eventuality and that meant maintaining strict discipline, either when patrolling on foot or moving about in vehicles.

It appeared to be the same farther west at Cuntima, just south of another guerrilla base in Senegal at Faquina. In my view, from what I could observe across the way was that the only difference between the two camps was the number of vultures I saw flying around Cuntima and the dozens of scraggly bush paths leading away into the wilderness in all directions. At least that was the way it looked from the air. Like Sare Bacar, Cuntima was only a kilometre from President Leopold Senghor's border.

At both Sare Bacar and Cuntima the commanding officers told me, that as in the south around Cameconda and Guilege, most of the guerrillas who passed through their regions were more interested in getting through to the interior around Mansoa and Mansaba where there was a road tarring project in operation. Like Tite, this was also Balanta country, though there were Felupe tribesmen spread out along the border regions who did not tolerate any insurgent presence.[1] Of interest here is that Felupe militants often attacked PAIGC patrols with guns given to them by the Portuguese, but more often with their own primitive bows and arrows. Officers who had made contact with Felupe elders said that what had prompted that reaction was the fear among these Africans that guerrilla activities would eventually deprive them of Portuguese medical facilities if the authorities lost control.[2]

For this reason there was little serious action in the border zones. Tribesmen living in southern Senegal also resented guerrilla attacks along the border region, for they also made liberal use of free medical aid offered by Lisbon. Medical aid to potential enemies was regarded by the Portuguese to be of good propaganda value and they helped where they could.

Although the PAIGC was the controlling insurgent force in most of these areas, troops on the northern border of the enclave also had to contend with FLING (Frente de Luta pela Independência Nacional da Guiné) which was headquartered at Dakar. The difference between the two basically was that Cabral's revolutionary group was Marxist while the rebels operating from Senegal were pro–West.

FLING was comprised of seven breakaway liberation groups which operate out of the Senegalese capital, the oldest and largest of these the

---

1. There were numerous frontal assaults made by the guerrillas immediately after the author's last visit to the territory. These included mass attacks on Sare Bacar, Cameconde, Gadamael, Farim, Bambadinca in the central region and Cuntima, most of which took place in the latter half of 1972. The insurgents suffered heavy losses and continued to do so until the 1974 ceasefire.
2. Those fears were well grounded. After Lisbon had thrown in the towel and pulled its forces out of Africa, the rebel command went on to murder all tribal leaders who had sought succour with the government. Felupe families suffered similar fates, with the result that entire communities sought refuge in Senegal and at one stage the Senegalese Army was called out to prevent further massacres.

MLG (Movimento de Libertacao da Guine) formed in 1960 by a veteran anti-Portuguese campaigner, Francois (Francis) Mendy Kankoila, a Manjaco exile who lived most of his adult life in Senegal.

Another group was the URGP (Union des Resortisants de la Guinee Portuguaise) led by Benjamin Pinto-Bull, brother of Jaime who was killed in a 1970 helicopter crash. It is noteworthy that Benjamin and Jaime, long at political loggerheads, were the sons of an Englishman who had married a local African girl. They were well educated and were easily assimilated into Bissau's upper-crust Portuguese society.

FLING tended to draw most of its support from alienated Fulas, Manjacos, Mandingas and Papeis. There were also some Balantas, though this tribe maintained strong links with the PAIGC hierarchy in Conakry, obviously for good reason.

Captain Matos did mention that FLING, like the PAIGC, was partly hamstrung by the inability to establish forward bases in the arid north. They had mobile forward camps between Farim and Mansao but nothing permanent, very much as was expounded by Guevara, and for this reason there was a steady two-way traffic across the border. He was also convinced that although the guerrillas had much tactical mobility and flexibility of employment, the absence of forward bases was also their greatest weakness.

Insurgent logistics, except in border areas, he explained, had difficulty supporting sustained combat operations and the measure of Portugal's success in building her roads and villages in spite of substantial guerrilla reaction was underscored by the lack of these guerrilla facilities. His and other commanders' personal successes in managing to cut the flow in and out of the country to a minimum also contributed to the Portuguese war effort.

South of Sare Bacar, in the direction of Bafata, I was given the opportunity of visiting one of General Spínola's 'self-defence' villages. It lay about five kilometres off the main road in an area typical of most of the eastern portion of the enclave: undulating savannah country that had once supported massive herds of elephant, giraffe and antelope. There is little game left because wild animals had given way to the Fula and Mandinga cattle herds long before the colonial interregnum had suspended the natural course of history in these parts.

So it was that I arrived at one of the small shops at Sare Bacar whose drab walls were affixed with several posters that portrayed a simple message: *Juntos Venceremos*: 'Together we will win'. Underneath that large inscription a black hand clasped that of a white. An arid mile away, fringed with stumps of fat, grey-trunked baobabs and misshapen thorn bushes was the Senegalese border.

A new metalled highway ended abruptly at a sign attached to a chain stretched across the road. It read: 'Senegal'.

'Beyond is the enemy,' remarked the bald-headed, aquiline-featured Portuguese who had earlier introduced himself as Captain Manuel Medina Matos, also from Lourenço Marques – one of the surprising number of officers from Mozambique that I met in Portuguese Guinea. The tough, wiry captain, dressed in a faded green camouflage uniform which looked as if it had been through all three of Portugal's African wars, said there was a brace of enemy machine guns a few hundred metres into Senegalese territory, running parallel with the frontier. His intelligence network had informed him of the positions. They had also told him that the guns were placed in a defensive deployment 'just in case our troops decide to wander about too far into Senghor's country.'

The wind was blowing from the south and with a wicked glint in his eye the captain pulled out a box of matches and set a few tufts of grass alight. He explained that the fire would carry through into Senegal and help to clear the bush and perhaps force the machine gunners to evacuate their posts.

'We often play games like this with each other. When the wind blows from the north they try and set us alight. They almost succeeded once and that is why we have cleared the area around the camp for hundreds of metres.'

Camp Sare Bacar, about a kilometre from the village, was not like most of the other military concentrations I had seen elsewhere in the country. It was a hexagon, about ninety metres to a side, with observation posts at three of the points nearest the border. Not a tree sheltered the 165 men who lived in this bare and desolate corner of the country, nor a blade of grass poked its way through the loose red soil which seemed to creep in everywhere as the light wind churned our steps into dust and followed our jeep in thick vermilion layers three metres high. Sare Bacar was a lonely outpost in Europe's most enduring African empire.

Captain Matos explained that the men with him had been there a year and had another nine months to go. During their twenty-one-month sojourn at Sare Bacar the officers – but not the men – were allowed to visit Bissau every six months or so for a few days' break. In a way, he said, the African draftees were the lucky ones. Had these troops not been posted overseas their period of conscription would have been extended by another year.

All the same, I observed, it was an isolated, austere existence for men used to an Iberian environment where the family is always on call and social life centres on the village *barra*. Guinea's remoteness hardly helped the morale of the metropolitans and conditions were exacerbated by the monthly PAIGC attack, when they hurled rockets and mortars at the Portuguese from across the border.

Anyone with a modicum of individuality, I could see, was soon driven to distraction by the rusty routine which went on unbroken for almost two years. Even among the officers, young accountants, lawyers, engineers, architects, lecturers and scientists – each one of them thrown together in the farrago of army life – there was much lacking, though these men had each other for company. I would have thought the lonely circumstances would have lent themselves to homosexuality, as it had with United States troops in Indochina. But it had not, apparently, though all commanders were conscious of this possibility and watched for it keenly. By all accounts, a homosexual offence was a rare event among these devout Catholics, though obviously it happened and among the men such things simply had to be tolerated. The Senegalese women, many of them, tall and angular and quite beautiful like Nigeria's Fulani women, who came regularly across the border with only their bodies for sale, undoubtedly had something to do with that.

The majority of troops when not out on patrol or on guard duty were generally left to their own devices. For this reason quite a few of the young officers and NCOs had sought succour in matching wits with the enemy. Several had become accomplished killers who often learned to know the jungle and bush around them as well as their own locally born scouts. Some had earned reputations for themselves in the enclave and beyond and quite a few had substantial prices on their heads in Conakry and Dakar. To these men the fact that they were 'wanted' by the PAIGC was an ample measure of achievement and they seemed to relish the notoriety.

Peculiarly, there were also those troops – probably on both sides of the front – who eventually came to love the war and many of its gory ramifications. I was to meet a few of them while wandering from one unit to another and almost to a man they would say that yes, they had problems, but these would be faced when it all ended, when the killing was over and they were forced to return to an ordered society where atavistic urges had to be kept in check.

And when that time came, said one of them, 'we will be as far out of our element as an advertising executive in a steelworker's blue denims.' Others routinely compared their condition to what was going on in South East Asia at the time, though they hardly had the picture since almost no military bases outside Bissau had TV.

I was taken by road from the north to Bafata, second city of Portuguese Guinea, along a straight tarred highway that led through country whose dozy monotony could easily have nodded an army off to sleep had the trip gone on long enough. Our Jeep travelled ahead of a Unimog looking more like an armoury than an escort vehicle. The region had once been hotly contested, my aide told me, but since the road had been completed, the enemy had lost the initiative, mainly because the guerrillas' main means of inflicting damage – landmines – had been neutralized. Nevertheless, the headquarters could take no chances, and it was only when reached Contubael, about halfway between the border and Bafata, that our escort left us and we travelled alone into the inchoate dusk, colours spraying across the western sky toward the Atlantic.

I found Bafata to be a quiet town, situated on a row of hills overlooking the river. It was cleaner and quieter than Bissau and the climate manageable, although it lay near the headwaters of the same river which eventually wends its way murkily past the capital. All roads appeared to run either up or down the high-lying ground with few connecting in between. We arrived shortly before dinner which was held with great ceremony in the officers' mess, a low bungalow near the middle of town – a special occasion in honour of the visiting journalist. Whisky again, and, as usual, too much of it.

We were then taken to a football match at the town stadium where the Bafata garrison was defending its honour against the up-country champions from Farim. Like all Portuguese games it was a rowdy, rumbustious affair with the referee coming in for as much barracking from the spectators as the players. Africans from miles around had converged on the field, crowding the stands and every available standing space. Others peered over the high walls or hung precariously from branches of trees which surrounded the stadium. Farim took the honours, but it was an unpopular decision although the up-country players obviously had the edge on the home team. Hoots and boos echoed through the night.

Later that evening I was taken to a Madinga ceremony a short distance out of town, beyond the airstrip. A group of youths and young girls had recently been circumcised and this was to be their 'coming-out' ceremony after having been in isolation for forty days. The period obviously had a religious significance which went back a long way in tribal lore (to Jesus Christ's forty-day fast in the desert?). The ritual was every bit as serious as a pontifical mass, although the final night was given over to a frenzy of festivity and palm-wine drinking which, I was told by one of the local doctors who was interested in African traditions and customs, would go on until morning.

We visited the village in one of the army station wagons. Only when we had left the lights of Bafata behind us did I realize that not one of the men was armed. The only precaution they took against a possible attack was to remove their shoulder tabs so as not to be immediately recognizable as officers. The village loomed up suddenly in the dark. We could hear the drums a long way off but there were no lights, only a low smoky fire around which the novitiates danced. All of them – there were about two dozen boys and girls – were naked and covered in a dull white paint which made them look in the shadowy light like *pierrots* out of a French pantomime act. Their ages ranged from about eight to eighteen.

Now that the necessary rituals had been performed, the medical officer assured me, these youngsters would be ready to take their place in society as adults, but it would take months for their genital wounds to heal and the possibility of infection was real enough to sometimes cause death, about which nobody talked. There was nothing lascivious about these young people mixing together unashamedly in the nude. The traditions of centuries had instilled in them the gravity of a tribal custom on which all future male–female relationships would be based and in which their children in turn would take part. Indeed, we were warmly welcomed by the villagers after they had recognized our doctor guide, who was obviously a regular visitor. They certainly did not resent our intrusion as I had expected they would, for it is not often that the white man is allowed to enter the esoteric domain of tribal custom. We were offered the choice of palm wine or soured goat milk mixed with fresh blood taken from a cow which had been sacrificed earlier that evening. We opted for the wine and left, as we had arrived, quietly, about an hour later. For a long while the dull throb of drums followed us down the long track back to town, distinctly tribal but appealing.

'This is part of that irresistible urge which has brought generations of explorers and settlers back to Africa, time and again,' said the lieutenant doctor. The mysterious lure, he reckoned, was a powerful one and probably one of the reasons why there are today almost five million white people living and working on what some still like to refer to as the 'Dark Continent'.

Chapter Eight

Principal Adversaries: Cabral and Spinola

U ntil he was assassinated by his own people, guerrilla leader Amilcar Lopes da Costa Cabral led from the front. All major decisions regarding his fighters came either directly from his desk or had to be cleared by him personally before they were put into action. He was both the brain and the moving force behind this insurrection and few could fault the majority of his decisions.

It obviously helped that he was not bound by any financial constraints. His PAIGC forces were given everything in the way of military hardware, expertise and training that he demanded. Portugal in contrast, one of Europe's poorest nations, had to pay in hard cash for what they needed from their NATO allies.

General António de Spínola, his opposite number was also a hands-on operator, to the extent that some of his staff in Bissau sometimes commented on the fact that he hardly slept. If he wasn't in his office working on detail, the next day's operations, or in his command centre in Bissau discussing detail with his commanders, he was out in the field inspecting troops, defences, talking to the men and, more salient, to his black civilian population and their leaders about ways to handle their defences.

A stickler for both order and discipline, quite a few military careers were abruptly ended at his behest, especially those officers who did not live up to expectations and were ordered back onto the first plane to Europe. Military headquarters in Bissau – and the numerous Portuguese Army bases in the interior – were tough environments in which to survive, but at the same time, he richly rewarded those officers who went that extra unasked-for mile.

Yet, it all came at a cost. Ahead of all others in Lisbon's military and political establishments, this fighting general played a seminal role, not only in turning around a failing war in Portuguese Guinea, but also winning the trust of many of the local leaders who fell within his administrative domain.

General António Sebastião Ribeiro de Spínola was in his mid-fifties when he was appointed to command Lisbon's forces in the West African enclave. A shrewd, erudite tactician who used his time with German forces monitoring Wehrmacht movements during the encirclement of Leningrad (Portuguese volunteers having been incorporated into the Blue Division), he went on to become the fourteenth president of his country.

In my discussions with Spínola, both on and off the record, I discovered a man who, while echoing many of the sentiments expressed by the Lisbon hierarchy, had a very distinct agenda of his own which he implemented with a determination that was fierce and forthright. The first was to ignore the tenets of Lisbon's traditional colonial policy and that meant appointing promising black soldiers to commissioned rank. The illustrious Captain João Bacar was one of those. The second was to ignore Lisbon's efforts to interfere in his war: he knew what he wanted and was capable of getting it, no matter what.

His role, he would always stress, was a 'civilizing' one. While abstruse, he did intend to crush his enemy and hopefully, in the process, destroy Amilcar Cabral and was well on his way to doing so. Indeed, by the time of my last visit early 1971, Spínola had actually succeeded in reversing the course of the war. There was even a subtle air of optimism among some of the senior functionaries whom I met in Bissau, reflected subsequently in the first of my books on the Guinea war.

But that was before Soviet SAM-7 Strela ground-to-air MANPADs were issued to the PAIGC. This was probably Moscow's retaliation for Washington supplying the Angolan rebel leader Jonas Savimbi who headed UNITA with the same Stinger missiles then being issued to the mujahedeen fighting the Soviets in Afghanistan. Still, even with the infusion of more advanced East European armaments, which included missiles and a vast range of landmines, BM-21 'Grad' multiple rocket systems and the rest, Lisbon was still far from losing this war, though it had almost done so in the past.

American historian and academic Douglas Porch maintained in his book, *The Portuguese Armed Forces and the Revolution*, a comprehensive assessment of Lisbon's military adventures in Africa that although Spínola's own work, *Portugal and the Future* was only published in 1974, it was already written by 1971. That suggested that he was probably working on the manuscript or had just finished it while I was in Bissau.

In our face-to-face meetings, Spínola hardly seemed the man who was later to say that 'an unwinnable war' was at the root of the Portuguese problems, or that 'the future of Portugal depends on an appropriate solution to the problems raised by the war which, by consuming lives, resources and talent, increasingly compromises the rhythm of development which we must have to catch up with other countries'. Indeed, I could not have met a more determined or articulate exponent of traditional hard-line tactics and, as we have already observed, his approach toward the PAIGC was uncompromising.

I quote his response from one of my interviews: 'You ask whether a military victory is possible for the Portuguese in this province? I say to you that we are already achieving victory with our forces in that we are guaranteeing and underwriting the security of the Guinean people.'

He accused the PAIGC of kidnapping young people to feed their war machine, of a meddlesome Soviet Union trying to implicate others in the struggle and a conflict that already involved East and West for the domination ... of parts of the south Atlantic and West Africa as a whole. In any other context, Spínola might have been a spokesman for the American State Department of the day.

The book was widely read by Portuguese officers. It was immensely popular and bought by the container-load throughout the country, although it was banned in the overseas provinces. But even there it was smuggled into colonial messes and surreptitiously circulated.

For the Young Officers' Movement, the MFA, *Portugal and the Future* was a godsend. It provided the likes of Major Vitor Alves and his comrades with a fundamental political guideline and there were many people who cited the general's book as one of the single most important political catalyst of the movement.

That was contested by Otelo Saraiva de Carvalho, another officer whom I got to know quite well because he was the general's ADC while I was in Guinea and I spent some good time with him. Later imprisoned by his fellow revolutionaries because of activities which fringed on anarchism, de Carvalho reasoned that Spínola was not radical enough. In contrast, before the coup, the MFA was regarded thoroughly 'Spinolist', both in doctrine and in leadership.

Then, to the surprise of us all, the Armed Forces Movement having failed to achieve their ends, the young officers now in power, ditched the eminent general as abruptly as they had embraced him. Within a year Spínola was forced into exile in Brazil. In Portugal itself, the general was bitterly castigated by the extreme left and labelled a traitor by many, even though nobody disputed that he was one of the most resourceful and competent leaders that the country had produced that century. For all that, he never disguised his contempt for what he termed 'that bunch of hermits in power' in Lisbon.

Looking back, it is interesting that prior to the army putsch, many of the young MFA officers felt that in order to succeed, they had need of a general to lend prestige to their revolutionary movement. First they tried to entice to their cause General Kaulza de Arriaga who, though he had botched his efforts to win the war in Portuguese East Africa (Mozambique), seemed a likely candidate. But, as we were aware, de Arriaga was a staunch rightist and while accepting that change was necessary, there was very real possibility that he would end up using their radical stance to take over himself instead of them using him. So the MFA opted instead for Spínola, whose book, of course, was the cherry on the top of all this subterfuge.

One of the interesting sidelights of what he wrote was the attitude of the then prime minister, Marcello Caetano, who shared a common thread with the Pretoria regime in detecting the sinister hand of international Marxism just about everywhere. General Francisco Costa Gomes, who succeeded Spínola as president in September 1974 (and was one of the brains behind the revolution) sent Caetano a copy of the book.

In *O Depoimento* (which was later published in Rio de Janeiro after Caetano had himself sought sanctuary in Brazil) he wrote: 'On the 18th I received a copy of *Portugal and the Future* with the friendly dedication of the author. I could not read it that day, nor the following one, which was taken up by the council of ministers. Only on the 20th after a tiring day did I pick up the book after 11 o'clock at night. I did not stop reading until I reached the last page. And when I'd closed the book, I believed that I understood that a military coup d'état, which I sensed for some months had been brewing, was now inevitable.'

Next day Caetano called both Spínola and General Costa Gomes, then Chief of the General Staff of the Portuguese Armed Forces (and a powerful adversary) into his office 'for the most serious and disagreeable conversation of my life.'

As Caetano recalls, General de Spínola's book contained a critical opening section 'which could not fail to influence the desire of the armed forces not to continue to defend the overseas provinces, and to weigh on public opinion, which would have a severe effect on international affairs and reduce the already narrow margin of manoeuvrability open to my government in its foreign policy.' Written by the vice-chief of the general staff and approved by his superior, it opened a breach between the prime minister and the highest chiefs of the armed forces, Costa Gomes especially.

'It would be impossible to continue to govern with an insubordinate officer corps and discordant military chiefs,' wrote Caetano.

In an obituary notice published in the *The New York Times* on 1 August 2001 and headlined 'Francisco da Costa Gomes, 87, General Who Led Portugal', it stated that it was General Costa Gomes who ended Portugal's involvement in Africa that began in 1415, granting independence to Angola, Mozambique, the Cape Verde Islands and São Tomé and Príncipe and Guiné-Bissau, then Portuguese Guinea.

Although Spínola preferred a more gradual disentanglement from Africa, Costa Gomes favoured a rapid exit. Internationalized civil war followed the departure from all three of Lisbon's African colonies while Indonesia annexed East Timor, a south Asian colony that had been briefly independent. The obituary goes on:

General Costa Gomes, nicknamed 'The Cork' for his remarkable ability to stay afloat in crises, dealt with considerable political and social instability. In 1975, nearly a million people had to flee to Portugal from the former African colonies, followed by the new revolutionary government itself nationalizing much of the economy, including banking, transportation and the media.

In parts of southern Portugal, peasants expropriated large farms and started communal farms, while strikes in cities became widespread. An uprising by pro-communist officers in the army was crushed in November 1975.

General de Spínola's early life makes for compelling reading because there was much interest, both while he was involved with the Guinea war and after the Carnation Revolution. While not directly where he was involved, it took place very much as a result of the book he wrote.

Paul Montgomery of *The New York Times* declared immediately after the army mutiny that 'General Spínola was married in 1922, and is known as a family man. Observers often call him Portugal's de Gaulle – a man of the right who can effect a disengagement from colonial ties without causing political chaos or beginning a civil war.'

In Lisbon today, curiously, the generations that followed that country's travails in Africa continue to show interest, not only in the fighting that took place in Angola, Mozambique and Portuguese Guinea, but also in the more prominent participants, on both sides of the fence.

The son of a wealthy family, António de Spínola's father was Inspector General of Finance and Prime Minister Salazar's chief of staff in the Ministry of Finance. In 1920, he joined the Military College in Lisbon and enrolled at the Escola Politécnica de Lisboa and soon afterward entered the Colégio Militar, beginning a most successful army career. At the academy, the records declare that he stood out as a young and promising cavalry officer.

The late 1930s and early 1940s offered this young officer a number of opportunities – the first being, with Salazar's blessing – he fought as a volunteer with Franco's Fascist forces in the Spanish Civil War and received German training during the Second World War when Portugal remained neutral. It was then that he went into the Soviet Union as an observer with the German Army during the battle for Leningrad. That experience alone must have had an enormous influence in his thinking as a career military officer.

With the start of the war in Angola, he volunteered and organized Cavalry Group 345. His first mission in that territory was in the region of Bessa Monteiro and later in the border region of São Salvador do

Congo where he remained on active duty until 1963. It was in Angola that Spínola appeared to have become aware that to in order to win the guerrilla struggle the solution rested largely on political issues, something he communicated to his contacts within government back home. This might have been the reason that he was called by Salazar to serve as governor and commander-in-chief of the armed forces in Portuguese Guinea, positions for which he would later be reappointed in 1972, which he did not accept due to the lack of support from the central government. During this period he continued to practise a range of initiatives in the ongoing conflict, from clandestine meetings – he secretly met with the president of Senegal, Léopold Sédar Senghor at one stage – to armed incursions within neighbouring states which included Operation Green Sea, a hugely successful maritime rescue of Portuguese troops held in the Republic of Guinea.

On 25 April 1974, as a representative of the MFA, he received from Prime Minister Marcello Caetano, head of the Portuguese government (which had taken refuge in the Carmo army barracks), the surrender of the government. Although the general did not play an important role, Marcello Caetano insisted he would only surrender power to Spínola. This allowed him to assume an important public place as a leader of the revolution, although that was not what the MFA had originally intended. The formation of the Junta de Salvçãao Nacional (National Salvation Junta), formed in the days following the army revolt allowed Spínola to take on the role of President of the Republic.

Spínola met with President Mobutu Sese Seko of Zaire (the Democratic Republic of the Congo today) on 15 September 1974, on Sal Island in the Cape Verde archipelago in a bid to craft a plan to empower the Angolan rebel leaders to formulate a plan to take over the government.

During his relatively short term of four months in power in Lisbon, he had the unreserved support of the moderate faction of the MFA but was opposed by all the others (communists, socialists, anarchists). He was ousted soon afterward and went into exile.

In February 1987 all was forgiven and returned home to be inducted as Chancellor of the Old Military Orders, and handed the insignia of the Grand Cross of the Military Order of the Tower and Espada, for 'feats of military and civic heroism and for having been a symbol of the April revolution and the first President of the Republic after the dictatorship'.

A versatile writer for much of his career he wrote several books including *For a Better Guinea* in 1970, *Line of Action* and *On the Path of the Future* during the two subsequent years and in 1973, *For a Renewed Portugality*. It was his last book, *Portugal and the Future*, that changed history in Portugal and resulted in the army revolt as well as the end of Lisbon's wars in Africa. The work took Portugal by storm, which was remarkable in a country where political debate, and particularly debate about the colonial wars, had been stifled for decades. The debate about the book, between right and left continues in some quarters among Portugal's military and political veterans.

Which brings us to the revolutionary guerrilla group PAIGC that was certainly the most successful and destructive of the three major guerrilla groups Lisbon faced at the time: Agostinho Neto's MPLA in Angola and Samora Machel's FRELIMO in Mozambique.

I met Portuguese Guinea's guerrilla leader Amilcar Cabral only once very briefly in Addis Ababa during the 1971 Summit of African Heads of State while he was strolling casually through the Press Centre prior to the start of the third day's session. His grey suit of distinct continental cut contrasted readily with the more conservative styles of a few of the delegates around him and the plain-clothed Ethiopian security officer who was tasked to follow him around the building. I gathered later that this man was there more for his own safety than for any insurrection he may have contemplated while in Emperor Haile Selassie's capital.

Like General Spínola, the Portuguese commander that was committed to defeating him, Cabral epitomized the nature of his movement. A small, ascetic-looking man with a burnished complexion and still in his early fifties, he had the piercing eyes that characterized so many of the more prominent African leaders. His bold chin was offset by a thin ring of salt-and-pepper beard. Even in camouflage uniform, which he donned when he occasionally crossed the border and ventured into enemy territory, his dress was tidy. He reflected the bearing of a senior staff officer, although in reality, his military training behind the Iron Curtain had been fragmentary. His manner was informal when I stepped forward past his minder and introduced myself. Only a short while before I had been with

Captain João Bacar, one of Portugal's most successful commando officers in the jungles of Portuguese Guinea, very much intent on hunting his men. I told him so and he was genuinely interested. He translated what I had said for the benefit of one of his aides, who was also present. Like most African guerrilla leaders, Cabral spoke fluent Portuguese and a passable English.

'We must talk,' he said. 'There is obviously much that we could tell each other.' Not for a moment did the easy affable smile leave his lips.

After a few minutes he excused himself in order to enter the debating chamber in the almost-regal Africa Hall. My immediate impression was that his personality exuded forcefulness and authority: effectively, one could say, he was manifestly the brainchild of the war. Personality-wise, he was affable and blended easily with an undeniable old world charm that one so rarely encounters among some of the African or American dignitaries one meets these days. An American might have described him as Mister Nice Guy. In the words of a Scandinavian colleague who was with me at the time, Amilcar Cabral was very much the 'complete individual – unquestionably a leader of men.' Yet, said a Cuban intelligence officer who came to know him well, Cabral was no communist.

He told Piero Gleijeses, 'He was a progressive leader with very advanced ideas and an extreme clarity about Africa's problems.'[1]

Amilcar Lopes Cabral was born in Bafata, one of the larger centres of the enclave that lies well into the interior of what was then known as Portuguese Guinea. His parents were of Cape Verde stock and of mixed blood, which is one of the reasons why his complexion was tawny rather than the jet black of so many of his fellow party members, including his leading combat fighter, General Niño.

From the start young Amilcar distinguished himself at school. He was always at or near the top of his class and this prompted local authorities to take more than a passing interest in this brilliant young *mestico* who showed promise in just about everything he did. *Assimilado* status followed as a matter of course: Cabral became one of eleven young men who were that year politically assimilated into the all-white ruling establishment

---

1. Piero Gleijeses, 'First Ambassadors: Cuba's Role in Guinea-Bissau's War of Independence' in *Journal of Latin American Studies*, Vol. 29, No. 1, February 1977, pp. 45–88.

in the country. Which was why, shortly after the end of Europe's war, he was awarded a scholarship to the Institute Superior de Agronomia, a technical university in Lisbon. He graduated in 1950 with honours as an agronomist, or what the Portuguese might call an agricultural engineer.

Political awareness must have come early. Already in 1948 Cabral, the student, was exchanging views at the subsequently banned Casa dos Estudantes do Imperio with such men as Agostinho Neto, who was to become head of the Angolan liberation movement, as well as another African exile, Mario Pinto de Andrade, a poet of renown. Pinto had studied in Frankfurt and Paris and, according to Portuguese sources, was recruited by the radical Portuguese underground and French communist parties.

Shortly after heading back to West Africa, Cabral made his first serious political gesture by forming an African political movement known as MING, the Movement for the Independence of Guinea. Meanwhile, he was employed by the government Agronomical Office in Bissau. His work during this period (1952–54) entailed travelling throughout Portuguese Guinea to make contact with the local citizens at all levels, which would have allowed him contact with his African comrades from every possible strata. His approach was always sympathetic. Local peasants confided in him, while the more outspoken demanded that he help them right their wrongs, which, at the hands of the Portuguese authorities of that period, were many. Quietly, systematically and with diligence, he built up a list of reliable, mostly clandestine supporters; the more militant were told to bide their time. They were assured that forces were in the making to bring power to the black man; the pattern was not unlike that followed by many of the young political aspirants in other West African colonies of the time   future leaders like the Gold Coast's Nkrumah or Sékou Touré of Guinea.

Cabral made his mark during this period. Long after the guerrilla war started, many Portuguese and local blacks still recalled that he was an astonishingly energetic young official who would do as much work in a day as most Portuguese managed in three. He even gained favourable notice from the government. One of the agricultural reports drawn up by him at the time recommended certain measures which should be taken

Portuguese soldiers give the general salute at one of the garrisons taken over by PAIGC guerrillas after the 1974 coup.

His characteristic monocle always in place, General António de Spínola was the disciplinarian who turned the war around in this West African enclave.

Portugal's long-serving Prime Minister Salazar refused to follow Britain's and France's decolonization trend of the 1960s.

Italian-built Fiat G.91s lined up at Bissau's Bissalanca military air base prior to operations in the interior.

In places the jungle was an ambush gift for the guerrillas.

Head of the PAIGC guerrilla movement, Amilcar Cabral, during one of his forays into the beleaguered Portuguese colony.

Approaching Bissau, a view of the capital of Portuguese Guinea from the air during the war.

Waiting for helicopter casualty evacuation, troops attend to one of their comrades injured in a landmine blast.

An aerial view of the Bissalanca military air base on the outskirts of Bissau, 1966.

The first Portuguese fort along the Guinean coast was built at Cacheu in the north of the country five centuries ago.

One of Portugal's most respected war heroes, Captain João Bacar wears his country's highest decoration for valour.

A PAIGC guerrilla squad at one of their camps in the interior of Portuguese Guinea.

One of the Portuguese Air Force planes shot down in Portuguese Guinea by a Soviet SAM-7 Strela surface-to-air missile.

An Alouette III helicopter arrives at a bush camp to evacuate a wounded soldier.

A protected village, an *aldeamento*, in the interior under the watchful eye of a helicopter gunship.

An ominous warning at a Portuguese Army bush base: landmines half a pace away.

Portuguese marines – *Fuzileiros* – during operations along the Guinean coast where fighting was often intense.

Portuguese Navy support ship *Montante* deployed in Spínola's rescue of his imprisoned troops held captive in Conakry.

Portuguese Air Force World War Two-vintage T-6 Harvard ground support aircraft with distinctive underwing rocket pods, at an airstrip in Guinea.

The enigmatic guerrilla leader Amilcar Cabral became a good friend of Fidel Castro's as the war progressed.

The supreme commander in Portuguese Guinea, General António de Spínola, addresses a public meeting on the outskirts of Bissau.

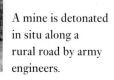

A mine is detonated in situ along a rural road by army engineers.

Impressive frontal view of a Soviet Komar–class torpedo boat of the type that operated out of Conakry where Spínola launched his seaborne rescue effort.

The Portuguese Navy gave solid support during attacks on guerrilla positions, especially among the offshore western islands.

Loading an artillery piece in preparation for an attack on a suspected guerrilla position in southern Senegal.

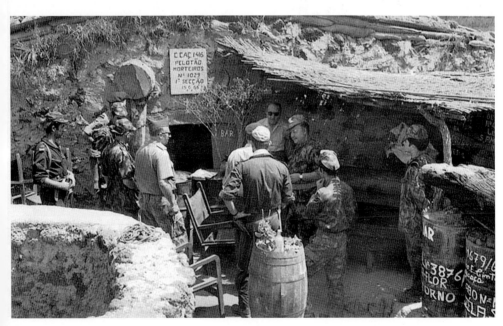

Bunkers in a Portuguese Army camp in the interior of the enclave, underscoring the intensity of guerrilla attacks which invariably featured mortars.

A PAIGC guerrilla unit on parade: well-drilled and smartly turned out, in spite of their ragged uniforms.

A Portuguese Air Force helicopter gunship with a 20mm cannon mounted to port in this West African guerrilla war.

Approaching Tite's gravel strip in a PAF Dornier. This base, not to be confused with Tete in Mozambique, was hit often and hard by the rebels.

Jungle camouflage over an army armoured vehicle; such efforts rarely fooled the enemy.

Guerrillas on the march in Portuguese Guinea, with the ubiquitous Soviet RPG-2 very much in evidence.

Remains of a Portuguese Air Force jet fighter brought down by a Soviet-supplied Strela missile in 1974.

Bombing-up one of the American jet fighters deployed by the Portuguese Air Force to West Africa for service in the counter-insurgency war.

Fuzileiros deploying from one the naval frigates in counter-insurgency operations off the coast of Africa.

Portuguese Air Force G.91 fighter-trainers provided excellent ground support during the Guinean war, until four of these jets were shot down by Soviet missiles.

Fuzileiros operational along the Cacheu River in the north-west of the country, adjacent to Senegal.

Marine *commandante* Alpoim Calvão (front right) leading a squad into action against guerrilla elements on the islands.

A trio of Portuguese Navy warships in Guinean waters. A lot of effort went into interdicting insurgent groups trying to infiltrate from the Republic of Guinea.

A Soviet instructional diagram for the TM-57 anti-tank landmine, a much-favoured guerrilla weapon in the insurgency.

Взрыватель МВЗ-57

1. Ось заводной пружины
2. Шпилька
3. Шарик
4. Ударник
5. Медная срезная чека

6. Втулка
7. Защелка
8. Боевая пружина
9. Шайба
10. Шток толкателя

11. Корпус
12. Втулка
13. Капсюль - детонатор
14. Гайка
15. Оттягивающая пружина
16. Кнопка
17. Корпус

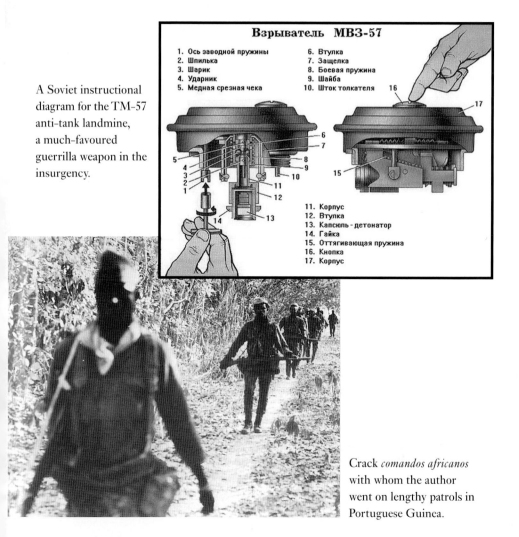

Crack *comandos africanos* with whom the author went on lengthy patrols in Portuguese Guinea.

Another victim of the grim guerrilla war.

Discipline during road convoys into the interior became lax towards the end of the war. The Portuguese Army was 'war weary' after more than a decade of fighting.

Portuguese Navy patrol boat at Cacine. The author returned to Guiné–Bissau decades later to find this fighting vessel reduced to a rusting hulk abandoned on the beach.

A pair of T-6 Harvards heads back to base after a sortie in the bush.

A nondescript bunch of
PAIGC guerrillas hosting a
visiting media group from
Conakry.

Some of the most difficult
patrols were on water.

Landmine casualties
on unsurfaced roads
in the interior were
bound to have a serious
effect on troop morale:
the guerrillas knew it.

Portuguese Navy patrol boat travelling at speed in offshore waters.

The author with Portuguese marines on river patrol close to the border with Senegal.

The army was ill-equipped with troop-carrying vehicles: the men sat back-to-back and there was no real protection against either ambush or landmines.

Aircrew back at base after a sortie over hostile terrain.

A Portuguese squad in the bush, including a medic.

Portuguese Navy ship and spotter plane off Como Island, south-west of Bissau.

Ongoing counter-insurgency operations along the fringes of the colony's islands which were always regarded as 'disputed' territory.

Memorial to a long-forgotten Portuguese Army unit that was based at this remote bush camp for much of its two-year deployment in Africa.

to improve conditions in the interior and was adopted by the governor. It was still in force when the war ended.

At the same time, his revolutionary talk did not go unnoticed. Gradually reports filtered through to the headquarters of the Portuguese secret police in Bissau that the young Cabral was a revolutionary. However, he was well liked and invariably the rumours were scotched because it was believed he was an ambitious, hardworking fellow who was eager to make his way to the top. This was his way of doing it, one report read.

It is interesting that at the time, the 1950s, the concept of political maturity among the indigenes was so remote, even in more developed colonies such as Kenya and the Gold Coast – soon to become Ghana – as to make revolution unthinkable in most official white African circles. But matters came to a head early in 1954 and Cabral was given the choice of ending his activities or leaving the country. Wisely, he took the latter option and returned to Lisbon, stayed a while and, fearing arrest, returned to Africa where he spent the next three years establishing the political structure which was eventually to bring his movement to maturity.

A powerful speaker, he addressed a variety of political conferences in Africa, Europe, Asia and the Americas during the course of his career, such as the first Tricontinental Conference of the Peoples of Asia, Africa and Latin America held in Havana in January 1966. He rarely pulled punches, as illustrated by his opening paragraph:

If any of us came to Cuba with doubts in our mind about the solidity, strength, maturity and vitality of the Cuban Revolution, these doubts have been removed by what we have been able to see. Our hearts are now warmed by an unshakeable certainty which gives us courage in the difficult but glorious struggle against the common enemy: no power in the world will be able to destroy this Cuban Revolution, which is creating in the countryside and in the towns not only a new life but also – and even more important – a New Man, fully conscious of his national, continental and international rights and duties. In every field of activity the Cuban people have made major progress during the last seven years, particularly in 1965, Year of Agriculture.

We believe that this constitutes a particular lesson for the national liberation movements, especially for those who want their national revolution to be a true revolution.

Speaking to an American journalist, David Andelmann of *The New York Times* about the period, Cabral explained his approach:

We decided initially to try peaceful coercion as a means of obtaining independence. The Portuguese use of massive force to crush a dockworkers' strike in Bissau harbour – named the Pidgiguiti Massacre – was decisive in prompting our movement to change its tactics.

In the beginning we thought it would be possible to fight in the towns, using the example of the experiences in other countries, like Algeria. But it was a mistake. We tried strikes and demonstrations but after the dockside massacre we realized that would not work. The Portuguese used force of arms, lots of it, so there was no choice; we had to do the same.

It was at this point that Cabral was finally convinced that he had to create a guerrilla organization that would concentrate on armed insurrection.

Chapter Nine

War in the Air

What was clear from the beginning of the war was that the Portuguese were obliged to fight their wars very differently compared to how other nations handled theirs. For a start, it was age of the 'whirly-bird', but Lisbon was never able to afford the kind of helicopter support the Americans enjoyed in Vietnam. They had Alouette gunships to start with – hardly comparable to the utility Bell UH-1 (Huey) choppers fielded in vast numbers by the Americans in Vietnam. Toward the end of the war, the PAF (Forca Aerea Portuguesa, the Portuguese Air Force, or PAF) acquired Sud-Aviation SA330 medium-lift Pumas, but those troopers only saw cursory service in Africa and never flew in Portuguese Guinea.

For all that, a pair of French-built helicopter troopers, each with a capacity of fifteen paras or commandos and protected by one or more gunships, could quickly put thirty men into action on the ground and were extremely versatile. Some Pumas were to have been sent to Portuguese Guinea, but during the attack on the Tancos Air Force base near Lisbon, several newly delivered machines were destroyed by a clandestine Portuguese Communist Party strike force in March 1971. It was a spectacular night raid that stunned the nation.

For almost all of Lisbon's African campaigns, Portugal – unlike France, which bolstered its aircraft industry after the Second World War – had to rely heavily on obsolete American fixed-wing aircraft for many of their counterinsurgency operations. Portugal inventoried 125 F-84G Thunderjets and sixty-five North American F-86F Sabres when the revolution started, of which a fair proportion were deployed in Africa. But there were problems.

The American jets were supplied by the US after the country joined NATO, with the stipulation that they would not be used anywhere outside Portugal. But Lisbon in its routine double-talk about the colonies always referred to its African possessions as provinces and were thus integral to the nation, which was why the PAF began to deploy some of its Sabres to Angola and Portuguese Guinea. Not fooled, Washington exercised heavy pressure and forced Salazar to withdraw most but not all of its fighter jets from the overseas territories.

Portugal then opted to buy surplus Fiat G.91s from Germany, again on condition that the planes would only be deployed in Europe. But in the end, Rome was not as insistent as Washington and turned a blind eye when some of these jet fighter/trainers ended up on African combat missions, in Portuguese Guinea especially.

With helicopters, PAF Aerospatiale Alouette IIs were superseded by the more sophisticated Alouette IIIs and used in all three conflict zones, but since the country was struggling to balance its budgets, Lisbon's military commanders thought long and hard before deploying these valuable assets. No matter what the purpose, a helicopter would need a very good reason to be committed to a specific operation.

In Portuguese Guinea, the PAF had its work cut out. In larger operations in the Alouette phase, Special Force units such as the Caçadores Paraquedistas – literally Hunter-Paratroops – would be taken in by the gunships (referred to in the lingo as *Lobo Mau* or, more appropriately, 'heli-cannons'). Though fitted with all-purpose 7.62mm GPMGs in the earlier stages, the gunships eventually came equipped with 20mm cannons, mounted – as with both the Rhodesian and South African air forces – on the port side. These special units were customarily based on groups of twenty men and under 'normal' circumstances, a clutch of helicopters would each uplift five paratroopers at a time. There were also an awful lot of 'abnormal' operations.

On the offensive side, the Portuguese Air Force took a while to make effective use of these machines. When these helicopters first arrived in Africa, some unit commanders would try to squeeze six men on board, even though this remarkably resilient little gunship was designed for a maximum two (crew) plus four (troopers). French technicians attached to the Portuguese armed forces warned early on that excess weight could result in the gearbox being stripped, so numbers were afterward reduced.

When the liberation war started in Angola in 1961, the PAF had almost 400 aircraft and more than 22,000 personnel on its books. There were roughly 150 military aircraft deployed in the three overseas provinces, including North American T-6 Harvards, Lockheed PV2 Harpoons, and Lockheed Neptunes (bought from the Royal Netherlands Navy) as well as the more modern Republic F-84 Thunderjets and North American F-86G Sabres. The transport air arm included the Noratlas-2501, Douglas C-47s and C-54/DC-6s and later, Boeing 707 transports. More modest aircraft included Austers and the German/Spanish-built Dornier Do 27s.

For counterinsurgency purposes, the T-6s Harvards proved admirably capable workhorses, armed with machine gun pods and light bombs and were much in evidence in and out of Bissalanca. In spite of their relatively low speed, these plucky little snub-nosed support planes proved to be useful in providing back-up at critical moments during contacts and I would sometimes see them returning from sorties in pairs, with the pilots waving at us as they drew level.

Considering the duration of the war – eleven years in Guinea – coupled to the number of contacts registered annually, relatively few planes were lost in action. Even more remarkable was the fact that for about eighteen months early on, the only strike capability came from the T-6s because more advanced jet fighter/ground-support aircraft arrived later.

Napalm soon became a feature of many of the raids into the interior – first in Angola, and afterward in Portuguese Guinea and Mozambique, though when I raised this issue at official briefings, nobody 'knew' what I was talking about.

Tracking rebel groups from the air in some of the most difficult jungle and bush terrain in the world – in Guinea's swamplands and coastal regions especially, was always serious issue. While government forces obviously enjoyed some success, especially among groups cornered in isolated patches of bush, Lisbon was aware that even though Washington had deployed squadrons of B-52s – and routinely pounded Viet Cong and North Vietnamese infiltration routes (like the Ho Chi Minh Trail) – that kind of interdiction had had no real effect on the ultimate outcome of the war.

In reality, the PAF also had no real resources to fight a 'rich man's war', like the United States did in South East Asia. On the contrary, Portuguese operations abroad were fought on the proverbial shoestring – further hampered by debilitating and often obsolete military thinking.

In South East Asia there would be damage, of course, and the flow of arms would be temporarily interrupted, but then everything would go forward as before after the holes had been plugged. Something similar applied to Africa, though with significant differences. First, the Portuguese Air Force was a lightweight when it came to delivering tonnage because they had very little heavy stuff to start with. More importantly, much of the terrain in which battles were being fought was in regions that had always been sparsely populated. That meant there were hundreds of paths that were neither mapped nor identified by either side. It also suggested that there were no set or detailed infiltration routes, and anyway, Amilcar Cabral had learned early on to vary both his routines and access routes.

The Portuguese Air Force eventually managed to partially solve the bomb-load problem by acquiring surplus B–26 'Invaders', quite a few on a 'nudge-nudge' basis from the Americans who would supply the planes without end-user certificates. Those responsible would usually look the other way when the B–26s were flown out of holding bases in Arizona and elsewhere by Portuguese nationals on false flag missions. The initial acquisition of these COIN-type aircraft was clandestinely handled by international arms salesmen in Europe, largely because sales of B–26s tended to raise eyebrows: the bombers had already been linked to a spate of illegal operations in Central and South America (including the Bay of Pigs debacle), Vietnam, Laos as well as the Congo, where they were flown by squads of Cuban émigrés living in Miami, originally hired by the CIA. There were still more problems before they could be taken into active service in Africa because almost all were past their prime. The aircraft were acquired at a time when the B–26 fleet worldwide had been grounded following a series of wing-spar failures, though this impediment did not apply to newly remanufactured Mark B–26K 'Counter-invaders', then finding favour in South East Asia.

The Portuguese Air Force went ahead anyway and with the kind of improvisation for which this nation became known, they took these ageing bombers in hand and solved most of the problems.

A number of B–26C models were converted for strafing use in ground-support roles that eventually proved successful and, in a sense, these were modest European forerunners of what was already referred to in Vietnam as 'Puff the Magic Dragon'. Similarly, C–47 Dakotas were deployed in this role, but on a more limited basis when overwhelming suppressing fire was required for a specific operation

For all that, the Portuguese Air Force always had a limited role in interdicting insurgent presence, especially in regions with heavy natural forest cover. Aircraft did play a valuable supporting role throughout the wars, but when push became shove, it was men on the ground that achieved results. Those who have experienced this kind of warfare know that a single large tree can easily hide six or eight soldiers from prying eyes hovering above.

Areas of aviation responsibility were divided up between Portugal and the African colonies and every large settlement throughout Portuguese Africa had at least one airstrip that could handle light planes. Maintenance facilities were restricted to the regional capitals, with modest secondary repair units at a few outlying airports. Unlike Rhodesia and South Africa, if a plane crashed in the interior, it would not be hauled back for repair, even if this was feasible. It happened, of course, but most times the wreck would be stripped of anything useable and left where it had come to rest.

As the war progressed, the Aeritalia G.91 (also known as the Fiat G.91 and nicknamed 'Gina') was an Italian fighter intended to serve as standard equipment for NATO air forces in the 1960s; and while it was a first-class operational aircraft, it was eventually adopted by only three countries – the Italian Air Force, West Germany's Luftwaffe, and the Portuguese Air Force, but enjoyed a long service life that extended over thirty-five years.

Throughout the war Lisbon always tended to be secretive about losses, but, as I was to see for myself, they were relatively light. A Sabre fighter was destroyed when it overran the runway during an emergency landing, and another was shot down by ground fire in 1963 (the pilot ejected and was rescued).

It is worth mentioning that in February 1973, a decade after the Guinea war started and with hostilities in full swing, a PAF G-91 jet fighter was shot down by a SAM missile. The pilot, Almeida Brito, was killed and it was only after two more were lost that the Portuguese started to follow the South African example to fly at treetop level. The damage came when the PAIGC introduced to service SA-7 Grail MANPADs, which made things more complex for the PAF and obliged the Portuguese to introduce a series of urgent measures – including over-painting most of their aircraft and helicopters in 'IR-suppressive' green as well as instituting a reorientation of operational tactics.

While the G-91 replaced Lisbon's F-86 Sabres, the F-84 was to continue flying operationally for some time, probably because Washington believed them to be obsolete. Thus, Portuguese G-91s continued providing tactical support to ground forces until Lisbon's total withdrawal from Africa in 1975 and were finally phased out in the PAF in 1993 and Italy in 1995.

It is interesting that other Italian warplanes were involved in several African conflicts. Italy supplied the South African Air Force with more than a hundred Macchi MB-326 jet fighters under a contract that included a squadron of underpowered single-engine prop-driven reconnaissance/ spotters.

According to Robert Craig Johnson, F-86F Sabres were sent to Portuguese Guinea in 1961. 'Eight aircraft – as Detachment 52, operated out of Bissalanca Air Base having flown 577 sorties, using bombs, napalm, and Matra and HVAR rockets.' The Portuguese, as with the Americans in Vietnam were not averse to using defoliants to achieve certain strategic aims.[1]

During my visits to Portuguese Guinea, I would often see the Fiats lined up on the runways, but was always steered clear of them 'for reasons of security'. There was no comment on their role, or their weapons. The G-91 – a modest-sized aircraft that was able to operate under Third World conditions that might mean landing on a road or on dusty strips – probably had the most lasting effect in this series of counterinsurgency campaigns. In Portuguese Guinea they saw service with 121 Squadron (nicknamed *Tigres*). Armed with a variety of weapons, they came with four .50-calibre machine guns instead of the usual 30mm DEFA cannon which the Germans mounted. It says a lot that their need in Guinea Bissau was so urgent that when they first arrived in Africa they still displayed their Luftwaffe markings.

In Mozambique, where the Portuguese had complete air dominance, the G-91s subsequently flew numerous reconnaissance missions

---

1. Robert Craig Johnson, 'COIN: The Portuguese in Africa 1959–75' at www. worldatwar/chandelle/v3/v3n2portcoin.html.

equipped with K-20 camera-pods mounted up front. In the process, a large part of this East African country on the Indian Ocean was mapped. Not so in Portuguese Guinea, where the fighting was too fierce to allow for anything diversionary.

There were few in Lisbon who were under the illusion that the air force would be able to operate unchallenged forever. In 1973 the strategic emphasis switched rather dramatically once the PAIGC were provided with Soviet-supplied SAM-ground-to-air MANPADs.

We are aware that in March 1973, three PAF aircraft were lost over eight or nine weeks but by September the PAIGC claimed to have downed twenty-one Portuguese war planes, which was pushing the credibility envelope. That was customary with most insurgent groups, particularly those operating in Africa: in Guinea, if you count the number of kills the guerrillas claimed in their routine communiqués, there would have been tens of thousands of Portuguese soldiers killed.

To quote Tom Cooper and José Matos in their report on the deployment of G-91s in Africa, the disappearance of the air force from the skies as a consequence of repeated missile strikes was a heavy blow for the morale of the Portuguese Army troops.

> These [troops] now knew they would get no helicopter support for casualty evacuation, nor for gunfire support, and also the appeasing sound of the Fiats flying CAS-sorties would not be heard overhead. Moreover, the Portuguese morale was in decline after the departure of General de Spínola in 1972. These negative developments finally enabled [the guerrillas] to attack and capture Guiledje, an important military base commanding supply routes.[2]

Then there were conflicting reports about the military wing of the PAIGC having formed its own air force that included MiG-17s, ostensibly flown by East European pilots and based in Conakry. Intelligence intercepts suggested that five MiG-17s and two MiG-15s had been delivered. The threat was considered serious enough for all the G-91s to be wired for the carriage of AIM-9B Sidewinder AAMs, also a NATO weapon.

---

2. Cooper, Tom and José Matos, '*Ginas über Afrika*' in *Fliegerrevue Extra*, Vol. 24.

The reality was that these were Nigerian Air Force jet fighters, supposed to be flown by Nigerian pilots. But even that report didn't make sense since the Nigerians used South African, British and Egyptian mercenaries to fly their aircraft for the duration of the Biafran War. But the Portuguese did take these threats seriously enough to install a battery of anti-aircraft missiles at Bissau. This French Crotale system was identical to the Cactus missile, which South Africa funded through development and production.[3]

Shortly before the Lisbon coup, Portugal was talking to the French government about buying of a squadron of Dassault Mirage III interceptors, similar to those acquired by South Africa. Had the war continued, these would probably have been stationed in Portuguese Guinea.

During the Guinea campaign, the Portuguese Air Force was far more active against the guerrillas than in Angola and Mozambique for the simple reason that Amilcar Cabral's PAIGC was both more active and aggressive than either the MPLA or FRELIMO. It was certainly better motivated.

Some of the sorties involving American-built jet fighters verged on conventional warfare there were so many of them. Tom Cooper gives us an illuminating insight to some of these operations, all of which started and ended at Bissau's Bissalanca airport. As he tells us, even with its limitations in communication and cumbersome coordination leading to an alerted enemy, F-86Fs in service with the Portuguese Air Force in Guinea proved extremely effective. This was particularly so during August 1963, as they executed various assignments against PAIGC installations on the islands of Como and Caiar and in bush country adjacent to Tombali and Catió. Things were not easy because the PAIGC had introduced heavy anti-aircraft machine guns to protect its encampments in these areas, and it was these weapons that had to be eliminated. On 21 August that year

3. In 1964 South Africa placed a development contract with the French company Thomson-Houston (later Thomson-CSF) for a mobile, all-weather, low-altitude surface-to-air missile system. Pretoria paid 85 per cent of the development costs for the system which it called Cactus, the rest coming from France for what it termed the Crotale missile. Obviously South Africa must have played a role in some of the missile platoons being sold to Lisbon.

F-86Fs attacked and silenced two anti-aircraft redoubts next to Incassol, and at the end of that month, in the area of Cachaque Balanta, attacked various guerrilla encampments with napalm. Both of the latter were on the Quitafine Peninsula.

The PAIGC complained internationally about the use of napalm and was able to re-ignite American pressure to return the F-86Fs to Europe. George Ball, the Under Secretary of State, made this point on his visit to Lisbon the following August.

A month later, F-86Fs attacked bases along the banks of the Corubal River in the area of Xitole, in Campeane and in Caulaca, and shortly afterward provided close air support in Exercise Sabre, an operation where government forces attacked PAIGC encampments in the region of Enxalé and Malafo and again on Como Island. In this case a French-built Broussard acted as an airborne forward command post (*posto de comando avançado* or PCA) to overcome the lack of an air–ground radio in the F-86F as well as to coordinate air–ground operations.

Also during September that year, in response to the widening war, the PAF Chief of Staff conducted an inspection tour and determined that Bissalanca needed solid augmentation to form a more balanced and enhanced force structure. He recommended the following changes:

- 10–15 Alouette III helicopters (only three Alouette IIs were operationally assigned at the time of his visit)
- 12 F-86F Sabre fighter jets (only eight assigned)
- 20 T-6G Harvard trainer-fighters (eight assigned)
- 12 Do 27 observation aircraft (four assigned)
- 3 C-47 Dakota transports (three assigned).

Additionally, he recommended an urgent resolution to the air force's weak photo-reconnaissance capability, an expansion of Bissalanca's runway as well as exterior lighting of the buildings to improve security. Finally, he assigned Lieutenant Colonel Manuel Barbeitos de Sousa as commander of the Bissalanca air base.

Barbeitos was an experienced F-86F pilot who had a thorough grasp of its gun and ordnance systems and its tactical employment. He became intimately involved in Detachment 52 operations from that November onward, and throughout was an important factor in revitalizing mission profiles of both the F–86Fs and T–6Gs as well as the adoption of new procedures for close air support.

The shortage of spare parts for the F–86F engines and brake systems continued to plague operations. Even with these impediments, in mid-December that year, the Sabres undertook a series of missions against targets in and around Darsalame where the PAIGC defiantly continued to fly its flag. These operations during the closing months of 1963 were precursors to Operation Tridente.

Following Tridente, keeping the F–86Fs operational became increasingly difficult: their constant use, consequent heavy maintenance demands and the scarcity of spare parts all seemed to work against expanding their role. Consequently, faced with underutilized F–86F pilots, the commander decided that the ten of the jet pilots were to fly other types of aircraft assigned to the base. These would have been the T–6G Harvards as well as the Dornier 27s.

The F–86F and the T–6G (being Second World War American cast-offs) proved both slow and vulnerable in combat and prompted consideration as to their replacements. Available alternatives were the North American T–28 Trojan (series), the Chance Vought F4U–4 Corsair, and the Douglas AD–4 Skyraider, all of which were available from French surplus stocks with the 1962 conclusion of the Algerian war. Another alternative was the purchase of sixty-five Sabres manufactured in Canada and sold to West Germany. Bonn had replaced its Sabres with the Lockheed F–104 Starfighter and Lisbon became a willing buyer for the now-surplus aircraft. However, complications arose with the sale as both the United States and Canada sought to honour the United Nations arms embargo on the African conflict.

The search for a stop-gap aircraft continued, and ultimately Germany offered to sell Portugal forty of its Fiat G.91/R4 attack aircraft, which would be free of UN embargo complications. The Fiats had been retired in 1965 and were available from storage for deployment as soon as they were refurbished and experienced Portuguese pilots had completed their conversions.

As 1964 advanced, F–86F operations began to wind down, and the final mission with these fighters was flown on 20 October that year. The aircraft were subsequently dismantled and put aboard ships for their return to the *metrópole*. For the next eighteen months the always-reliable but ageing Harvard T-6G would be the primary fire support platform, until the Fiats arrived in May 1966.

The F-86F inventory in Portuguese Guinea was about eight aircraft for the three years they operated. There were some strikes (losses) and these were replaced to maintain a steady eight F-86s. Maintenance problems inevitably reduced the numbers, so there were six more or less available at any one time.

A final word about the French-built Alouette helicopter, without which Portugal's wars in Africa would have ended much sooner. It is of interest that helicopters as an extension of the military fighting arm only came into its own not that many years before, something I deal with in some detail in my book, *The Chopper Boys*: *Helicopter Warfare in Africa*.

While the British initially formed the Far East Casualty Air Evacuation Flight in Malaya with three Westland S-51 Dragonfly choppers in 1950 – an unsuccessful venture, as it transpired – it was the French in Algeria that first strapped men onto litters on either side of the fuselage of helicopters to deliver support fire in the mountains that fringed the Mediterranean. While it was a decidedly primitive means for what it was supposed to achieve, it worked. From then on the French worked vigorously toward the implementation of the helicopter gunship as we know it today and apart from their own needs in Africa, some of the early Alouette IIs were delivered to the Portuguese.

Like the South Africans and the Rhodesians in their bush wars, the Aerospatiale SA-316 Alouette III was arguably the most successful counterinsurgency machine ever built outside the United States. Lightweight, underpowered and saddled with a comparatively low speed, these tiny choppers could take a remarkable amount of punishment from triple-A ground fire yet, more often than not, still manage to return to base, a few times with their tail booms or a partially crippled rotor hanging by a thread.

Although almost half a century old, there are still Alouettes operational in both military and civilian sectors in scores of countries around the globe, which might be expected since there were almost 1,500 units built by the time production ended in 1979 (apart from another 500 built in India and Romania under licence).

It is interesting that one of the first Alouette IIIs to come off the production line landed and took off in July 1960 with seven people on board and reached an altitude just short of 5,000 metres in the French Alps near Mont Blanc. Speak to some of the 'fly boys' who piloted their 'Alos' through a variety of attacks and onslaughts across the length and breadth of Africa – including Angola, Mozambique and Portuguese Guinea – and you will begin to understand why these were such fine helicopters.

Chapter Ten

Cuban and Soviet Involvement

'As the rebels of Guinea-Bissau fought for independence from Portugal, Cuban military instructors stood by their side and Cuban doctors treated their wounds. Joining the rebellion in 1966 and remaining through to the war's end in 1974, that was the longest Cuban intervention in Africa before the dispatch of Cuban troops to Angola in November 1975 [to fight in the civil war]. It was also the most successful,' the Guiné-Bissau newspaper *Nõ Pintcha* declared, adding, 'Cuban solidarity was decisive for our struggle.' Professor Gleijeses's observation was only one example of Cuban support for various insurgencies in Africa. There were others who also highlighted Castro's involvement in those conflicts, yet curiously, very little in Portugal itself, both during the war and after it ended as ignominiously as it did.

In order to understand the extent of Soviet – and in particular, Cuban – involvement in Portugal's colonial wars in Africa, one has need to review a tranche of documents that emerged in Havana a few years ago. These were not officially released, but came from an unnamed whistleblower who had defected to the United States.

What becomes immediately clear is that from the 1960s and thereafter, both the Soviet Union and its Cuban surrogate had been actively fomenting their own brand of a 'people's revolt', geared for the communists to take over in some African countries, very much as Fidel Castro had in his own. Moreover, it had been going on for many years, with Angola – because of its enormous natural resources and strategic position in the South Atlantic – being top of the pile. More salient, both Moscow and Havana were supported, most times clandestinely, by radical fellow-travellers within the Portuguese armed forces and the government. Some, like Admiral Rosa Coutinho, was already being referred to in Lisbon's inner circles – and at the highest level of state – as 'the Red Admiral'.

The subversive arrangement within the African framework between the Soviets and Cuba worked very well, with Castro's people doing much of the ground work and Moscow providing the wherewithal for conducting three wars – in Angola, Mozambique and Portuguese Guinea. Essentially, what took place in Angola eventually also came also to be echoed within PAIGC corridors of power.

One of the most significant series of documents that emerged were those involving Castro's emissaries to the Angolan rebel leader Agostinho Neto: many are dated early 1970s, which suggests a few years before the Portuguese capitulated. Written by Raúl Diaz Arguelles, a Cuban leader of what was termed The Tenth Direction and marked for the attention of the Minister of the [Cuban] Revolutionary Armed Forces, it reported on a visit to Luanda where conversations were held with Agostinho Neto, chairman of the MPLA, its Politburo as well as the head of the Angolan army. Subjects covered included military training for Angolan revolutionaries in Cuba itself and links to both FRELIMO (the Mozambique liberation group) as well as to Cabral's PAIGC. Also dealt was the supply of weapons and other matériel with which to fight 'enemies of the people' as well as strong condemnation of the forces of imperialism and capitalism and the rest. Not long afterward Cuban troops were being clandestinely flown into remote northern Angolan airstrips by Soviet planes, in much the same way they were being shipped to Conakry in the Republic of Guinea to assist in the war against the Portuguese.

This new development involving an acknowledged communist state with clear African aspirations immediately illuminated the Kremlin's long-term intentions. Cuba had already been involved militarily in Africa for several years: in the Congo, Somalia, Eritrea, with Egyptian forces in Yemen and Algeria, and with the Polisario Front against Morocco in the Western Sahara.

In these two ventures – the wars in Angola and Portuguese Guinea, thousands of tons of Soviet arms and equipment were airlifted by aircraft flying regular shuttles from Eastern Europe. There was also movement of military hardware by ship to Dar es Salaam in Tanzania for use by liberation forces in both Mozambique and Rhodesia and obviously stuff was also coming from communist China. Clearly, all three guerrilla movements were getting much more economic support from a variety of hostile states than Lisbon was receiving under the table from NATO.

All this subterfuge was coordinated (in conjunction with Soviet allies) by Moscow, whose commissars divided training and support needs between participating countries like Tanzania, Ethiopia, Algeria, Libya, Guinea (Conakry) and several Soviet states that included Bulgaria, Czechoslovakia, Romania and others.

Gradually Cuba came to head the list, underscored by a memorandum from the Centro de Informacion de la Defensa de las Fuerzas Armadas Revolucionarias dated 22 November 1972. Compiled by Major Manuel Piñeiro Lozada to Major Raúl Castro, Fidel's brother, it was headed: 'Shipment of Comrades to Africa':

> For some time now we have discussed the possibility of entering Angola, Guiné (Portuguese Guinea) and Mozambique with the objective of getting to know the revolutionarily movements in those countries.
>
> These movements have been a mystery even for those socialist countries that provide them with considerable aid. This research would help us give more focused aid to those movements.
>
> I don't consider it necessary to delineate the strategic nature of these countries [of what is taking place]. It takes only pointing out that a change in the course of events of the wars that are developing in both countries could signify a change in all the forces on the African continent.

By the time that Cuba and the Soviet Union became involved in these African liberation struggles, the PAIGC was already waging a highly efficient guerrilla campaign in Portuguese Guinea against government forces from its rear bases in the Guinea Republic, with a major operational headquarters in Conakry. Amilcar Cabral's insurgent army was to prove itself the deadliest of all the movements militarily active in Lisbon's African colonies.

However, the guerrillas had their problems. For a start, they started out dismally ignorant of proper know-how and combat skills related to the use of sophisticated equipment like artillery and mortar deployments which would obviously have been useful to harass the Portuguese garrisons located near the border. Many anti-Portuguese fusillades were actually fired from across the border and it was rare that any cross-border follow-ups would result. Cadres also had to be taught how to use landmines to maximum advantage and by all accounts, they learned this discipline very quickly because it was straightforward.

Consequently, the first advisers of the Misión Militar Cubana en Guinea y Guinea-Bissau (Cuban Military Mission in Guinea and Guinea-Bissau, or MMCG) arrived in Conakry on 8 May 1967. Thereafter, the MMCG included between fifty and sixty operators in Guinea-Conakry, mostly artillerymen. Furthermore, Cuban advisers were responsible for training PAIGC fighters in the use of a bunch of new weapon systems delivered by the Soviets or other Eastern Bloc countries and from time to time, Cuban specialists even crossed the Guinean border to direct their students how to use indirect fire to maximum effect.

Spínola did not remain altogether unresponsive. His forces had already been fighting the enemy on the offshore islands, Como especially. In November 1971 his forces launched a raid that, in retrospect was extremely risky but also remarkably well coordinated against Conakry, to rescue soldiers that had been taken captive. For once, Lisbon demonstrated a willingness to conduct operations against an enemy that had become overly secure within the confines of a hostile host nation. I deal with this action in some detail later.

Also, the Portuguese Air Force by then had deployed Fiat G-91 fighter-bombers in Guinea-Bissau, and the relatively small Guinean Air Force was clearly unable to provide a credible deterrent against potential Portuguese air raids, noticeably because its squadron of MiG-17Fs lacked qualified pilots while low maintenance standards resulted in equally low availability rates. For these reasons, only one Guinean MiG-17 managed to take off during the November 1971 raid and failed anyway to attack the retreating Portuguese ships. A short while later, Nigeria loaned Conakry some of its pilots to fly available MiG fighters who, even Lagos had to admit, were not the most competent aviators in Africa. Nigeria then was experiencing one of the highest aviation accident rates in the world, one of the reasons why Nigerian Airways passenger jets were eventually banned from entering American air space.

Obviously, something had to be done, and this situation triggered a doubling-down of Cuban involvement. Accordingly, eight pilots from the Cuban Revolutionary Air and Air Defence Force (Defensa Anti-Aérea Y Fuerza Aérea Revolucionaria) – commonly abbreviated to DAAFAR – arrived in two groups in February and May 1973 together with a small detachment of technicians. Thanks to this support, the Guinean Air Force was soon able to keep a pair of MiG-17Fs on standby for take-off around the clock, while frequent combat air patrol (CAP) missions were flown along the border with Guinea-Bissau as well as along the coast. Meanwhile, Cuba helped to extend the runways of Conakry, Kankan and Labé airports and erected several P-37 and P-12 radars.

Despite several Portuguese air strikes on Guinean territory, Soviet-supplied MiGs and Lisbon's Fiats never actually engaged in air combat. The closest they came to reality was in September 1973 when a pair of MiG-17s, piloted by a Cuban and a Guinean, crossed the border to make a visual low-altitude reconnaissance of a Portuguese garrison before returning to base. As a result, the Portuguese scrambled a pair of G-91s from Bissalanca, but failed to intercept the Soviet jets which had withdrawn at high speed.[1]

It is worth mentioning that Fidel Castro's intent to become militarily involved in Portugal's African wars became clear shortly after Belgium granted independence to the Belgian Congo in June 1960. The country was then renamed the Democratic Republic of the Congo, but carnage in all major centres ensued within days of Brussels's hasty retreat back to Europe. The country at that stage – with a population of millions – had only six university graduates and, clearly, was totally unprepared for managing its own affairs. This state of affairs resulted in the Congo's army and police force mutinying and with nobody effectively in charge, chaos resulted, especially in the bigger northern cities like Leopoldville, which was eventually renamed Kinshasa. The same with Stanleyville farther east, which became Kisangani. It was then that the first group of mercenaries was hired to restore order, but they were a rough bunch of European ruffians.

---

1. Piero Gleijeses, pp. 189-97 & 209; José Matos, www.Ecured.cu/Mikoyan-Gurevich_MiG-17.

Late in 1965 – a few years after many more African countries had been handed full independence by Britain, France and Spain – the Argentine-born revolutionary Che Guevara spent time in Africa on an assignment backed by Castro himself. The intent was to study revolutionary options in several countries still under colonial rule and, in particular, the recently independent Congo, Angola's nearest neighbour. By then Guevara had been made a member of Havana's Politburo and all three wars in the Portuguese territories were in full flow. Somebody in the Cuban capital must have believed that prospects on the 'Black Continent' for revolution were good for expanding the Marxist credo among the 'uninitiated'. Using Dar es Salaam as a base, Guevara spent months in the eastern reaches of Mobuto's Congo, a good part of it with Laurent Kabila, who was eventually to become president of this vast country. On his return home, Guevara reported that there was excellent reason for Moscow and its surrogates to become involved in Africa's troubles, the first being strategic and the reasons are basic: being a part of the Soviet intention to attempt to convert all of Africa to communism.

There was another reason, linked to Moscow's Cold War interests: by bringing large tracts of Africa within its domain, the Soviets would have derived invaluable strategic and economic advantages from a take-over of Angola and also Mozambique, which fringed the littoral of the Indian Ocean. In the broader picture, hostilities would then expand southward, the idea being to eventually cripple South Africa politically, militarily and economically. In theory, it made very good sense: Moscow was already well ensconced in the Republic of Guinea – which bordered on Portuguese Guinea – and documents uncovered after the break-up of the Soviet Union suggest that the Kremlin always intended expanding its interests southward, which would ultimately allow Moscow to eventually dominate the oil route around the Cape, the biggest single conduit of oil supplies between the Middle East and Europe.

In this regard hostilities in Portuguese Guinea (and Angola and Mozambique) became integral to Moscow's strategic planning, one of the reasons why the conflict in the tiny colonial West African enclave became the most intense of Lisbon's three African campaigns, all of which had already become an enormous drain on Portuguese resources.

A good deal of this subterfuge was coordinated by the Politburo, whose commissars divided training and support needs between participating states like Tanzania, Ethiopia, Algeria, Libya, Congo (Brazzaville), Guinea (Conakry) as well as several Soviet states that included Bulgaria, Czechoslovakia and Romania. There were also informal links with Beijing but with time, Cuba's revolutionary efforts in Africa came to head the list.

The bottom line with regard to all these developments is that none of it would have happened had there not been solid and ongoing collusion with radical influences within the Portuguese government and armed forces, not only in Lisbon but in all three of Portugal's troubled African possessions.

We can observe this from what took place once the new revolutionary military leadership in Portugal – after the 1974 military putsch in Lisbon – formally declared that all metropolitan troops would be withdrawn from Africa. Angola quickly became the focal point of this policy, in part because the group of officers who headed the coup declared that the best course of action would be to cooperate fully with the most of effective of the three revolutionary movements. This was the MPLA or Movimento Popular de Libertação de Angola, which, like Bissau's PAIGC, had been a Soviet surrogate for more than a decade.

That was the official version. What also emerged was that Admiral António Alva Rosa Coutinho – the man effectively running the show in Angola – was a full-blown, card-carrying communist. The fact that he had been appointed to the topmost position in Angola, Portugal's largest and wealthiest African colony, suggests that there must have been others who shared his sentiments. Documents that emerged from Havana's CIDFAR (Centro de Informacion de la Defensa de las Fuerzas Armadas Revolucionarias or Centre of Information of the Armed Forces) also make it clear that the admiral was not only aware of Cuban political aspirations in Angola but actually helped realize them. For a start, he knew about clandestine groups of Castro's people entering the country – anything from sixty to 100 trained personnel at a time usually flown into remote air strips in the north of the country in Soviet transport planes. Similarly, he would have been party to secret arms shipments landed along the coast north of Luanda.[2]

2. 'Conflicting Missions: Secret Cuban Documents on History of Africa Involvement', former CIA Station Chief on Angola Conflict interview with Piero Gleijeses, National Security Archive Electronic Briefing Book No. 67 edited by Peter Kornbluh, 2002.

Something similar was taking place in Portuguese Guinea, but launched from Guinean soil to the south of the enclave. Cuban involvement in Portuguese Guinea gained considerable impetus after the PAIGC leader Amilcar Cabral attended the radical Third World Tricontinental Conference in Havana in 1966; word has it that he made a strong impression on Fidel Castro and the two men went on to become good friends, confidants even, some say. As a result, Havana agreed to supply the rebel movement with a range of military experts that were well versed in the use of artillery, landmines, logistics and training. Medical personnel and technicians to assist in the independence struggle followed.

The head of the Cuban Military Mission in Guinea (Conakry) was Victor Dreke, a rather unusual Soviet-trained *eminence grise* with good experience in intelligence and subterfuge. Dreke was close to his boss, Fidel Castro, to whom he personally answered while abroad. One report states that as a result, the PAIGC had carried out almost 150 attacks on Portuguese barracks and army encampments roughly a year after Dreke had taken command, and it was claimed (but never substantiated) that the rebels effectively controlled two-thirds of Portuguese Guinea. In my own view, having travelled widely throughout the Portuguese territory on my missions to gather material, I would have put their control at about 10 or 20 per cent, none of it fully liberated, with the exception of some of the offshore islands.

The following year, with the arrival of General Antonio de Spínola, Portugal – as a matter of great urgency because of the awareness that the situation could turn – began a new and more intensive campaign against the guerrillas which, apart from the military effort, included a great deal of civil action. Spínola launched programmes to build new schools, hospitals, housing complexes as well as improving the road system in the country. He also initiated a vigorous campaign to incorporate more Africans within the armed forces and in the process established the all-black Special Forces *comandos africanos* unit, which served with distinction until Lisbon pulled its forces back to Europe in 1975.

But long before that happened, General de Spínola, now in total command of the country in both civil and military roles, inculcated within the Portuguese forces in the enclave a new determination to halt the PAIGC's efforts to overrun the country: in this he achieved some remarkable results within a comparatively short time. There is also evidence that he orchestrated gaining access and making use of some of the weapons the Americans had introduced into Vietnam, which included napalm and defoliants.

On the Cuban side, Victor Dreke had the appropriate background to achieve results in an African colonial war. During Castro's Cuban revolution and thereafter, he was one of the commanders of the so-called *Lucha Contra Bandidos* (War Against Bandits), a series of battles against CIA-backed anti-communist forces in the Las Villas province of Cuba. He also spent time in the Congo, serving as a deputy to Che Guevara, after which he was appointed head of Cuba's diplomatic mission in Conakry.

Following his return from Zaire, Dreke headed Cuba's UM 1546, the unit in Havana's Ministry of Interior that oversaw the military training of foreigners and of Cubans preparing to go on military missions abroad. He was reported by a source to have commented to one of his aides: 'Fidel told me: "You must take charge of the military mission in Guinea."' The Cuban leader also urged Dreke to take with him to the West African war some of the men who had been with him in Zaire. 'The best' were Castro's words.

There was much evidence of Cuban and Soviet activity in Sékou Touré's Republic of Guinea. These included numerous radio transmitting stations, monitoring bases, as well as Soviet spy ships operating quite blatantly off Bissau's coast, as they were too, quite flagrantly off South West Africa (Namibia today), Angola and Mozambique.

In Guinea's interior there were several training camps and in Conakry itself a technical centre staffed by Russian technicians whose job it was to teach the intricacies of some of the more sophisticated Soviet hardware to aspiring guerrilla enthusiasts. They were assisted by personnel seconded to West Africa from other Eastern Bloc states.

It is notable, as detailed in a lengthy report written by Piero Gleijeses, that as long as Amilcar Cabral headed the PAIGC the Cuban military presence would remain a secret. That was why, Gleijeses explains (quoting Luis Cabral, his brother), 'he asked Fidel that the technicians [sent from Cuba] be blacks ... but it soon became public knowledge that the men who were driving the PAIGC trucks were Cubans; they were the only people in Conakry who smoked cigars!'

He goes on: 'It wasn't only the cigars that gave away the Cubans. The PAIGC fighters in Guinea-Bissau soon knew that Cubans were operating their artillery. One of the men from Havana wrote in his diary that Amilcar Cabral himself told a group of PAIGC combatants':

> 'Meet the Cubans' and he asked us to introduce ourselves. He then explained that we had come from a distant country, a revolutionary country, that we would play a very important role in their struggle, and that we had foregone the advantages of the Cuban revolution to join them.
>
> Furthermore, on several occasions the PAIGC captured Portuguese soldiers, held them in camps in which there were Cubans, and later freed them. And, as Galarza points out, 'our ships docked openly in Conakry with supplies and combatants — there was no way people wouldn't see every Cuban ship.'

Accordingly, in February 1967, Portuguese military communiqués began mentioning a distinct Cuban presence, that Castro's advisers were operating with the guerrillas, and a month later the CIA wrote that 'there are at least 60 Cubans ... reportedly engaged in PAIGC training at the present time'.

Curiously, even though the secret was out, Washington did not respond. The American ambassador in Conakry from October 1966 to August 1969, remarked: 'The State Department was not particularly concerned with the Cuban presence ... it was not a big preoccupation for us.' This complacency, reckons Piero Gleijeses – which contrasts starkly with the American reaction to even the rumour of Cuban combatants in Latin America – characterized Washington's reaction to Cubans elsewhere in Africa: 'US officials were confident that a handful of Cubans could not be effective in distant, alien African countries ... this belief was strengthened by the failure of Guevara's column in 1965 to save the rebels in Zaire.'

Also, in discussing communist subversion in Africa, the CIA barely mentioned Cuba:

The Cuban Military Mission in the Republic of Guinea and which also dealt with Guiné-Bissau (MMGG), which handled Cuban assistance to the PAIGC, was indeed a small mission, but it had a very important military role: it was the PAIGC's only artillery.

It was headquartered in Conakry, in a house provided by that country's Marxist President Sékou Touré and reported directly to Cuban intelligence (M) in Havana, and in particular to Ulises Estrada, head of M's Dirección 5, which covered Africa and Asia.

Apart from Cuban involvement in that West African conflagration, it made good sense for the Soviets to get involved in General Spínola's war, very much as Moscow did on the periphery in Vietnam while the Americans were fighting there.

Of all the states in West Africa during the 1960s and 1970s, the Republic of Guinea, formerly a French colony that rejected French overtures to become part of Paris's extended multinational Francophonic community in Africa, might arguably have been the Soviet Union's strongest supporter in Africa. Ghana under Kwame Nkrumah ran a close second, but this political favourite of the already-radical London School of Economics overstepped the mark by fomenting revolution among his neighbours and he was soon removed in a putsch by ambitious Ghanaian army officers.

For Moscow, Conakry at that time might have been equated to the United States military base on the Indian Ocean island of Diego Garcia, for both had great Cold War tactical value. The Republic of Guinea was not only an essential electronics monitoring hub for the Soviets, it also became a refuelling stop for Soviet ships and aircraft keeping tabs on Western shipping as well as American missile launches from Cape Canaveral across the pond.

Indeed, the Cold War was a harsh reality of the times and much of what took place was both strategic and contained a measure of potential dominance of regions that would ultimately become solidly linked to the Soviet Bloc. A significant presence in both the northern and southern reaches of the Atlantic was all part of it: from their African bases, Soviet Tupolev TU-95 'Bear' bombers and TU-l6 'Badgers' presented a long-term threat to the sea routes that stretched from the oil-rich Gulf to Europe.

What did emerge after the collapse of the Soviet Union was that for several decades Soviet strategists viewed much of Africa potentially as a constructive extension of Moscow's global interests, a remote and expansive new *lebensraum* for the great socialist empire originally envisioned by Lenin. Naturally, financing revolutionary wars in distant lands did not come cheap and these adventures in Africa, the Middle East, Central America and elsewhere – all vigorously opposed by the West – were costing the Soviets billions of dollars a year. Coupled to a hopeless guerrilla struggle in Afghanistan that lasted from December 1979 to February 1989, all these factors combined eventually crippled the nation and led to the collapse of the Soviet Union.

Chapter Eleven

Landmines and Other Weapons of War

I saw it often enough, an unmistakeable, almost palpable apprehension in the eyes of some young Portuguese Army conscripts designated to travel at the head of a column of troops. It was usually that way with youngsters about to tread unfamiliar ground in Africa and leading the pack was not everybody's idea of fun, especially when ambushes and landmines was a fairly well-entrenched modus operandi of the enemy, in Portuguese Guinea especially.

The order for the next day's work would customarily come from the command post the evening before, the basics of who, what, when and how ... but hardly ever a 'why'. It was rarely necessary because there was a war on the go.

The half-dozen or so most important details would head the list: the names of those who would lead patrols in the immediate vicinity of the camp, long-range sorties, expected visitors, usually senior officers on routine rounds (more often than not they would come in by air, followed by convoy duties and the weekly airdrop of the mail, without which nothing functioned properly. Destinations would usually not be posted until the following morning for security reasons, but that was not always the case because in remote parts of the bush or jungle there was only one road leading in and out of the base. What did matter to the men was who would be involved as well as the name of the NCO or officer who would be leading the patrol, who would already have been briefed about destinations or objectives and handed the latest intelligence about what areas were the most active and, crucially, the probability of encountering landmines. It was all for good reason.

The specific positions of individual troops in convoys – either foot patrols or on the road – were usually worked on a rotational basis. If you travelled at the head of a column on the last convoy, you got to end up at the rear, probably on a truck or armoured vehicle the next time round.

It was axiomatic, therefore, that if you had not done 'sharp end' duty for a trip or two, your lot would almost certainly be somewhere up front, or 'point' as American GIs liked to call it in. While the concept might seem mundane, where you were placed on convoy duty in the African bush always had an effect on the morale of the soldiers involved. So did the possibility – always hopeful, almost never a certainty – of being airlifted out by helicopter if you were wounded and/or should your vehicle detonate a mine. The situation was tenuous because emergency evacuations were sometimes not possible because of distance or perhaps the base commander regarded calling in a chopper unnecessary.

The farther away from any one of the air force operational bases that an incident took place, the less likelihood there would be of an airlift out to get you behind the lines to hospital. In the argot of various fighting groups it is usually referred to as a medevac or a casevac (medical or casualty evacuation). Some areas where the Portuguese Army was engaged in counterinsurgency warfare – parts of eastern Angola and north Mozambique especially – were so far removed from air support that it could take days to get a casualty to safety (and then only by road) never mind a proper medical facility with doctors and nurses.

The essential truth about Portugal's wars in Africa – particularly in the vast regions of Angola and northern Mozambique (the former is double the size of France, while Vietnam will easily fit twice over into the East African province) – was that requesting a helicopter to return a wounded man to safety, even if within flying range, was not going to happen. It cost money and Lisbon's coffers were empty for most of the thirteen years that Portugal was active militarily; the result was that most times, it simply did not happen, unless, of course, the casualty was an officer.

Portuguese Guinea was different. The country was small and General Antonio de Spínola made it his business to see that troops under his command – officers and men – got what they were entitled to and to his mind, medical evacuations were a priority. Indeed, getting injured troops back to base was as important as keeping the morale of the average fighting man at top level. Expensive or not, if it were possible to send up an Alouette helicopter or one of the Dorniers to bring a wounded man back to safety, it was done – one of the many reasons why so many of the men under his command went the whole nine yards when commanded to do so.

Most times, if the wounds were serious, the general would see to it that the aircraft was sent out with one of his 'angels of mercy' – para-trained combat nurses who were sent in to tend to the wounded. Such things counted immeasurably when any kind of threat became real. Landmines – both anti-tank and anti-personnel – very quickly emerged as the single biggest threat to life during the course that guerrilla war.

Nor did it take very long for serious consideration to be given to counter the mine threat. Portuguese engineers commenced the herculean task of tarring the rural road network, which made the laying of landmines a more difficult task for the guerrillas. It was easy to see whether the surface of the road had been disturbed when it was permanently surfaced. Also, mine detection was accomplished not only by electronic mine detectors, but also by employing trained soldiers (*picadors*) walking abreast with long probes to detect non–metallic road mines.

From the early 1960s, an enormous range of landmines was hauled across the borders of Lisbon's three colonies in Africa from almost a dozen neighbouring states. Not all of these countries were hostile: for years Malawi played the guerrillas off against the Portuguese (and vice versa) while several nations, if not allied to Lisbon's interests, were decidedly friendly, among them South Africa, Rhodesia and South West Africa (Namibia to be).

While some effort was put into developing mine-resistant, or mine-protected, vehicles by Portuguese engineers back home, the average trooper from the *metrópole* serving in Africa was almost permanently stuck with the troop-carrying 2.5 Unimog, an all-terrain, all-purpose vehicle developed by Mercedes Benz for military use that was admirably suited for Third World conditions. Soldiers sat back to back behind the driver's cab when out on the roads, their rifles at the ready to counter ambushes or the occasional sniper. The undersides of these vehicles – eventually assembled in their own country under licence – offered sparse protection from the kind of blast that came from detonating an anti-vehicle mine, which was designed to be immensely destructive.

It is worth mentioning that the blast of the average Soviet TM-46 (or the more sophisticated TM-57 anti-tank that came later) contained more than six kilograms of TNT, TGA (usually RDX/TNT/Aluminium) or MS (RDX/TNT/Aluminium/Wax). On detonation the bombs generated temperatures of up to 3,000° Celsius. Fuses were usually pressure-detonated or could incorporate the MVSh-57 tilt system which came with MD019 detonators. Some of those mines proved extremely difficult to lift because they were designed with that option. The result was that the majority were usually destroyed in situ if encountered during road checks.

Almost throughout the war as hostilities progressed, many of the Portuguese improvised troop carriers were reinforced by replacing sand bags with steel plating, but this had little effect in effectively limiting blast. But then, as some of the men would say, every little bit helps. It was different in Africa's far south.

One of the first of many dedicated tasks tackled by Ian Smith's government in Rhodesia was to design vehicles that would offer his soldiers some kind of protection from bombs hidden in the ground. Until that happened, Rhodesian Army Bedford trucks, like Portuguese Army Unimogs relied on sandbags. Considering Salisbury's limited financial and engineering resources, the Rhodesian Army proved astonishingly successful in developing several prototypes, though never in any number because that former British colony was perpetually broke.

The Rhodesians made serious efforts at countering large numbers of anti-vehicle mines that insurgents were laying on their country roads, to the extent that some their innovations were eventually incorporated within the expansive South African anti-mine programme that cost millions.

South Africa also went ahead and constructed several of the most outstanding mine-protected military vehicles, every one of them which went on to save lives. That programme resulted in some of the best counter-mine measures to date and several variations of these remarkable machines – like the Casspir (originally for a police role in an insurgency and one of the best infantry fighting vehicles ever built) as well as the Mamba and the troop-carrying Buffel, all already decades old – are still to be seen in many United Nations or national peacekeeping operations. All have seen service in many of the Middle East wars and even in Sri Lanka during its internecine conflict.

Like the Portuguese, the Rhodesian Army was faced with the threat of Soviet TM-46s, as well as Yugoslav TMA-3s (also called the cheese mine, because it looks like a traditional rounded Dutch or Swiss cheese roll). This blast bomb is distinctive because of its three fuse wells, with a fourth to fit an anti-lifting device if needed. There are about a hundred different types of anti-tank mines listed by journals published by Britain's Jane's Information Group and many of these found their way into Africa's wars. Even Cuba was involved: its AT-8 was a square green plastic-cased anti-tank mine (actually a scaled-up version of Castro's anti-personnel mine that contained eight kilograms of explosives). There were also Chinese metal-cased Type 72s as well as a catalogue of others. The insurgents even acquired from Libya some British anti-tank mines of Second World War-vintage that had been lifted in the desert and recycled and some were laid by Robert Mugabe's cadres in Rhodesia.

Moving about the embattled regions with Portuguese units was not as dangerous as most would make it. If a convoy proposed using a specific route the engineers would try to ensure that it had been checked for mines. But when travelling about on unsurfaced roads in your own vehicle, as I did often enough in Mozambique and Rhodesia (several times with my wife), the threat was palpable.

One trip, from the city of Tete on the Zambezi northward to the Malawi was memorable. Our convoy of about a hundred vehicles – almost all large freight carriers headed for Zambia or the Congo – was sometimes spread out along the route for several kilometres. We set out at dawn and travelled at almost walking speed for some of the way. Every possible suspect area was checked by Portuguese Army engineers who accompanied our column, these men moving about on foot. That created additional risks because of much smaller anti-personnel mines which were customarily laid by the guerrillas in clusters of anything between three and six.

A common tactic was to plant a single large anti-vehicle mine in a roadway bordered by obvious cover – an irrigation ditch or a culvert – and seed the depression with anti-personnel mines. Detonation of the vehicle mine would cause Portuguese troops to deploy and sometimes seek cover in the ditch, where still more mines might have been secreted in the dirt and cause further carnage.

Having chosen a relatively secure position somewhere toward the middle of the column, we followed the established pattern after the lead truck had detonated an anti-personnel mine, which required two hours to replace a wheel. Even so, we did do our best to carefully follow in the tracks of the vehicle immediately ahead, the theory being that if his wheels hadn't detonated a bomb, nor would ours. Every few miles or so the column would halt and we'd watch the troops scratching the dirt or digging holes in the road. We were always required to remain in our stationary vehicles while this went on: the area had not been cleared until the entire road had been checked. It was an utterly boring, time-consuming process, which resulted in us taking almost two days to cover the less than 200 kilometres between Tete on the Zambezi and Mwanza in southern Malawi.

It did not take long for things to happen. The first blast happened shortly after we left the turn-off to the Moatize coalmine, and toward dusk another explosion followed, much heavier than before; our escort said something about it probably being anti-tank. It was possibly a TM-46, he suggested, the Russian version of the wartime German Tellermine 42. Word came down the line that it had been detonated by a Berliet heavy truck in the lead squad and there had been a couple of casualties.

So it went: inevitable stops and starts of an insurgency centred not so much on the people who laid these bombs – though they were around, of course – but on landmines. In between, we were sniped at by the guerrillas who had taken up positions in the thick bush all around us, but nobody was hit even though hundreds of rounds were fired. So much for insurgent range work.

We'd come upon holes in the road that had been caused by earlier convoys using the same road, some quite expansive and perhaps a metre deep. Others were barely larger than potholes. Or perhaps they *were* potholes, somebody would quip. Occasionally we'd spot scraps of steel and rubber scattered about the fringes of the road, tell-tale evidence of previous mayhem. There was never talk about casualties, though obviously it happened. One area, near a bridge that had been partly demolished by guerrillas, provided a few disturbing answers. The remains of a burnt-out truck – its cab ripped apart by what must have been a strong blast, almost certainly anti-tank – lay on its side by the road. Alongside the dusty track – metres away – were the wrappings of a bunch of field dressings, together with empty plastic plasma bottles and wadding, some of it tinged black with coagulated blood. There were flies everywhere. The dressings were relatively fresh, which suggested that whatever it was might have taken place a day or two before, probably on the southbound convoy before the last rains, which would have washed away all this evidence before us.

It was the same in Guinea, though more often than not one or two of the soldiers would sit gung-ho on the bonnet of the lead truck in a bid to detect signs that the road ahead had been disturbed by enemy mine-layers. Heavy undergrowth sometimes almost covered the road, so there was really very little the men at point would be able to see anyway.

The system that the Portuguese Army employed to clear mines was basic, though not without risk. Once an alarm had been verbally sounded and the column halted, a number of trained soldiers – black and white – would spend several minutes assessing the situation on the road ahead. If it was felt that the surface might conceal mines, a stick of four men would disembark and walk slowly ahead, using their steel-tipped wooden lances, about the length of a golf club, to probe the soil. It was soft, freshly disturbed soil that would customarily indicate mines. The lances were named *picas*, after the Portuguese bullfight probe, a curious anomaly at a time when there were any number of electronic mine-detecting devices available. Yet, I was to see that throughout all of Lisbon's conflicts in Africa, these primitive handheld staffs were always regarded the most reliable means of detecting under-earth bombs.

It was interesting that all our road convoys actually had on board a variety of electronic systems for the purpose, all labelled with NATO designations. But this equipment, one of the officers told me later, was rarely unpacked from their bulky, suitcase-sized containers because they were all but useless along roads where huge amounts of metal debris lay scattered about. That included cans, tinfoil, spent cartridge cases, eating utensils, spare parts and the rest – all discarded over the years by minor armies of transients like us.

In Portuguese Guinea, Soviet landmines included the very popular PMN (called the Black Widow in some handbooks but often referred to by those at the receiving end as 'widow makers'), as well as a host of others. Even amphibious mines such as PDMs were used, along with numerous homemade anti-personnel wooden box mines and other non-metallic explosive devices. The MON-50 anti-personnel mine, a Soviet version of the American M-18 claymore, a directional fragmentation mine, also came into play in the hands of guerrilla cadres and even a Vietnamese anti-personnel mine about the size of a tennis ball that was mounted on a stake for use with a tripwire or sometimes buried just below the surface and set off by pressure. There is no question that the impact of rebel mining operations, in addition to causing casualties, seriously undermined the mobility of Portuguese forces. Most times it involved diverting troops and equipment from security and offensive roles to convoy protection and mine-clearing missions.

It is a harsh reality that landmines remain as much of a threat today in some parts of the globe as they were half a century or more ago and that more than fifty years after those wars ended, there are still internationally funded mine-clearing operations actively trying to make safe the misdeeds of earlier generations of fighting men.

Over several decades, the Soviets and their allies shipped billions of dollars' worth of military hardware to Africa while these wars of liberation lasted, much of it to counter Lisbon in its three provinces. This included not only firearms and enough ammunition to start ten similarly sized conflicts, but a variety of more sophisticated weapons that had their origins in Moscow's war with Nazi Germany.

Shipments channelled through ports like Dar es Salaam in Tanzania, Pointe Noire in Congo (Brazzaville) and Conakry included the full range of mortars (light and heavy), RPG-2 rockets and their launchers, as well as shiploads of POM-Z stake-mounted, anti-personnel fragmentation grenades much favoured by the guerrillas. Also taken in were Soviet BM-21 multiple rocket launchers, good for mass attacks but which often made more noise than causing real damage, as well as the B-10 recoilless rifle, a Soviet 82mm smoothbore recoilless gun which could be mounted on the rear of BTR-50 armoured personnel carriers.

Every possible variation of vehicles then manufactured in the Soviet Union also went to Africa, including the all-popular GAZ truck or troop carrier which included models such as the GAZ-52, GAZ-53A and GAZ-66. The majority of these vehicles were inferior to anything similar produced in the West, though they burned easily when captured and set alight, which happened quite often, particularly in South Africa's Border War.

We have already seen the kind of air support that was given to the PAIGC, not directly, but through the offices of the group's major benefactor in Africa, Sékou Touré's Republic of Guinea. But very little has been written about the Soviet naval effort, though this was covered in part by the American historian John P. Cann in his book *Brown Waters of Africa: Portuguese Riverine Warfare 1961–1974*. What emerged is that without maritime support the guerrillas would have been largely ineffective in moving men and war supplies around, not only onto landing points in mainland Portuguese Guinea, but also among the offshore islands which were a vital component to the insurgent war effort. Early on Cabral's people captured four Portuguese motor boats, the *Mirandela*, *Arouca*, *Bandim* and *Bissau*. These were not sophisticated vessels but adequate for the job intended, which was to transport troops and supplies northward from Conakry, the Guinean capital and major Soviet transit points at the time.

As the war progressed and at the behest of the Kremlin, the military wing of the PAIGC, the Forças Armadas Revolucionáras do Povo, extended operations and started laying mines in the approaches to Bissau. For this, the rebels were handed four patrol boats, of which several were sunk or damaged in the General Spínola's 1970 'Green Sea' rescue operation.

More Soviet naval craft – three P-6 patrol boats – arrived in 1972, two of which were hijacked by Amilcar Cabral's assassins when they tried to evade capture but they were apprehended a day later by the Soviet destroyer *Bivally* anyway. There was no trial: the men were tortured to reveal the names of accomplices and shot.

There were two other weapons fielded by the guerrillas which were generally a lot more lethal than mines, both Soviet heavy machine guns, which I have seen in action in many wars and, several times, been at the receiving end. The first is the DShK 1938 (*Degtyaryov-Shpagin* Large-Calibre) with a V-shaped 'butterfly' trigger that fires a 12.7mm cartridge. It is nicknamed *Dushka* (a dear or beloved person) in Russian-speaking countries. Seen in action in many wars up to the present-day level, British forces experienced its wrath in Al-Almarah, Iraq. In Syria, rebels mounted the gun on pick-ups and claimed to have destroyed forty cars on a highway in Aleppo and six in Sael on the same day. In Portuguese Guinea the *Dushka* was a hot favourite with the guerrillas because it was both handy and easily transportable. In the field it comes with a tripod, can fire 600 rounds a minute and is said to be smallest anti–aircraft gun by calibre on the open market. When flying operationally with Neall Ellis in his antiquated Mi-24 helicopter gunship, we regularly took fire from this weapon and though we were comparatively safe in the gunship's titanium bath which surrounded our vital parts, a hit in the hydraulics or the tail rotor would have been the end of it. Apparently there were a few Portuguese Air Force casualties in Africa resulting from contacts with rebels armed with this weapon.

The second, far more lethal heavy machine gun that the Soviets supplied to the PAIGC was the KPV 14.5mm with a range of 3,000 metres horizontally and which can make mincemeat of most armoured cars. During my time with Charlie Company, a South African Parabat unit where I was embedded during the attack on the rebel base at Cuamato (and which later turned out to be a crack Angolan army unit), the South Africans lost two men killed and six wounded to this formidable machine gun which was being fired directly at our positions until taken out by air force Impalas. What places the air-cooled KPV in a class on its own is that its cartridge can be used with high-explosive incendiary tracer (HEI-T) or armour-piercing incendiary (API) bullets, and these have approximately twice the energy of a 12.7mm (.50 BMG) projectile. Obviously, any force deploying a bunch of these heavy-duty weapons – as Coalition Forces found in Iraq during the course of those hostilities – more often than not, cost lives. The gun is also a favourite of Islamic State: worse, they know exactly how to use them to maximum advantage, in large part because the distance at which the bullet retains lethal force is eight kilometres.

During the course of Lisbon's African wars, the Russians pumped all manner of weapons into the revolutionary wars they backed, from landmines to heavy machine guns, multiple rocket launchers, BRDM amphibious armoured cars and any variety of devices to kill or maim. Booby traps involving explosives became a speciality with Cabral's people, laying them in approaches to bunkers (often on steps leading down to them) or on paths leading to their camps.

Top of the pops in all these wars among the insurgents was always the ubiquitous Kalashnikov AK-47, which claims as its designer the celebrated Mikhail Kalashnikov. In truth, he was not an inventor but rather a peasant with no engineering training. In reality, the AK- 47 is the improved and greatly modified brother of the world's first assault rifle, the MTG-44 created by Hugo Schmiesser, the Third Reich's celebrated engineer and weapons' designer. Though not generally credited, it was he who devised one of the most remarkable instruments of war of the last two centuries, at least since Alfred Nobel invented dynamite in the mid-1800s.

No question, the AK-47 is a most remarkable weapon. It has made it into the Guinness Book of Records as the most widespread weapon in the world, with 100 million Kalashnikov rifles currently in use. Military and Special Forces around the globe are armed with them and I was to see some of this when some South African Reconnaissance Regiment squads during the course of that country's Border War preferred the gas-operated AK with its 7.62×39mm calibre to the locally produced R4 which is based on the Israeli IMI Galil with its 5.56×45mm NATO calibre. It suggests really solid quality when one considers that Russia (and the Soviet Union before) has not only distributed the Kalashnikov rifles all over the world, but also licensed its production in over thirty other countries, including China, Israel, India, Egypt and Nigeria.

As the weapon of choice by so many countries, it is no surprise, maintains one reliable source, that over nearly seven decades, the AK-47 has caused more deaths than all the artillery fire, airstrikes and rocket attacks that have taken place in this period combined. Somebody else mentioned that an estimated quarter of a million people are gunned down by bullets from Kalashnikovs every year and while it would be impossible to verify, it does tell you a lot. It actually goes a lot further. The guerrillas' AK-47 rifles and its variants were highly thought of by many Portuguese soldiers, as they were more mobile than the m/961 (G3), while permitting the user to deliver a heavy volume of automatic fire at the closer ranges typically encountered in bush warfare. Also, the AK-47s ammunition loads are lighter.

The average rebel battling Lisbon's men in the field could easily transport five thirty-round magazines with 150 cartridges (in 7.62x39mm calibre) on his person during bush operations, compared to a hundred

7.62×51mm rounds (five twenty-round magazines) which were typically hauled by a Portuguese infantryman on patrol. A common misconception is that Portuguese soldiers liked to use captured AK-47s, but this was only true of a few elite units for special missions because they moved about clandestinely and anything out of the ordinary like a G3 would immediately have given them away. Like American forces in Vietnam, ammunition resupply difficulties and the obvious danger of being mistaken for a guerrilla when firing an enemy weapon further precluded their use.

Though not as popular with the insurgents, there were also many Soviet SKS semi-automatic rifles within the guerrilla ranks, but they were usually only there because nothing else was available and would be discarded when more AKs came along.

Armaments employed by nationalist groups came mainly from the Soviet Union, China, Cuba and the Eastern Bloc. However, they also used small arms of American manufacture such as the Thompson sub-machine gun which chambered the 45 ACP cartridge. There were also many European weapons that arrived in Portuguese Guinea from neighbouring states sympathetic to their cause, with British, French and German weapons predominating early on, but later replaced by AKs.

Rebel forces made extensive use of machine guns for ambush and positional defence and these included the RPD light machine gun which found favour just about everywhere as well as the Mauser MG 34 general purpose machine gun or, more commonly, the GPMG. In this category the RPK (Kalshnikov hand-held machine gun) could also be regularly spotted, popular because of its bipod and distinctive seventy-five-round drum magazine.

On the anti-aircraft front the 14.5x114mm AAA cannon was the most widely used, but by far the most effective was the Strela-2 missile or MANPAD, first introduced to guerrilla forces in Portuguese Guinea in 1973 and in Mozambique the following year by Soviet technicians.

Clearly, while the Soviet Union was a willing participant in these confrontations, the financial outlay became an enormous drain on Moscow's economy, certainly not helped by Washington, then under Ronald Reagan, making every possible effort to counter every move by the Soviets. The Kremlin was by then supporting more than a dozen wars in Africa Central America, the Middle East and, of course, Afghanistan, which it invaded in 1980 and ended becoming the ultimate nightmare for the Soviets. All of it cost money and when the crunch finally came in the final decade of the twentieth century with the collapse of the Soviet Union, it did not surprise us all.

Chapter Twelve

Operations Green Sea and Tridente

O peration Green Sea – *Mar Verde* in Portuguese – says former US Marine aviator Captain John P. Cann was a bold, daring and successful rescue of 26 prisoners of war from a prison deep in enemy territory.[1] The maritime-based raid which penetrated the defences of Conakry, capital of the Marxist Republic of Guinea and resulted in the destruction of PAIGC naval capability, was an unqualified success from a military point of view. It was the first of its kind ever undertaken by Portugal, and it again proved the capabilities of a relatively small group of elite troops and the effectiveness of a well-planned, covert strike with limited objectives.

Portuguese operatives stormed a bastion in a city relatively far from their base of operations and relied on surprise to achieve the success necessary for a safe withdrawal. The bottom line was an ingenious plan that ably addressed limited resources, unique operational security requirements as well as an incomplete intelligence picture.

Today nearly half a century later, when one visits Conakry, recalls Cann, the imprint of the strike remains indelible. The locals still talk about the Portuguese 'invasion' with great emotion and will point to where the raiders came ashore. The operation was a brilliant, one-of-a-kind event in which total surprise was the vital ingredient.

The concept of the mission was to send an overnight raiding party from Portuguese Guinea by sea to Conakry and to launch an operation that would shatter both the ability of the PAIGC to continue its assault on Portuguese Guinea and the ability of President Sékou Touré, Moscow's staunchest ally in West Africa, to support the PAIGC.

---

1. John P. Cann, *The Fuzileiros: Portuguese Marines in Africa, 1961–1974*, Helion, Solihill 2016.

Its primary objectives were to free the prisoners, destroy Touré's fast Soviet-supplied patrol boats moored in Conakry harbour and disable the six to eight Guinean MiG-15 and MIG-17 jet fighter aircraft at the airport. Secondary objectives would be addressed as opportunity allowed.

Destruction of the boats and aircraft was essential, primarily as a defensive measure, because the raiding party, having to return to home base in daylight hours on an open ocean would be vulnerable. The Portuguese vessels were considerably slower than the enemy strike craft being targeted, were more lightly armed and being far from home, lacked effective air defences against hostile aircraft. Portuguese air cover from its primary base of Bissau did not extend to Conakry, and thus the returning vessels could not be protected when exposed during the return leg of what was clearly an extremely risky venture. Essentially, the operation relied on complete initial surprise to enable a small and unprotected Portuguese force to gain the initiative and realize all those vital objectives.

The idea for some of the finer details of the attack – including the threat of Soviet vessels in Conakry harbour – had initially come from a Portuguese marine officer Commander Alpoim Calvão, a Special Forces veteran trained as a scuba-sapper. He suggested to General Spínola that the warships could be neutralized with limpet mines laid by frogmen under his command. Both Spínola and the Chief of the Navy, Vice-Admiral Armando de Roboredo, agreed to the operation on the stipulation that the watchword would be total secrecy.

The problem then was that Portugal had no limpet mines of its own, but the South Africans did; some very advanced versions of their own design which were later used against Soviet and Cuban ships in Angolan ports. That meant that the commander was soon headed to South Africa, where he negotiated the sale with several senior military officers attached to the Bureau of State Security in Pretoria and returned with the bombs secreted in luggage he checked in on a commercial flight to Lisbon.

The project would also need updated maps of Conakry harbour, some of which were found when several merchant ships calling at Bissau were discreetly raided. Though outdated, the charts told the Portuguese planning group what it needed to know.

At the same time, in order to update the situation, a large surveillance boat, the *Cassiopeia*, was disguised as a PAIGC ship and stationed off Bissau near the island of João Vieira where the mission was being prepared. The sailors on board were all African, with not a white single white face among them and they wore PAIGC-style uniforms and hats. The ruse worked perfectly.

By midnight on 17 September, the ship found itself in Sangareya Bay off Conakry, having taken up a position between the distinctive peninsula that makes up part of the city and the islands of Loos. Everything that went on to the immediate east was monitored by radar, including a variety of details of the port's infrastructure, including berthing jetties.

In Lisbon meantime, several senior members of Salazar's cabinet began to get the jitters and expressed doubts as to the validity of the operation. The strongest dissent came from the Overseas Minister, Joaquim da Silva Cunha, because at that stage the focus of the raid was entirely on crippling enemy ships in Conakry harbour and possibly destroying Soviet-supplied MiGs at the airport.

At that point, in Bissau, Spínola – in consultation with his naval commander Calvão – came up with the idea that since they were sending a raiding force all the way down to coast to the capital of the Guinea Republic, why not use the opportunity to free more than twenty Portuguese soldiers then being held in the city's main prison. That issue was also submitted to Lisbon and approved, with nothing more heard from da Silva Cunha.

However, a number of other issues arose. Apart from the MiG-15s and MiG-17s, some of the boats in Conakry harbour included an unknown number of Soviet strike craft: these included both Komar-class and P6 missile ships, the former having already proved itself a formidable adversary. Egyptian Navy Komar-class missile boats had destroyed the Israeli destroyer *Eilat* on 21 October 1967 in the first combat use of Soviet P-15 Termit anti-ship missiles. It was also the first time that a warship had sunk another using guided missiles.

Still more work on the raid was nearing completion in Lisbon, with a special batch of uniforms being prepared which were very different from those issued either in the Portuguese armed forces. Hats too, received attention, a local company producing a number that were similar to the Soviet-origin tropical model and customarily worn by PAIGC cadres. From hats to boots, nothing would indicate their Portuguese origin. To complete the charade, all white Portuguese military involved in the operation were required to blacken their faces and exposed limbs so as to appear African.

The operation was kept basic, hence its unparalleled success. As Spínola had stressed from the start, it had to be easily executable, as it was the first such event in the modern period in which a colonial African force was to invade the hostile capital of a neighbouring country that everybody was aware was bristling with Soviet weaponry. Indeed, once done, success was so complete that it prompted Alpoim Calvão, organizer and commander of the raiding party, to observe afterward that 'At nine in the morning I held the city in my hands.'[2]

Not totally unexpected, there was much confusion in the Guinean capital after the raiders had departed. Reports of suspicious activity and Portuguese spies under every other bed proliferated and hundreds of people were arrested. Quite a few were summarily executed, based solely on hearsay evidence. Many reports declared that President Sékou Touré was in full control, but other reports mentioned plans being made, while the attack was taking place, for him to seek asylum in the Soviet Embassy should he need protection. This was all strongly denied afterward.

According to Radio Conakry, a second attempt to invade Guinea was made late on 23 November but was also foiled, which was nonsense. It was admitted the same day, however, that, although the invaders had failed to occupy the airport, they had captured the Camayenne prison and released political prisoners, including Colonel Kaman Diaby, Touré's former army chief of staff who had been condemned to death in 1969 and that the attackers had wrecked the local headquarters of the PAIGC. A day later it was confirmed that Amilcar Cabral was 'safe and sound'.

While no reliable casualties figures were available, it was announced in East Berlin that Dr Siegfried Krebs, deputy consul at the East German Embassy in Conakry, had been killed in the fighting and Herr Helmut Fischer, commercial attaché, seriously wounded. In Bonn, the death was

---

2. José Freire Antunes, "*Calvão evoca Conakry: Às 9 da manhã eu tinha a cidade nas mãos*" [Calvão remembers Conakry: "At nine in the morning I held the city in my hands."], *Semanário* (10 December 1988): 16.

announced of Count Ulf von Tiesenhausen, a West German national who was employed by a German firm in Conakry.

President Sékou Touré meantime alleged that it was European mercenaries trained in Portuguese Guinea who had been involved in the attack. He declared that the group was headed by Colonel Jean Schramme, formerly a mercenary leader in the Congo and associate of French Colonel Bob Denard (who might also have been implicated). Lisbon pointed out soon enough that Schramme had been a poultry farmer in Portugal for two years and was still in that country while Denard was elsewhere in Africa.

Days later Radio Conakry announced another attack, stating that a third group of 'mercenaries' had been repulsed and that hostile foreign ships were still patrolling the coast. According to reports from Dakar in Senegal 'hundreds of people' had been killed during the three days' fighting. Adding to the aftermath of the confusion, the French publication *Jeune Afrique* published what it termed an 'eyewitness report' on 1 December stating that the raid had been planned and carried out by exiled Guinean Army officers and not by the Portuguese. Its failure, it stated 'was due to a sudden power cut and difficulties in communication in Conakry that fateful night' and that the struggle for 'the liberation of Guinea from Sékou Touré's dictatorship' would be continued, as about a million exiled Guineans were waiting to return to their country. The report added that a Portuguese offer of aid to these dissident elements made two years earlier (through Senegalese intermediaries) had been turned down by a majority of the writer's group. In an open letter to U Thant, the UN Secretary-General, from the Regroupement des Guinéens en Europe (RGE), published in *Le Monde* at about the same time, it was claimed that the Conakry events had been the work of the 'armed forces of Guinean liberation', that only Guineans and no mercenaries had been involved, that 450 prisoners had been freed in the action and that General Diane Lansana, one of the 'sinister torturers' of Sékou Touré s regime, had been shot dead.

On the other hand, the Liberian Ministry of Information announced that a Portuguese soldier, Francisco Gomez Nanque – then under arrest in Monrovia – had declared that he had been a member of a parachute unit instructed to invade the Republic of Guinea, and that the invasion had been started from Bafata in Portuguese Guinea. He had escaped, he told the police in Monrovia and been picked up by a Dutch merchant ship, the *Straat Bali*, whose master confirmed later that he had rescued the man.

To that variety of vignettes was added a declaration from General Antonio de Spínola that Portugal was in no way involved in the action. Concurrently, the Portuguese government declared in Lisbon: 'We positively deny this accusation, which has not the slightest foundation. Portugal has enough trouble already in her African territories, because of its neighbours, and therefore has no interest in creating more.'

The other notable operation, which took place on Guinea's offshore islands the guerrillas had effectively penetrated in force, took place some years before. As with the Conakry strike, it has gone down as one of the most important campaigns of Lisbon's African wars. Several large guerrilla groups were involved with the strategic Como Island, the most important target. John Cann's maritime history, *Brown Waters of Africa: Portuguese Riverine Warfare 1961–1974*, is instructive because this joint army, navy and air force operation encapsulates many of the problems faced by the colonial authorities.

By early 1964, and year or so after that war had started, the border area with the Republic of Guinea and the coastal areas around Catió and Cacine had become so badly corrupted by PAIGC insurgents that a serious Portuguese challenge was long overdue. The navy, in particular, had long voiced concerns that without such action its access to Catió would be restricted. Accordingly a joint operation, styled Operation Tridente, would combine Portuguese army, navy, and air force resources to isolate and sanitize the familiar islands of Caiar, Como, and Catunco, which were bounded by the Atlantic Ocean and the Cumbijã, Caiar, and Cobade rivers. Caiar had been the scene of an earlier December 1962 action, which had been a sweep through the island and had had no lasting effect.

The expanded area of operations for Tridente nominally covered roughly 200 square kilometres of land (Manhattan, by comparison is sixty square kilometres) of which only a portion was usable because of mangrove swamps and tides. The three islands were characterized by large tracts of rice paddies with successions of intricate dyke systems, and alternatively by vast areas of dense and impenetrable grasslands and swamp forests. Clearly, much of this inhospitable terrain provided good cover for insurgent groups, as the troops involved in the strike found passage through them difficult going.

The operation obviously had its work cut out, since it was to be the first such joint services operation in any of Lisbon's African theatres of war and would last for more than two months. From the naval perspective, it would be supported by a substantial portion of its resources operating in the enclave and, over time, many naval vessels including the two frigates *Vouga* and the *Nuno Tristão* as well as landing craft and patrol boats were committed to the operation.

Como and its adjacent islands were considered important both to the insurgents and the Portuguese command structure, for quite obvious reasons. For the guerrillas it was regarded as a perfect staging point because the offshore region was remote. Also, its isolation brought with it comparative security. Como could easily be supplied by sea from the sanctuary of the Guinea Republic mainland in the south, roughly forty kilometres distant or a few hours, at most, by boat. There was also the reality that the islands provided an excellent springboard for PAIGC subversive operations deep into the heart of the Portuguese territory.

From Lisbon's point of view, the island threat was perceived as being at the core of insurgent activity and an unwelcome subversion of its population in a prime rice-growing and a very modest cattle-grazing region. The insurgents, in turn, diverted the crops and livestock to their own ends and established themselves as a relatively permanent fixture within the local population. It was classic modus operandi in the Mao concept of guerrilla warfare. Portuguese intelligence estimated the PAIGC force on the three islands to be about 300 fighters, including roughly fifteen military advisers from the Republic of Guinea.

Integrated into Spínola's headquarters was the Special Operations Corps which was commanded by Lieutenant Commander William Alpoim Calvão (Marines), the same officer who had helped mastermind the Conakry raid. He had prepared and performed a series of actions against the naval assets of the PAIGC, which consisted of river ambushes mounted by marines in floats, which took several PAIGC ships by forced assault. In the process his men destroyed two PAIGC ships involved in the war, including MV *Patrice Lumumba* that had been ferrying men and military supplies between Conakry and the offshore islands. For Lisbon, the operation had five objectives:

- Secure the Portuguese riverine lines of communication in the south.
- Protect the population from PAIGC subversion and intimidation.
- Reinforce Portuguese administrative authority over the island.
- Improve the economic well-being of the population and the area.
- Inflict a grave loss of credibility and prestige to the enemy.

The naval concept in this effort was firstly to isolate the area by securing the surrounding waterways of the Caiar, Cobade, and Cumbijã rivers, followed by the disembarkation of land forces in their sweep for enemy troops and, secondly, to secure maritime and riverine lines of communication so that a permanent presence could be maintained in the area. To this end the navy established three zones to control the inland waters around the target area.

All three forces, with the aid of aerial reconnaissance in the form of a dated but capable P-2V5 Neptune aircraft would prevent insurgent escape from land forces sweeping the three islands by killing or capturing the fleeing insurgents and destroying their boats.

Finally, the operation was divided into three phases. The first began on 15 January 1964 with the landing of between 1,100 and 1,200 troops at various sites on the islands. The landings were given close air support by a single air force T-6 Harvard, coupled to artillery fire from a support base in Catió some ten to fifteen kilometres distant. As might have been expected the guerrillas mounted a series of challenges of their own. A string of canoes was soon identified by the patrolling Neptune, which vectored surface craft to their locations for destruction. Then one of the larger navy ships came under fire as it patrolled about 500 metres offshore, followed by one of the frigates coming to its aid, and subduing enemy machine-gun fire. A Portuguese Navy radioman was wounded, with a rubber boat and a PRC-10 radio destroyed in the process. Then a group of insurgents was dispersed by fire from one of the ships, with a larger group taken on by frigate fire before it too fled.

So it went over the several days during the course of that initial phase and into the second, with shore landings encountering sporadic resistance from the insurgents and their local recruits while they tried to flee the islands in canoes or on foot, or to hide in the swamp forests.

The second phase followed, centred on patrolling the three islands to establish a wide presence, flush out insurgents, and gather intelligence.

Following the landing and establishment phases, the third phase lasted two months and involved lengthy periods of intense fighting throughout the main island of Como. More exchanges took place in the area of Uncomené near the river of the same name that separates the islands of Como and Caiar, as well as the Cachil swamp forest on Caiar where the insurgents suffered seventy-six killed, fifteen wounded and nine taken prisoner, a casualty rate of around 30 per cent. These numbers did not include insurgent losses from artillery fire and close air support. Captured correspondence between PAIGC leaders subsequently confirmed a besieged and desperate state among the rebel defenders and several urgent calls for reinforcements.

The Portuguese forces suffered nine killed and almost fifty wounded in the seventy-one-day operation, but these numbers do not reflect the toll on troops from the tropical climate and poor diet. There were an additional 193 personnel evacuated because of sickness.

The routine for troops in the field in that campaign was to survive on combat rations for an initial period, after which hot meals were ferried in, usually from the ships. A major problem faced by the commanders was drinking water was contaminated if not purified. A doctor observed that in one company of 151 men, he treated 132 for related tropical illnesses of one form or another.

Once the campaign had ended, taking stock of what had taken place was vital if any future operations were to be contemplated. It had always been accepted that seizing territory from the enemy during the course of an insurgency was rarely critical and usually irrelevant. In essence, the struggle was focused more on the loyalty of the civilian population. Consequently, Operation Tridente could only be considered to have achieved something of a Pyrrhic victory. However, it did assert Portuguese sovereignty over an area where its presence was no longer paramount and it did disrupt enemy operations by denying the PAIGC a logistic base.

While a contingent of troops remained in Cachil as a caretaker force following the operation, it was eventually removed as not being worth the cost of policing the terrain. Indeed, it also tended to be an object of curiosity for the insurgents, as it was isolated from its support and seen as the proverbial 'target of choice'. Small numbers of insurgents consequently moved into the vacuum left by the departing Portuguese troops, while naval craft entering and leaving the Cumbijã River tended to give the islands a wide berth. Ultimately, none of the original goals of the operation was fully realized and General Arnaldo Schultz, the commander-in-chief of the armed forces in Portuguese Guinea (and Spínola's much-maligned predecessor because the man was out of his depth in dealing with the PAIGC), had limited results in his bid to treat the insurgency with conventional solutions.

As if to underscore the shortcomings of Tridente, Amílcar Cabral held his famous Cassacá Congress during February 1964 at his base near the settlement of that same name on the Quintafine Peninsula, which extends south of Cacine. Its purpose was to reorganize the PAIGC war effort and consolidate his independent commanders into a national army to be called the FARP (Forças Armadas Revolucionárias de Povo) or Revolutionary Armed Forces of the People.

With time though, numbers of both local inhabitants as well as insurgents remained modest in the Como Island region and it gradually lost its importance as an area of local support and for the guerrillas. Alpoim Calvão confirmed this when he returned to Como five years later in Operation Torpedo with DFE 7 and discovered only token resistance.

The PAIGC moved progressively northward onto the peninsulas of Quintafine and Cantanhez, adjacent to the Guinean border and proceeded to isolate the local market towns of Catió and Bedanda. However, both ports of these besieged towns maintained secure links with the capital Bissau through numerous coastal waterways.

For all that, these moves did position the PAIGC to advantageously subvert the interior of the colony, as lines of communication from its Guinean sanctuary through these two peninsulas became increasingly secure from Portuguese interdiction. For Bissau, this proved to be one of the grand operations that from time to time punctuated what might have been an otherwise sound and patient strategy of counterinsurgency in Africa.

It was interesting that at that stage of the war, this kind of large-scale conventional manoeuvre seemed to hold an attraction for local commanders as, to their minds, it seemed to be a means to end the war quickly. In reality, it was the reverse and objectives inevitably fell short. While many weapons were generally taken, and insurgents captured or killed as well as bases destroyed, the enemy tended to melt into the terrain or disappear into the local population.

None of these security efforts could be concealed because of scale, it also meant that other areas of Portuguese Guinea were denuded of troops. In the end, large operations were regarded as not viable because they left the bulk of the population elsewhere vulnerable. Tom Cooper's Air Combat Information Group (acig.org) provides valuable information on many of these operations, including Operation Tridente. During the course of that campaign, he tells us, the Portuguese Air Force flew 851 combat sorties, listed as F-86Fs: 73; T-6 Harvards: 141; Dornier-27s: 180; Austers: 46; Alouette III helicopters: 323; PV-2 Neptunes: 16; C-47/Dakotas: 2.

Cooper also discloses that in October 1964, following powerful pressure from Washington, the Portuguese Air Force was obliged to pull out all its Sabre jet fighters stationed at Bissalanca. The Americans complained – with justification – that Lisbon was endangering NATO defences. The planes were intended to protect Europe's western flank, not Portugal's African possessions, was the view of the American government.

Curiously, ACIG also reminds us that 'the USA did not make an issue about the deployment of former USAF Sabre jets to Angola, but the presence of these fighters [in the war in Portuguese Guinea] was obviously worrying to Washington for tactical reasons, no doubt due to Bissau's proximity to Marxist Guinea where the Soviets maintained significant air and naval installations'. Cooper continues:

> The Portuguese experienced similar problems with deployment of their P2V-5 Neptunes. These were originally obtained to replace their ageing fleet of PV-2 Harpoons as maritime patrol and anti-submarine aircraft. Due to pressure from the United States they could not be permanently deployed in Africa, and were based in

Portugal. Nevertheless, small detachments were sent to Portuguese Guinea and Angola as and when necessary.

One of best known such deployments was Operation Resgate, undertaken in December 1965 when two Neptunes that had been forward-deployed at Sal (Cape Verde) and were tasked to proceed to Bissau loaded with 350-kilogram bombs in their bays.

After delivering successful attacks against PAIGC positions, both planes had to return to the Montijo air force base in Portugal, again due to adverse American reaction.[3]

---

3. www.acig.org.

Chapter Thirteen

Casualties of War

Compared to the kind of casualties we have seen in Iraq and Syria in recent years – and those suffered by countries like Portugal, South Africa and Rhodesia – the mainly white tribes of Africa did a good deal better for instance than some of those involved in some Middle Eastern conflicts. Estimates of deaths in Syria's civil war – give or take 100,000 after almost a decade of hostilities – vary somewhere between 367,965 and 560,000, depending on whose side you are on.

South Africans killed in action during the course almost a quarter century of conflict in its Border War which was restricted to regions immediately south of Angola (together with a sliver of neighbouring Zambia adjacent to the Caprivi Strip), claimed 715 SADF lives. Roughly three or four times that number were wounded.

Rhodesia did almost as well considering that that landlocked country was surrounded by the enemy on three sides of four. That guerrilla campaign lasted fifteen years, though only the last five or six years were intensive, with Robert Mugabe's guerrillas making total use of an independent (and by then Marxist) Mozambique to infiltrate the former British colony. Officially, about 3,000 Rhodesians of all races died trying to protect their country, though some talk of a final tally being about 5,000 KIA.

While casualties in Portugal's African wars in the 1960s and 1970s were relatively modest compared to modern-day horrific casualties, they appalled the nation. There was barely anybody who did not know somebody who had either been killed or wounded in the three overseas provinces, especially since conscription had been nationwide from the start and every family was involved in one way or another. Obviously casualties were one of the most significant causes of disaffection within the populace, something that could hardly be missed by those organizing the 1974 military putsch. The 'Young Officers' used these losses to good advantage to appeal to the nation to end the struggles, especially since almost 9,000 soldiers and airmen who lost their lives in a nation of only nine million had consequences.

Another factor was the quality of medical treatment in the field, which was often lacking. The wounded were obviously treated by those responsible, but it was quality rather than quantity that suffered. As I was to see for myself in Mozambique, there were often serious lapses in getting the wounded back to the kind of hospitals were survival was paramount.

In Portugal today, medical institutions like the Hospital of the University of Coimbra, Lisbon's Hospital of São José and a host of others that are world-class. There is also the Hospital das Forças Armadas (HFAR) or Armed Forces Hospital and it is notable that HFAR absorbed, in a single hospital structure the hospitals of the Navy, Army and Air Force.

But at the height of the war, those few scribes who were able to put a foot inside some of the military hospitals in Portugal's African domains were in for shock, especially if these medical establishments were outside the mainstream. While conditions in military hospitals in places like Luanda, Bissau, Beira, Nova Lisboa (Huambo), and Lourenço Marques (Maputo) were exemplary, these were the showpieces of Lisbon's wartime effort and all were kept in exceptionally good nick; the same could not be said of some the others.

It would be simplistic to suggest that conditions in much of the interior were appalling, but I went through some of them and indeed, they were. They were dreadful, not only in terms of medical attention, or lack of what was being rendered to critically injured troops, but also in modern medical methodology, hygiene, sanitation, equipment, inattentive staff – including doctors – and the rest.

My interest in these issues extended beyond my reporting duties. I was personally interested in what was going on because I was involved with an organization in South Africa that was raising funds to provide ambulances and medical supplies for the Portuguese war effort, run by Cape Town's Doreen Jones. Her committee was particularly interested to learn how things were going in the war and whether the vehicles and very substantial amounts of medicines and drugs were being put to good use.

Speaking personally, I was not pleased with what I discovered during my travels, specifically in Mozambique. One of my reports described conditions in some outlying hospitals as barbarous. In fact, the hospital at Tete was rated by one American observer who travelled in my party as 'symptomatic of another epoch, probably pre-First World War'. We would emerge from some of these establishments and talk about the experience afterward in whispers.

The consensus among one and all, was that only God could help you if had the misfortune to take a hit out in the field and ended up in one of those wards. Worse if you were to lose a limb from a mine.

There were exceptions, of course, especially in the bigger centres, but much of what we were able to look at from up close made the sort of thing that the American TV series *M*A*S*H* look like the Mayo Clinic by comparison.

In almost the entire country malaria was endemic and in spite of quinine, it took a steady toll in lives lost. Many soldiers went down with hepatitis, again because of abysmal hygiene in the cooking places and latrines. This, after all, was Africa, and flies are always a pest, but no one seemed to care. In some places there were inadequate supplies of fresh water.

Portuguese Guinea, it seemed, offered a far more efficient medical service to those serving there, in part, one suspected, because the commanding general took a personal interest in what was going on around him. Unannounced and most times unheralded, General Antonio de Spínola – always the stickler for military correctness – would arrive at any one of the hospitals or clinics under his command. There he'd spend an hour or two not only talking to those in charge but doing the rounds of the wards, the kitchens, emergency rooms and the rest. If he found something wrong, the offending party would be made to answer. He probably would not be put on the next plane home – there were far too many Portuguese soldiers simply hoping for that option – instead, the individual would be charged and likely as not put on double duties. If there was a second offence, it might even be the brig, which in that enervating climate – coupled to short rations and no mosquito nets – was tantamount to a 'brief spell on the original Devil's Island', one officer was heard to comment.

The fact that Portuguese Guinea was only a fraction the size of either Angola or Mozambique made a huge difference. General Spínola could – and often did – hop onto a chopper and meander to the Guinean frontier along eastern reaches of his territory within the hour. Also, he seemed to run a more efficient war machine.

It was while covering the war along this stretch of the West African coast that I met a Portuguese Army nurse, Natercia de Conceicao Pais, a rather lovely young woman of 26, who with a dozen others, served with General Spínola's command in the minuscule enclave. The troops and airmen called them Angels of Mercy. The women were all members of a female parachute corps. While it rarely happened, if at all, the idea was that if things became desperate, she or her colleagues would be dropped into one of the beleaguered camps in the interior to tend to the wounded. Her main role while I was in Portuguese Guinea was hauling out some of the worst casualties from camps in the interior, almost always by helicopter. Nurse Pais had her own reasons for joining the army. She was young, charmingly ebullient and erudite enough in English for us to get along fine. By her own admission, she'd never been seriously in love, though that didn't prevent her from getting about three or four marriage proposals a week, which I suppose, was to be expected since single Portuguese women were a premium in these tropical wars.

'Why did you join?' I asked her.

She was evasive at first. Then it came out. 'I had a brother in the army and he came home with some terrible stories about the war, especially here in West Africa. One of his friends had been badly wounded. Although they did their best for him, it wasn't enough. The last word he spoke before he died – he was just 18 – was "Mama".'

She hesitated briefly to gather her thoughts before she went on. 'That's when I thought that I might be able to do something. Until then I had been working as a doctor's receptionist, so I had a smattering of a medical background and that was four years ago. This spring, I've been here for about two years and frankly, I'm glad I came.'

Para-nurse Pais wasn't part of any select group of propagandists brought out to impress this transient hack. We'd met by chance; she and her patient were on a flight from Bigene to Teixeiro Pinto, the tiny country's second largest town. With her was a man who'd almost been stung nearly to death by bees. He'd survived only because somebody had a few antihistamine pills on hand that he'd kept aside for his own allergies. The patient had more than a hundred stings and his face and arms were like pumpkins.

It was while transiting Mozambique that I was to observe some of the worst of these excesses. During a visit to the military hospital at Tete in February 1973, we discovered one young soldier alone in a ward with terrible leg and abdominal wounds caused by a mine. The stench was something else: it hit us like a foul, wet rag when we entered the ward.

The boy, perhaps 18 years old, was obviously in terrible distress. His pain must have been indescribable because he blacked out twice in the short time we were there and even to this inexperienced observer it was obvious that gangrene had set in. I was with a group of South Africans at the time, some of them nurses, and we said as much to the Portuguese doctor who accompanied us. He dismissed the suggestion with a shrug, but we persisted because it was obvious that something had to be done. On pulling back the bedclothes, we could see that part of the boy's upper thigh that had not been wrapped in bandages had turned an evil shade of green. For that poor soul it might have been a better fate to have got a bullet in the head than to suffer the inevitable lingering death to which he was condemned.

Of course, there were other Portuguese soldiers present who shared the experience, but it would not have been worth the odds to have countermanded an officer. One sensed that such things must have had a debilitating effect on morale, and worse, word does eventually get around.

There were many reasons why wounded Portuguese troops sometimes suffered serious shortcomings in the military theatres in which Lisbon was involved during its African struggle. The first, and arguably the most significant was money. Portugal simply did not have enough funds to maintain three fully equipped and deployed armies in the field, almost across the length and breadth of the African continent. Apart from formidable logistical problems in keeping its more than 100,000 troops stationed in Africa adequately supplied, there were many other needs, air support among the most pressing. In this role the Portuguese Ministry of Defence was enormously underfunded.

Elsewhere I make the point that either New York City or Los Angeles probably had more helicopters on their books than were serving at the time in the entire Mozambique. While that may be an overstatement, I am not far wrong. The same situation would have applied to Angola and, to a lesser extent to Portuguese Guinea (because it was tiny compared to the two other provinces).

What that did mean was that Portuguese Air Force helicopters were sparingly used and if the casualty evacuation of a Portuguese soldier could be avoided, it was. In turn, that resulted in land travel for the wounded, never a healthy prospect for a man with serious battle injuries in the tropics, especially if a unit commander in an isolated and dangerous area was going to be stripped of his only medic in order to attend to the patient.

Last, the average Portuguese Army medic, while more than adequately trained to handle emergencies such as run-of-the-mill injuries or combat casualties, probably knew very little about serious trauma, especially if a wounded man had an internal injury or had perhaps lost a limb. Every soldier serving in Africa was aware that in the tropics an untreated gut wound invariably result in septicaemia setting in within half a day and that death would almost follow soon after.

Obviously, there were many serious casualties that were airlifted out to safety. There were also a lot that were simply beyond the range of the average Alouette helicopter. But then these tiny choppers had a gunship role to fulfil and unit commanders were loath to remove them from the combat area for any length of time, especially if there was a threat of attack. The larger and faster Puma troop carriers would have been better suited for the purpose, but then they only entered the war in Angola in the final years and were never deployed in Portuguese Guinea and in Mozambique only sparingly.

There was one other important factor that played against more efficacy on the part of military medical personnel. Most university graduates – including doctors, dentists, nurses and so on – deeply resented having to be called up to complete their requisite period of service in a conscript army. Many, having graduated, slipped quietly out of the country to find work abroad. But the majority did what was expected of them, signed up after graduation and were drafted to Africa, often in remote corners of a continent that few had ever seen before and probably would have had little interest in visiting of their own volition anyway.

The consequences were manifest. These professionals did what was required of them in their respective military fields but there is no question that with many, their hearts were really not into it. They hated the conditions under which they lived and, more to the point, despised the war and the regular forces under whom they served. The results were pretty obvious: when presented with serious casualties, some with life-threatening injuries, those poor souls were cursorily dealt with, as was the case, I would imagine, with the gangrene-afflicted wound we encountered at the Tete military hospital.

Although my role as a correspondent was largely as an observer covering the war, at Tete I took it upon myself to make a case for the fellow who was obviously in excruciating pain, as is always the case with gangrene. It was as clear as day that if something was not done, and soon, that the fellow would die. Though the doctor I initially accosted did properly react when we took up the wounded man's case, his initial reaction was little more than a pair of shrugged shoulders. He actually did not care a hoot until we threatened to make an issue of it all at military headquarters. There is no question that once we were out of the way, he would probably have reverted back to form, which was sad. In any other Western military establishment, in any other war he would have served time in the brig for dereliction of duties, as he actually should have. But conversely, that would have cut senior medical staff at Tete military hospital and he probably could not have been spared.

To be fair, that Mozambique incident was exceptional. In the broader shape of things Portuguese Army medical personnel that I encountered in many visits to all three African provinces were exemplary in doing what was necessary. During my visits, I was always shown the unit clinic, and in towns the hospital and I never again had reason to complain.

By comparison with other African colonial wars, Portugal did not suffer excessively severe casualties during its thirteen-year campaign in Guinea, Angola and Mozambique. While official figures from the book *Africa: A Vitoria Traida*, published in Lisbon by Intervencao soon after the coup, show that from May 1963 to May 1974 Portugal lost altogether 3,265 men killed in action in all three theatres of war. The balance to almost 9,000 is probably made up by road and other accidents as well as tropical illnesses of which malaria was the biggest factor.

All that bears little resemblance to the more than 2,000 men that France lost *annually* in Algeria over seven years. The number of deaths on Portuguese roads is not surprising, since the crazy driving of the Portuguese made you feel you were far more likely to die in some traffic disaster than from enemy action. The Portuguese have a name for this special kind of madness. They call it *loucara*, a fatalism or super optimism that I perceived was also reflected in the way they fought their wars. There was none of the regimentation or militarism of the Germanic races, but some Portuguese soldiers were often unusually brave, as I was to observe for myself.

The following figures were provided by official Portuguese sources some years after the war ended:

Casualties – Portuguese Armed Forces in Africa

	Guinea	Angola	Mozambique	Total	Avg/day
Deaths					
KIA	1,084	1,142	1,039	3,265	0.80
Other causes	791	529	755	3,075	0.76
Total deaths	1,875	2 671	1,794	6,340	1.55
Wounded					
In action	6,161	4,472	2,245	12,878	3.16
Other causes	2,167	6,595	6,279	15,041	3.69
Total wounded	8,328	11,067	8,524	27,919	6.86
(Disabled)				(3,835)	.94

Notes:
(a) The figures are listed from Guinea from 1 May 1963; Angola from 1 May 1961 and Mozambique from 1 November 1964, and in the three theatres of operations up to 1 May 1974.
(b) In the case of Portuguese Guinea, 4,016 days were used as a basis for calculation; 4,746 in Angola and 3,647 in Mozambique, giving an average of 4,076.
(c) From 1961 to 1973, the total number of troops in the three theatres of operations reached 1,392,230, which corresponds to an annual average of 107,095. The indices for this annual average and for the average duration of the war were calculated on 4,076 days.
(d) According to the Field Manual 101-10-1 (1072 of the United States Army and based on relevant figures for the Second World War in Europe), the indices corresponded to a theatre of operations in classical non-nuclear warfare. If these figures are applied to the total number of troops deployed throughout the duration of the war in the Portuguese overseas territories on a daily basis, it would be equal to 61,112 killed in battle, 240,083 wounded in battle and 707,154 casualties through accidents or sickness. The Second World War lasted seven years, while Portugal colonial wars went on for thirteen years in all.
(e) The number of medically processed Portuguese Army cases of combat and service accidents up to 31 July 1974.
(f) Figures relating to the Portuguese Navy and Portuguese Air Force were unobtainable.

Chapter Fourteen

What did Lisbon do Wrong?

T he majority of wars over the centuries – including some in the modern era – are like games of football: one team wins and the other loses. Sometimes the outcome of hostilities ends in a draw – as with the Korean War which ended in 1953 – or Israel's Yom Kippur War, where the Jewish state did very well but was forced to hand back Arab territories it had conquered in its appropriately named Six-Day War

Portugal's three African conflicts should have been the same, but in reality Lisbon was not defeated. Nor did it win, though the Portuguese Army came close to doing so in Angola by the time that war ended in 1974.

All three of Lisbon's military confrontations were settled by an army coup d'état in Lisbon that year and within a comparatively sort time, a bunch of young officers – inspired by a remarkable book written by one of the country's finest field commanders, General Antonio de Spínola – decided that hostilities must end and that everybody in uniform in Africa should return to the *metrópole*.

The relief within Portugal when the young officers took over was almost palpable. The measure of insecurity surrounding a series of ongoing conflicts in Africa had taken its toll and it was nobody's secret that the nation was war-weary and tired of never-ending communiqués of faraway skirmishes and the casualties that emerged with them. Worse, while hostilities raged, who could really be sure that the government was telling them the truth about what was really happening on a continent that so many of them had come to despise?

The fact that several senior military commanders were radically opposed to the wars and some, like Admiral Rosa Coutinho, actually espoused the guerrilla cause, hardly helped. Also, over a fairly long period, a situation had developed where some officers were actually helping the rebels to achieve their aims.

Those of us who have studied USSR and Cuban involvement in Africa's liberation wars were aghast at what emerged from Soviet archives after Gorbachev took over. While Soviet support for the rebels fighting the Portuguese cut deep into Lisbon's limited resources, there is no question that it cost the Kremlin billions. By the time the wars started, the Soviets had just emerged from giving North Vietnam just about everything it needed to counter America's major ally in South East Asia, followed by an extremely debilitating, almost-conventional war in Afghanistan which started well enough, but soon stressed Moscow's financial resources to the limit. Indirectly all these factors led to the end of seven decades years of Soviet rule. In a sense, it was almost a precursor for what was to happen to the Americans in that region a generation later.

The same with Cuba. There, too, some interesting facts emerged with regard to the Angolan civil war that only ended a decade and half after Lisbon had pulled out of Africa. Tom Cooper, the Austrian-based military historian acquired an enormous amount of information about Cuba's military adventures in Africa from a reliable source in Havana in 2017 and, with his co-author Adrien Fontanellaz, went on to publish an astonishing expose of the true extent of Castro's involvement in the three Portuguese wars.[1]

We had always believed – in fact, the figures came from official Havana handouts – that Cuba had something like 30,000 of its forces helping Agostinho Neto's MPLA guerrillas in Angola. I had heard differently and actually went into print suggesting a figure closer to the 50,000 mark. None of that was correct. Tom Cooper's Cuban files disclosed for the first time that the real figure with regard to Cuban troops deployed in Angola and fighting alongside the MPLA was in excess of 100,000. His Havana source suggested that it could possibly have been as high as 115,000.

Piero Gleijeses, a professor of United States foreign policy at the Paul H. Nitze School of Advanced International Studies (SAIS) at Johns Hopkins University and a specialist on Soviet military policy, has his own take on the extent of this activity on the part of Cuba, specifically

---

1. Adrien Fontanellaz and Tom Cooper, *War of Intervention in Angola: Angolan and Cuban Forces, 1975–1976*, Helion, Solihull, 2016.

where Castro's men were involved against Lisbon's forces in Portuguese Guinea.

To be sure, when the Soviet, Guinean and Cuban archives are fully opened, he declared some years ago, it will be much easier to respond. But in the meantime, he reckoned that we must make do with what there is. Since no available documents bear directly on the question, he can only offer an informed judgement, he declared.

Gleijeses goes on: 'There are two ways to address the question. One is to broaden the context to Cuban policy in Africa in the 1960s and early 1970s and its relationship to Soviet policy. The second is to analyze Cuban motivations.' In Africa, throughout the period under consideration, he says, Cuban and Soviet policies ran along parallel tracks:

> This was not a given: Cuban and Soviet policies could be at loggerheads — as they were in Latin America through the mid-1960s because of Cuba's support for armed struggle there. No such clash occurred in Africa.
>
> In Algeria, for example, the Soviets had no objection to Cuba's very close relations with Ahmed Ben Bella's regime and seem to have welcomed Cuba's decision in October 1963, to send a military force to help Algeria rebuff Morocco's armed attack. Similarly, in Zaire, the Soviets must have welcomed Guevara's column, since they were themselves helping the Zairean rebels.
>
> These parallel and often mutually supporting tracks are even more evident in the case of Guinea-Bissau. The Soviets began giving aid to the PAIGC in 1962, well before Cuba did. The Cuban military presence from 1966 onward complemented and enhanced the Soviet role, since the Cubans were in charge of the increasingly sophisticated weapons provided by the USSR.
>
> It follows, some will say, that the Cubans were the cannon fodder, but the fact that their policies ran along parallel tracks does not make Cuba an agent of the Soviet Union. In fact Cuba was following its own policy, a policy which dovetailed with that of the Soviet Union. The case of Algeria is illustrative. The Cubans began supporting the Algerian rebels on their own initiative in 1961 and Castro's decision to send the troops in 1963 was taken less than two hours

after a direct appeal by Ben Bella, making it unlikely that he would have had time to consult the Soviets even if he had wanted to. As in Angola in 1975, it was the Cubans who were pushing the Soviets, not vice versa.

Money – or the acute lack of it – was also at the heart of Lisbon's problems. Though indigent when compared to wealthier European countries like West Germany, France or Britain, the Portuguese military forces did remarkably well, but its forces in the field endured many privations because of a severe lack of critical equipment and military hardware. The very serious deficiency of operational helicopters stands at the forefront of these shortcomings for the simple reason that the Portuguese Air Force did not have enough gunships that it needed for actions that were taking place over vast regions.

It says a great deal if you do the sums: frontiers with hostile neighbours in Angola, Mozambique and Portuguese Guinea stretched more than 7,000 kilometres (more, if all the geographical kinks are taken into account). It was obvious that the military would never have been able to monitor all cross-border movements, not only by the guerrillas but also by civilians who might have shared an allegiance (family or otherwise) with the enemy.

When the liberation war started in Angola in 1961, the PAF had almost 400 aircraft and more than 22,000 personnel on its books, but by the time the PAF Chief of Staff conducted an inspection tour in Portuguese Guinea in September 1963, there were only three Alouette III helicopters operational at Bissau's Bissalanca airport. Because all these machines needed to be routinely serviced, that figure was quite often down to two. In comparison, Portugal had twenty-four Alouette helicopters available in Angola by the end of 1970, the majority with cannons mounted to port.

The figures for Bissau were augmented soon afterward, but shortages remained for the duration of hostilities and there is absolutely no question that with more gunships, Cabral's PAIGC would never have the striking capability it enjoyed.

The same applied to Sud-Aviation SA-330 Puma medium-lift helicopters, of which a bunch were ordered from France in the late 1960s with six on the way for Angola's ZML (*Zona Militar Leste* or Eastern Military Zone) in 1970. These troop carriers did well for the remainder of the war, but the Portuguese Air Force desperately needed more, which Lisbon simply could not afford. Two Pumas were said to have been scheduled for Guinea, until several were destroyed on the ground in a single overnight sabotage attack at Tancos air base shortly after being delivered from France in March 1971. Those claiming responsibility were several radical anti-war groups opposed to Lisbon's military presence in Africa though it was the Armed Revolutionary Action (Acção Revolucionária Armada, or ARA) linked to the Portuguese Communist Party that was responsible.

The loss of those Pumas apart, what it did mean was that there were usually only a handful of these helicopters in any of the theatres of African military activity, and only two for all of Mozambique.

Clearly, all these factors together had a severe effect on Portugal's ability to fight its wars effectively, as did the need for many more passenger planes on her inventory to shift troops between Europe and the colonies instead of sending them all by sea which could often take more than a month.

With the wars in Africa gathering strength and because of hostile neighbouring states, things simply could not go on the way they were. Something eventually had to give.

Something of a solution was found in the ability of the Portuguese Army to recruit locally. We have already seen that these black soldiers were not only outstanding fighters but, almost to a man, totally committed to the anti-insurgency cause. Naturally, as hostilities progressed, Lisbon gave orders to draw more heavily on locally recruited troops to pursue the struggle because African soldiers were not only cheaper to maintain than metropolitan troops but provided specific capabilities such as an intimate knowledge of the local terrain as well as the ability to speak local languages. They were also used for intelligence purposes since they could easily mix in with local communities that were prone to support the guerrillas. That information went on to save many lives.

The problem here, in hindsight, was that it took some years for the process of assimilation of black soldiers into the military to get into full swing. While Africans in the colonies were conscripted just like their white fellow-countrymen, Lisbon was tardy about overdoing their training to Special Forces level, as happened in Guinea soon after Spínola arrived. Many bureaucrats back home feared that they might use these skills against the government. Yet, when it was finally accepted that the role of African soldiers was invaluable, it went full pace. To take Angola as an example (the number of black troops in Guinea was higher), the proportion of locally recruited troops among the army manpower engaged in Angola increased from 14.9 per cent in 1961 to 42.4 per cent in 1973, all this taking place while the number of metropolitan troops increased from 28,477 to 37,773.

As the expatriate Maputo-based historian João Paulo Borges Coelho declared in his thesis submitted to the Eduardo Mondlane University, it was not surprising there that these readily available and often well-trained fighters were worth their weight in gold. The trouble was, he noted, 'once the Portuguese forces had left Africa these same highly efficient forces started killing each other.'

For our purposes, it is worth looking again at some of the basics of these multifarious African campaigns because numerous twists and turns emerged as hostilities continued, not least at one stage, that Amilcar Cabral's PAIGC guerrillas almost succeeded in driving Lisbon's army, navy and air force out of Portuguese Guinea. It was only a powerful rearguard action by General Antonio de Spínola that saved the day.

The new commander-in-chief introduced many changes including the way he preferred to conduct his war as well as implementing many new tactics. That included a more practical use of the few helicopters he had at his disposal as well as upgrading the intensity of search-and-destroy operations, very much along the lines employed by the Americans in Vietnam. Also, Lisbon agreed to send him reinforcements of another 10,000 men, bringing his complement to 35,000.

Spínola did manage to install a more flexible military strategy but also included a change of policy in his planning in order to face the PAIGC in this field. He went on to create civil self-defence groups within the various African ethnic groups, whose leaders he gathered together at a Supreme Council in the Congress of the People of Guinea, the idea being to win the loyalty of the population, or at least appeal to their potential neutrality.

The trouble here was that in any guerrilla war, be it Malaya, Rhodesia or the Congo, the civilian population caught up in the middle is often forced to provide succour to whatever force is present in their midst at the time. Not to do so would invite retribution and that could be terminal. It would be as crazy for a village in any disputed area to refuse to help a passing PAIGC patrol as it would be for them to turn their backs on a Portuguese Army group which might arrive only minutes after the guerrillas had left.

Nonethess, General Spínola went out of his way to manage and explore inter-ethnic rivalries within the tribes. That resulted in a subtle but effective undermining of the ground-level PAIGC support base. Eventually he concluded an alliance with the Fula ethnic group, one of the largest and most powerful tribal bodies in the country, many of whom ended up serving in the crack *comandos africanos* which we saw in action with Captain João Bacar in an earlier chapter. It was obviously a gamble, but Spínola was a shrewd administrator and familiar enough with the intricacies of African power-play to make it work. To carry out this plan, he replaced several senior officers, surrounding himself with a group of young, well-prepared officers who were regarded as experts in counter-subversion and psychological warfare operations. Referred to by their peers as the 'Boys of Spínola', this team constituted his praetorian guard who made good use use of revamped media and psychological tactics.

The psychological impact of Spínola was subsequently romanticized in national and international media, with the result that newspapers like the *The Washington Post*, *Der Spiegel* and London's *Daily Telegraph* began to take an interest in this monocled general in camouflage routinely accompanying his troops and sometimes coming under fire. Indeed, it was not long before Antonio de Spínola became something of an international figure.

It is of interest that the man appointed to handle the media at Bissau military headquarters, and who made a good job of his role as an intermediary was Captain Otelo Saraiva de Carvalho, who later went on to become one of the architects of the Carnation Revolution (*Revolução dos Cravos*) that ended up ousting Portugal's civilian government on 25 April 1974.

In achieving his aims, it was not lost on General Spínola or any of his colleagues who were battling insurgency in Africa that for centuries Lisbon had managed – most times with considerable vigour – to maintain the most dominant colonial presence on the continent of Africa. Also, it was not the first time government control from Europe had been challenged by powerful black warlords. Yet, by 1974, Lisbon went on to lose it all.

What is worth mentioning is that the Portuguese had also been instrumental in creating a powerful and loyal colonial following in Brazil from about 1500 onward (or roughly when Lisbon's agents first settled in Luanda). In 1815, after three centuries of Portuguese domination, Brazil was elevated to the status of a kingdom, alongside Portugal, as the United Kingdom of Portugal, Brazil and the Algarves. But there, too, dissension entered the ranks and a variety of private agendas emerged, some of which demanded an end to control from Lisbon. The final break came two centuries ago when Brazil declared itself independent of any Portuguese interests, though it says much that as with Angola, Mozambique and Guiné-Bissau, the language persists, proudly so, to this day.

Yet, for all their travails, these proud Lusitanians had a string of colonial responsibilities that stretched almost around the globe. Apart from the three *metrópole-províncias ultramarinas* in Africa (together with the adjacent islands of Cape Verde and the Azores, where the locals will tell you today they will always retain their Portuguese cultural and linguistic identity), there was Goa in India, Macau on the east coast of China and what was to become East Timor in Indonesia. None of these Asian dominions was of any size, but each required a presence, both civil and military, though Goa was lost early on when the Indian Army invaded in 1961 and promptly annexed the colony.

Additionally, the African conflicts were not centralized, such as with the wars faced by the French in Algeria or Britain in Kenya. Rather, Portugal was sucked into a half a dozen different rebellions on several different fronts in each of the African provinces.

One major military campaign in Angola's north became two when the ZIL (*Zona de Intervencao Leste* or Eastern Intervention Zone) was initiated, first by the MPLA and later by Savimbi's UNITA. Several smaller revolutionary groups, each eager for the slice of the pie operated out of both Congos – including FLEC which claimed historical rights to the Cabinda enclave.[2]

A similar situation existed in Portuguese Guinea with Amilcar Cabral's PAIGC constantly being undermined by the less radical Dakar-based Frente de Luta pela Independência Nacional da Guiné or FLING. Though largely ineffectual, these smaller revolutionary groups on the ground still required an element of muscle.

In contrast, a single large guerrilla group was responsible for almost all hostilities in Mozambique. Territorially, with a coastline north to south stretching almost 2,600 kilometres – this great landmass fringing the Indian Ocean is one of the biggest countries in Africa, and while the war started in the north, it soon moved to regions adjacent to the Zambezi Valley in the central regions, adjacent to Malawi and the Zambezi River.

Not one of these uprisings was small fry, even by today's standards. With irregular African service units, local militias and village protection cadres (including 'commando' forces at special rates of pay) as well as a police presence that was quasi-military anyway, multiracial Portuguese security forces in the three colonies numbered close to a quarter million men toward the end of hostilities.

Finally, leading the defensive thrust, the Portuguese Air Force – after South Africa and Egypt – did end up fielding the biggest air strike capability on the continent.

The actual numbers of operational aircraft were never constant because there were simply not enough technicians to keep them all airborne. That effectively meant that if the books reflected six or eight Douglas C-47 Dakotas on strength in Luanda at any one time, for instance, there might only be four or five that were actually airworthy. The same applied to a squadron or two of Italian-supplied Fiat G.91 ground-support jets, though these were operational only in Portuguese Guinea and Mozambique for the duration.

---

2. Frente para a Libertação do Enclave de Cabinda or FLEC has been active in the oil-rich enclave for half a century, much of this time operating from bases in neighbouring Congo (Brazzaville). It remains totally opposed to government control from Luanda. In 2010 the movement made headlines when it attacked a road convoy transporting members of the Moroccan national soccer team to a local venue and killed several people.

Cumulatively then, with concerted military activity spread over an enormous series of African regions, Lisbon needed an unending supply of manpower, something that became more acute as the conflicts dragged on. Things were exacerbated by many potential conscripts choosing to leave the country rather than go to Africa and fight for a cause that, as Europeans, they simply could not get to grips with. It was also one of the reasons why the Portuguese turned increasingly toward using their indigenes to assist with the fighting.

More significant, while a trusted member of NATO, Portugal's assets, as we have already seen, were embarrassingly sparse when compared to what her adversaries were getting from the Soviet Union and China. In a sense, this was an African version of Vietnam, only Portugal was no America.

The upshot here was that development of the overseas provinces remained pitifully slow. The accent when the wars started had been on cheap labour which, in part, meant keeping the populace relatively in the dark as to what was actually taking place and obviously, with the media in government hands, that helped for a while. But as in any small society, word gets out. Throughout, the government's propaganda machine laid great emphasis on what was termed the Great Society, but in reality there was little real authority vested in the provinces. Anything of importance was invariably referred back to Europe. Lisbon remained the ultimate authority, which, in any event, was dominated by a virtual dictatorship. Moreover, the African colonies were subject to the bidding of legions of functionaries who – with the military or the law just outside the door – oversaw everything, from local government, administration of the civil service, education, health, trade, commerce, industry to utilities and the rest.

In theory, Angola being an immensely wealthy region with great potential, there should have been an abundance for all its citizens, whatever their colour. In practice, Portugal's African population there, as well as in Portuguese Guinea and Mozambique, were relegated to a level of second-class citizenship that would sometimes make conditions in apartheid-ridden South Africa appear quite conciliatory by comparison. Forced labour was commonplace, as were public beatings. There were a lot of people that simply disappeared, but there is little reference to these war crimes in today's archives. At the same time, while the rule of government was not always brutal, it was certainly repressive and exploitative. Forced labour was exacted on a massive scale: many of the country's roads were built with prison labour.

The Portuguese secret police, PIDE, later replaced by the DGS, could almost be considered a government in itself. Its methods were thorough, cruel, and in some respects might compare with those of Iran's Sawak during the rule of the Shah.

Additionally, while everybody was supposed to be governed by a single, universal set of laws, there were very different criteria for Portuguese nationals and ethnic Africans. Blacks could be arrested at the whim of the local *chefe do posto*, often for trivial offences. Not paying the mandatory head tax or perhaps using bad language in the presence of a Portuguese female or juvenile could result in a jail term. Similarly, anybody encouraging labour unrest for better wages was charged with sedition and could be imprisoned. And since the entire country was ruled by decree, any kind of political activity, black or white was ruled illegal.

Harsh laws were imposed by bureaucrats who were sometimes vicious and uncompromising. Others were mindlessly brutal and were rarely made to account for their actions, even though lives might have been lost. Coupled to that, black wages in Angola, Mozambique and Portuguese Guinea were among the lowest on the continent. Yet, nobody starved. In so many ways, a similar political process was being played out in South Africa, Portuguese Guinea's distant neighbour. Only, Pretoria gave it a name: apartheid.[3]

Overall, in its African possessions, Lisbon did things a lot differently to how the French and British managed their African possessions. With time, Portugal's African colonies – on paper, at least – became what politicians in the metropolis would like to call 'one big happy, friendly family'. It was a splendid idea, except that the colonies were African, most times demonstrably so. The majority of people there had tribal origins that were impossible to ignore, something that was sometimes lost on those in charge because tribal animosity could be even more deep-rooted than an overriding hatred of Portuguese authority. Almost relentlessly, the deep-seated tribal system tended to generate its own laws of cause and effect and as those of us who grew up on this continent are sometimes made aware, these people have long memories. More likely, these sentiments would be ignored by European administrators who, more often than not used their African postings to accumulate as much money as possible in order to retire back in Europe. It is the same game played by legions of Europeans and Arabs who went into Africa for the money and, having made their pile, pushed off back to Greece, Portugal, France, Italy, Germany, Britain and elsewhere leaving nothing behind for those who helped to create this wealth. In so many instances it was exploitative in the extreme.

We are also aware that the system of government imposed on these societies could be insensitive to the needs of the ordinary man. While rarely as brutal as some of the excesses inflicted on the people in neighbouring Congo by the Belgians – the Portuguese, while not racists *per se*, could sometimes be inordinately harsh toward their charges, whatever their colour. Also, being Africa, things usually moved slowly, which meant that complaints could sometimes disappear between the cracks. *The Cambridge History of Africa* tells us that

> on the eve of the Second World War, the *Pax Europaea* was firmly established in Africa. At one level it was a seemingly tenuous peace, dependent on a handful of European administrators ruling over vast and populous areas with only a token force of African soldiers or para-military police at their disposal. Nigeria, for example, had only 4,000 soldiers and 4,000 police in 1930, of whom all but 75 in each force were black.[3]

It goes on:

> Just how thin on the ground the European administrators were, can be seen from the fact that in this corner of British West Africa in the late 1930s, the number of administrators for a population estimated at 20 million was only 386: a ratio of 1:54,000. And that included those in the secretariat.

---

3. Desmond J. Clark, Roland Anthony Oliver, J. D Fage and A. D. Roberts, *The Cambridge History of Africa*, Cambridge University Press, Cambridge, 1986.

In the Belgian Congo the ratio was 1:38,400 and in French West Africa 1:27,500. Also, it should not be forgotten that in parts of the European empire, the colonial imprint was still very light. Many Africans had never personally seen a white man, while in Mozambique parts of the territory were not even administered by the government but by concession companies.[4]

More salient, those same 'concession companies; were unfair and, obviously, motivated by profit. There were numerous exceptions, of course, but the human side of things would hardly begin to enter into their considerations, such as they were.

Despite these disparities, it took a while but the master–servant labour system in Portuguese Africa did become thoroughly entrenched and those poor souls who knew no better, accepted social dominance as the norm. Also, life in the so-called world beyond was unquestionably mixed, to the point that relations between the colonizers and the colonized gave rise to the old maxim: God made man white and God made man black, but the Portuguese made the mulatto.

There were many excesses exercised by Lisbon's cohorts over the indigenous population, some quite shocking. John P. Cann graphically lays it out in his thirty-page review 'Baixa do Cassange – Catalyst for Righting a Wrong', published in Lisbon in 2008 by Revista Militar. As he states:

> African villagers, some 150,000 people in 35,000 families, were hauled from their homes and forced to grow cotton on designated patches of land [in northern Angola]. There were no wages for this work, and when the crop was harvested at the end of the season, the Africans were forced to sell it to Cotonang as well as Lagos and Irmão at fixed, below-market prices, a value between five and six times less than the world price. The crop risk was assumed involuntarily by the impressed workers, who simply starved if there were crop failure and barely survived if it were a success.
>
> The concession companies thus took no commodity risk and purchased the crop from the growers with a certain built-in and

---

4. Ibid.

generous profit margin, a near riskless arbitrage. As with other similar enterprises, such as Companhia de Diamantes de Angola (Diamang), the diamond mining concession, the labourers earned a below-subsistence income, and the shareholders received an extraordinary return on their investment.

Many of those profiting could not even identify Angola on a map.

Then, quite suddenly, arrived the age of *Uhuru* – the Swahili watchword that shook East Africa 'as in a whirlwind', as it was once phrased by Nairobi's *East African Standard*. It signified freedom.

'Freedom of the masses', Kenyan President Jomo *Mzee* Kenyatta would proclaim with verve while he waved about his ubiquitous oxtail that also served as a fly swatter. Almost overnight a novel and thoroughly radical concept was being espoused from one end of Africa to the other, and it didn't take any of us very long to realize that African politics were in a state of flux, alarmingly so.

The 'wind of change' in Africa became a part of that equation soon afterward, and a plethora of independent states emerged: countries like Ghana, Gambia, Nigeria, Gabon, the Cameroons, Burundi, Chad and Sierra Leone. But not one under the Portuguese flag. Of all the European colonial powers, Lisbon proved the most intransigent: sharing power, simply put, was anathema to the minds of those who pulled the strings in Lisbon.

There were few people in the metropolis who were not of the opinion that no matter what, the nation would survive without any kind of political change. What was happening in parts of West, Central and southern Africa was referred to in the state-controlled press in Lisbon, Luanda and Lourenço Marques as a 'passing phase'. Portugal's African possessions, in contrast, they reckoned, were part of a culture and 'a great historical tradition'. For all its faults, ran the concept, Portugal and its overseas provinces had even eclipsed Iberian domination of the New World. Indeed, Angola at that time was regarded by quite a lot of its inhabitants – and many back home in Europe – as the 'future Brazil of Africa'. What Lisbon had not initially factored into the colonial equation was communications. What was going on elsewhere in Africa, could obviously not fail to have an impact on the peoples of Guinea, Angola and Mozambique. How else when Lisbon suddenly had to deal with a number of former British and French colonies that were now in control of their own affairs including several of their immediate neighbours? These included Senegal, Malawi, Congo (Brazzaville) as well as quite a few other countries, including Guinea, Tanzania and Zambia, all passionately opposed to the continuance of any kind of Portuguese colonial presence on the continent. Most of these countries were later to wage hostilities against Lisbon, some permitting armed revolutionary groups to operate from their soil.

Even this, some Portuguese colonists believed, they could deal with. And they probably could have, had those belligerent neighbours acted on their own. But the Cold War intervened because both Moscow and Beijing believed that there were some good prospects waiting for them in Africa.

Judging by that is going on in just about every black state in Africa today, that hope remains steadfast with the Chinese.

One of the principal architects of the African revolution that eventually changed the modern face of southern Africa from white to black was Julius Nyerere, an African academic who was always to be seen in his distinctive Maoist suit and who demanded that his people address him as *Mwalimu*, the Swahili word for teacher. Curiously, the demented Ghanaian despot, Kwame Nkrumah (he was ousted as president in an army mutiny while at a Commonwealth Heads of State meeting in Singapore), prefaced his name with *Osagjefo*. Loosely translated from his Akan native tongue, it means 'Redeemer', which is a lot better than Bokassa adding 'Emperor' to his list of grandiloquent designations. But then, as some of us have observed, unbridled power leads some African leaders to think this way. Or, as the aphorism goes, *absolute power corrupts absolutely*.

Julius Nyerere, a graduate of Kampala's one-time prestigious Makerere University, was awarded a scholarship to attend the University of Edinburgh in 1949, a remarkable distinction at the time because he was the first Tanzanian to study at a British university. Much to the chagrin of the British colonial authorities, the future East African head of state was already very much of a political factor in the old Tanganyika by the time the 'Revolutionary 1960s' arrived. He was abrasive toward the establishment, espoused a new form of African socialism which he called *Ujaama* and had the kind of chutzpah that could sway large crowds. Though he had been lionized by London's liberal society and made a great show of having a white secretary in his office after he came to power, the word in Dar es Salaam was that while he tolerated white people, he despised everything for which they stood. Of course that did not apply to his British education.

After numerous confrontations with London's representatives in Dar es Salaam, he led his country to independence to become first prime minister, and later President of the Republic of Tanzania. That name came from the amalgamation of Tanganyika and Zanzibar after the mainland army had mutinied. A terrified Nyerere went into hiding but was rescued by his nemesis, a British naval task force sent to East Africa by Whitehall to quell the rebellion, which it did in about forty-eight hours. Nyerere was one of many post-war African heads of state with strong academic and emotional links to the radical British left. Others were Kwame Nkrumah of Ghana, Milton Obote of Uganda, and Kenneth Kaunda of Zambia. It is significant that all four chose the Socialist path, usually through the good offices of the London School of Economics. Political sentiments apart, Nyerere ended up embracing every revolutionary who arrived at his door, including a good few from Angola and Mozambique.

Within a year, a dozen southern African revolutionary movements from Rhodesia, South West Africa and even a few that were not yet independent like Nyasaland and Kenya, had set up shop along Liberation Row in Dar es Salaam. The ultimate oxymoron, Dar es Salaam, in Arabic, means 'harbour of peace', but Nyerere was using his city to foster armed revolution. The Tanzanian president made no bones about wishing to see an end to white rule in Africa. He created an entire political and economic infrastructure to that end, first by supporting FRELIMO – the liberation movement in its war against the Portuguese in Mozambique – and, shortly afterward, Angolan revolutionary movements.

SWAPO, the South West African revolutionary movement and the ANC's Umkhonto we Sizwe (Spear of the Nation), soon followed.[5] Much of the military wherewithal needed by these radical groups, that still had

5. Umkhonto we Sizwe (Spear of the Nation), the armed wing of the African National Congress (ANC), was founded partly in response to the Sharpeville Massacre of March 1960. Its leader – Nelson Mandela – was arrested shortly after this manifesto was published and eventually sentenced to life in prison. With the end of apartheid looming, he was released in 1990.

some way to go before they became fully fledged guerrilla armies, was landed at Dar es Salaam harbour. Customarily, this matériel was moved first by road and then on the backs of human packhorses, often hundreds of kilometres into the interior. It was tough work.

A Soviet TM-46 anti-tank mine, for instance, weighs in at about twelves kilos and might have been hauled 300 kilometres overland by a minor army of porters by the time it was placed in a hole in the ground in Angola to await the next convoy out of Serpa Pinto. Like SWAPO, also fighting a war on the far side of the African continent, logistical problems in getting military hardware to the various fronts would often mean journeys that might last months. Weapons would sometimes cross several frontiers, including those of Zambia and, in later stages, Mobutu's Congo.

It was not long before South African revolutionaries established a secure base for their leaders in Dar es Salaam. Larger groups of political malcontents that had left South Africa, usually on foot, were housed in camps in the interior. With time, a revolutionary culture of its own began to evolve in Tanzania, together with a fairly distinct terminology. Tanzania resolutely preferred to call itself a 'Frontline State' even though the distance between Pretoria and Dar es Salaam is greater than between London and Athens. Zambia embraced the concept as well, but that was more appropriate because the country bordered on Rhodesia, and was at the receiving end of cross-border raids launched by Rhodesian security forces. Ultimately these forerunners were joined by Mobutu Seso Seko's Zaire – as well as Congo (Brazzaville) to its immediate north – with territorial interests in the oil-rich enclave of Cabinda.

While all this was taking place, there was a solid amount of truck between East Africa and the two most prominent revolutionary states on the West Coast, Ghana under Nkrumah and Sékou Touré's Republic of Guinea – not to be confused with today's Equatorial Guinea (formerly Spanish Guinea) or Guiné-Bissau (originally Portuguese Guinea). Irrespective of all this nomenclature, the Tanzanian connection was one of several major issues faced by Lisbon as these expanded colonial conflicts gathered momentum.

Looking back, we are now aware that Portugal's three military insurrections in Africa resulted in a powerful groundswell of anti-colonial hostility in Portugal itself – as well as elsewhere in Europe and North

America, especially among many of Lisbon's NATO allies. While the Portuguese hierarchy always made much about its historic and 'civilizing mission' in Africa, a good deal of that was dismissed by a younger, better educated generation as the cynical claptrap of a tottering dictatorship. As the historian and political commentator Kenneth Maxwell wrote: 'Portugal was the last European power in Africa to cling tenaciously to the panoply of formal dominion and this was no accident. For a long time Portugal very successfully disguised the nature of her presence behind a skilful amalgam of historic mythmaking, claims of multiracialism and good public relations.'

The reality, says Maxwell, was something very different. 'Economic weakness at home made intransigence in Africa inevitable. It was precisely through the exercise of [sovereignty] that Portugal was able to obtain any advantages at all from its civilizing mission. And these advantages were very considerable: cheap raw materials, large earnings from invisibles, the transfer of export earnings, gold and diamonds and protected markets for her wines and cotton textiles.'

Vietnam meanwhile, provided Europe and America with a fertile anti-war lobby which, when circumstances permitted, was conveniently switched to Africa. Not only Portuguese Africa became a target, but Rhodesia and South Africa also came under the hammer. This approach was adopted – though much less forcefully – by the educated classes in Portugal itself.

While popular stereotypes might be predisposed to depict Portugal as a stagnant backwater for almost three centuries, students, professional people, academics, the military, government officials and politicians became increasingly sensitive to the opprobrium that resulted from the reactionary policies of Prime Minister Salazar. Then he suffered a stroke in 1968. Optimists on both sides of the Atlantic hoped initially that under Marcello Caetano, his successor, the country would enter a more liberal phase and in a peculiar way, it did, though only marginally so. While some of the faces changed, the political system did not, though to be fair, much was done to bring education in line with the metropolis.

For instance, two major universities were established in the 1960s in Angola and Mozambique, the Universidade de Luanda and the Universidade de Lourenço Marques, and both offered a range of degrees from engineering to medicine and are fully functioning today, which is a lot more than can be said for Uganda's Makerere University, one of Britain's most cherished educational institutions abroad for many years. This was all the more notable since there were then only four public universities in all of Portugal, of which two were in Lisbon.

It wasn't surprising therefore that multiculturalism gradually took root, helped to some extent by the acceptance of the *assimilado* programme which actually encouraged Africans to accept Western values in preference to tribal ones. Here, sport was a touchstone, with many Africans encouraged to vie for top international slots. Among this tiny band of sportspeople was the footballer Eusébio – or more correctly, Eusébio da Silva Ferreira – originally from Mozambique, and who was embraced by soccer players the world over.

On the subject of Portugal's politics in Africa, the Brazilian political commentator Marcio Alves wrote: 'To hold on to the Empire was fundamental for Portuguese fascism. Economically, the African territories – and especially rich Angola – were so important to Portuguese capitalism that Caetano took over from Salazar on the condition that they would be defended.'

Part of the trouble was that in Portugal's African possessions, no political solution to the problem was either found or sought. If anybody stepped out of line, the only answer was the big stick ... or the gun. These people had centuries of reasonably successful African rule behind them and despite the rumblings and mumblings, things continued very much as in the past.

Matters deteriorated during the latter stages of this African conflict by an almost total break in communications in some areas between the security police and the Portuguese security forces. There were several cases in Tete and Nampula in Mozambique where liberal Portuguese officers informed FRELIMO sympathizers of future movements by PIDE officers into the interior. They knew that such information would be passed on to the revolutionaries and that good use would be made of it.

For all this 'dissension within the ranks', PIDE had a good measure of the enemies that the government was up against, and in all three territories. I know from practical experience that they got a lot of help from South Africa, which hosted an expatriate Portuguese community of about a quarter million, many former dissidents from the colonies.

Within the war zones, PIDE worked to a complex set of rules that involved thousands of informants that sometimes stretched all the way to rebel command headquarters in Dar es Salaam, Kinshasa, Conakry and Dakar. It was an expensive process, but it worked, as money always does in an unabashedly corrupt Africa.

Much more intelligence was derived from good old fashioned sleuthing on the ground, coupled to information brought in from patrols, cross-border travellers and captives, or possibly documents taken during or after contacts in the field. There was also limited air and naval reconnaissance that played a role.

As John Cann tells us, 'the Portuguese Army realized this critical need for effective intelligence and proceeded to build a productive network that helped its forces exploit weaknesses in the enemy.' He devotes a chapter that addresses the problems encountered with these operations in the field in selected areas and follows solutions adopted, comparing and contrasting them to the experiences of other countries with contemporaneous counterinsurgency operations that is well worth reading. 'These several adaptations were uniquely Portuguese and in keeping with the subdued and cost-conscious strategy,' Cann adds.[6]

While conditions in the field in impecunious Mozambique remained uncertain until the coup, things were a lot different in Angola which had good resources and was backed by a settler community that numbered more than 300,000. These people knew no other place but Angola as home and were prepared to fight and die for it.

Not so in Portuguese Guinea, where no real advance was possible for its few thousand white settlers because of the forbidding nature of the country: most of that country was pestilential swamp where the mosquitoes and bad water got you if the guerrillas didn't. In a population survey conducted in the 1930s, it was found that there were less than 100 Portuguese nationals living in the enclave who were not part of the government or security.

---

6. John P. Cann, *Counterinsurgency in Africa: The Portuguese Way of War 1961–1974*, Helion, Solihill 2012.

There was also little development, economic or otherwise in Portugal itself, with the result that by the time war ended, it was still rated the second poorest country in Europe. There is no question that a great deal of money was squandered in Lisbon's African war efforts because effectively, for almost as long as the conflicts lasted, there was no other way.

By 1970, the Portuguese colonial struggles were consuming about 40 per cent of Portugal's annual budget and at one point the government voted almost half the entire budget to the military, which, for many years during the earlier period was roughly the same percentage that Israel spent on keeping its society secure. But then Lisbon did not have Uncle Sam underwriting its military tab.[7]

Yet, there are still some who maintain that although Portugal was all but destitute when the war ended, it was not economic policies that eventually caused the collapse, because it was just as indigent when the insurrection started. Their argument was that the dictator Salazar was the real disaster. He had been trained as an economist, and in that he excelled. The problem was that he treated the coffers of the nation as his own, and in so doing, acted like the proverbial miser.

David Abshire and Michael Samuels wrote that during the wars, the Portuguese were able to maintain their gold and foreign reserves. In spite of increased expenditure on defence and the need for external borrowing, Salazar actually managed to *increase* Lisbon's reserves of gold and foreign exchange during the war years.[8]

Essentially then, as the wars in Africa progressed, the bean counters in the metropolis had absolutely no alternative but to cut the coat according to Portugal's tattered cloth.

---

7. Israel, like Egypt, still receives a bountiful $3 billion a year from the United States, originally agreed under the Camp David Accords, the framework for peace in the Middle East negotiated in 1978.
8. David Abshire and Michael Samuels (Eds), *Portuguese Africa: A Handbook*, Pall Mall Press, London, 1969.

Q and A Session on Portugal's African Wars

I n late 2015, shortly after my book *Portugal's Guerrilla Wars in Africa: Lisbon's Three Wars in Angola, Mozambique and Portuguese Guinea* had been translated as *Portugal e as Guerrilhas de Africa* and published in Lisbon, I was approached by José Sousa Dias, a senior writer with LUSA, Portugal's national news agency. He wanted to write about my bulky volume of almost 600 pages which covered Lisbon's three wars in Africa, conflicts that lasted almost twice as long as the American army fought in Vietnam. As a result I was presented with a list of questions. Dias, an old hand at the game because he had spent twenty years covering the African 'beat', was not one to waste words.

DIAS: Portugal was the first European nation to arrive in Africa and the last to leave. Was the Portuguese presence in Africa different from that of other European nations?

VENTER: During the decades that I covered Africa for publications as well as news and photo agencies, I was able to visit just about all of Africa and in the process, I made dozens of TV documentaries.

This appropriately termed 'total immersion' process gave me a fairly good insight as to how things were in the various African countries and how their respective governments worked. Obviously, there were enormous differences between those in the west and countries along the east coast of this vast continent. So too, between those countries whose nationals spoke English and the Francophone states, as well as the Lusitanian countries.

An awful lot had taken place in Africa after 1957, when the Gold Coast, the first of the British colonies to obtain self-government, was rechristened Ghana. Liberia for instance, though self-governing for more than a century, was actually more of an American colony than neighbouring British-run

Sierra Leone or the former French colony of Côte d'Ivoire. For as long as anybody could remember, Liberia currency had been the American dollar and it was only after President Tubman died (in his sleep) and some real troubles started, that Monrovia was obliged to establish its own currency. Until that happened, ties with Washington were so strong that Liberians could come and go to and from the United States as they pleased. Freed slaves had originally been the basis of it, but then Firestone got a grip with the rubber industry which became of strategic importance during two world wars. In the end, Firestone almost ran the country.

The two African colonial powers that really stood apart from the rest were Britain and France, both quite benevolent in their approach to imperial rule. France's mission was always to draw its colonies closer to what it termed the 'Motherland'. In turn, Africa provided France with much of the raw materials it needed as a commercial and industrial power. Obviously, all important matters were referred to Paris.

It did not take long after the end of the Second World War for the Elysée Palace to accept that these colonies would not remain subservient forever. A rebellion had already started in Indochina, which resulted in form of self-rule being implemented in places like Dakar, Yaoundé, Abidjan, Libreville, Bangui and elsewhere. It worked quite well because French rule of law prevailed and ordinary people were protected.

The British went a step further. Though they had their all-powerful governors in capitals like Nairobi, Lagos, Freetown and Dar es Salaam, Whitehall did not meddle in matters linked to tribal affairs. The eminent Lord Lugard had originally established what was referred to in Nigeria as 'indirect rule' for the Muslim people in the north and that meant that day-to-day government and administration was left in the hands of traditional Islamic rulers.

It is worth mentioning that when I met General de Spínola at his Bissau headquarters I had already observed his approach to local tribal leaders in Guiné (some of the photos here cover that aspect) and the 'Lugard' issue of a form of self-government had actually been raised. I got the impression that General Spínola had already considered that that might be the way forward because the war could not go on forever. I did sense that in raising the issue that I might be stirring muddy waters and he soon changed the subject.

My opinion is that if Spínola had time and resources on his side (which he did not), he could have made it work: the village self-defence concept was quite widespread in Portuguese Guinea and once in place, it operated quite well.

With regard to Black Africa generally, one must accept that Britain and France – as well as Spain, Italy and Belgium (and Germany before it lost all its colonies after the First World War) – were relatively newcomers to actually *colonizing* Africa. Though the French and the English had traded with the continent for a couple of hundred years, the British only annexed Lagos in 1861. Nairobi was established as the Kenyan capital in 1899. In contrast, Portugal put roots down on the African continent almost 500 years ago.

DIAS: Does that explain how Portugal could maintain a war in three African fronts for more than a decade?

VENTER: In trying to explain why Portugal fought so hard for more than a decade to prevent its provinces in the *ultramar* from being lost, one has to accept the reality that, like it or not, Lisbon knew and understood Africa and its peoples a lot better than any other European power.

Further, the rebellion in Angola's north in 1961 was nothing new. There had been many uprisings, rebellions and revolutions in the past, some quite minor and a few that needed a good deal of effort, time and manpower to quash.

When explaining reasons why Lisbon had reacted so strongly to the Angolan attacks in the early 1960s, Prime Minister Salazar said on numerous occasions that the provinces were, as he phrased it, 'an extension of Portugal itself', the idea being that if Angola was lost, all would be lost. 'All three African territories are part of the greater Portugal,' he once stated, adding that he was not going to allow centuries of historic 'civilizing' tradition to give way to radicals with guns. The consensus in Lisbon at the time was that this sort of thing had happened before and that things would eventually settle down.

Those in Lisbon who believed they were 'in the know' would remind the populace that some of the early rebellions in both Angola and Mozambique had been extensive. All had been put down, some quite brutally, particularly in regions adjacent to German South West Africa (before the First World War).

It is interesting that there are many recorded instances of South Africans having been hired to fight in some of the earlier conflicts in Angola, according to French historian René Pélissier; in fact, several dozen times the century before. But what is astonishing is that Portugal was able to rally the way it did when, for a time, all seemed lost in northern Angola in 1961.

One needs to recall that two or three thousand Portuguese civilians were slaughtered by the rebels (they were still a rabble, some reported, and not yet worthy of being classified as guerrillas) never mind tens of thousands of local people who were killed.

Portugal then was a nation of nine million people and, after Albania, the second poorest country in Europe, so obviously the impact of that rebellion was severe. One needs to accept too, that while the Portuguese were not battling the most sophisticated enemy on the planet, the guerrillas quickly evolved into a fairly effective fighting force and were kept very well supplied by the Soviets with the same weapons then being deployed against the Americans in Vietnam. Also, guerrilla cadres from all three territories were being trained in their thousands in military establishments behind the Iron Curtain, China and Cuba as well as in a dozen African states that enjoyed Moscow's support.

It is also true that the guerrillas trained by Eastern Bloc states were streets ahead of those funded by the West, with the single exception of UNITA which went on to control something like 90 per cent of Angola's rural regions at one stage of the civil war that followed Lisbon's exodus from Africa.

The Washington-supported FNLA, in contrast, was a token force by comparison, its morale and fighting capability destroyed in a single defeat immediately after independence in November 1975 at the Battle of Quifangondo, which became known among those who survived it as the 'Road of Death'.

It is also axiomatic that from the many guerrillas who were sent abroad for training, some brilliant and totally committed fighters would emerge and earned huge respect on both sides of the front line. Guiné's João Bernardo Vieira (*nom de guerre* 'Niño') was one of these combatants. Very much a 'hands-on' fighter, Niño demonstrated an utterly ruthless skill and daring while active militarily against Lisbon's forces, to the extent that his forces ended up controlling several no-go areas off the coast.

It was the same with the Swiss-educated Jonas Savimbi, who went on to become one of the favourites of the Central Intelligence Agency: they even ended up supplying his forces with the same Stinger ground-to-air missiles that were being issued to the anti-Soviet mujahedeen in Afghanistan.

It should be noted that in the post-independent phase, many of Savimbi's frontline troops were trained by South African military specialists and with American MANPADs, Savimbi's UNITA became a fearsome force.

It is ironic that those same South Africans were eventually recruited as mercenaries and hired by Luanda – their former arch-enemy – to destroy UNITA, which they did in a series of short, sharp campaigns.

DIAS: Can Portugal's wars in Africa be compared to US intervention in Vietnam?

VENTER: The Vietnam syndrome in relation to what was going on militarily in Africa at the time has been a subject of much debate. One has to recall that the first of the 'liberation wars' in East Africa was launched against Kenya's Mau Mau rebellion (it was referred to as 'terrorism' by Whitehall and the media) and very effectively put down by the British military, though it took a few years. Obviously Mau Mau tactics did not work, so a more conventional approach was adapted once the Angolan war got into stride, followed quickly by similar guerrilla struggles in Rhodesia and Mozambique.

What did subsequently emerge was that many of the instructors who put Angolan, Guinean and Mozambique insurgents through their paces had good experience of insurgent warfare in Vietnam. Also, identical weapons were deployed, both in Asia and in Africa: ubiquitous hardware like the AK, RPG-2s, the RPD light machine gun, the Soviet TM-46 anti-tank mine as well as a range of anti-personnel bombs like the POM-Z. With time, these weapons progressed to more advanced versions (RPG-7 and TM-57 among others)

Obviously, with the guerrillas being trained in Soviet Bloc countries, they were inducted into many of the systems employed by the Viet Cong veterans who had seen a considerable amount of action: being Third World and both regions largely undeveloped, it made good sense. Trainees were shown Viet Cong newsclips and propaganda films and seasoned battlefield commanders would come through and with the help of interpreters explain how they fought. There were actually a small number of Vietnamese troops that served along the guerrillas in both Angola and Portuguese Guinea, all volunteers.

DIAS: What are the reasons you believe that led Portugal military forces to a defeat?

VENTER: In the modern period – post–Second World War – there have been few wars that have been 'won' outright: that is, one side going in and victoriously crushing another. Most recent wars have ended up at the negotiating table and fairly clear victories have ended up with the 'winner' having to yield, often quite substantially. Cases in point include the Korean War (still undecided), Israel after the Six-Day War (the Jewish state having to hand back all of the Sinai Peninsula), American efforts in Vietnam, the Iraq-Iran War (one of the bloodiest) and South Africa's Border War. In most cases both sides claimed decisive victories.

The same with the Lisbon and its African 'provinces'. The Portuguese did not lose those wars in Angola, Mozambique and Portuguese Guinea, but then she did not win them either. Like all the others, everything eventually centred on politics and in Portugal's case the eventual outcome was driven by a disaffected military establishment that mutinied. But then the reality comes down to the fact that the people who challenged Lisbon's hegemony for their freedom in these overseas territories eventually got it.

At the same time anybody who was involved with these hostilities could see the writing pretty clearly on the wall: conflict in Lisbon's African dominions could simply not go on forever. The country was being bled dry by a war that pitted one of Western Europe's smallest and poorest nations against the might of the Soviet Union.

One also has to take into account that everything that happened was at the height of the Cold War, no small issue in the 1960s and 1970s. And with the Carnation Revolution everything changed.

Those who were there will tell you that the entire nation breathed a huge sigh of relief on the morning of 25 April 1974. Simply put, the nation was tired of conflict and the people were war-weary. Once large numbers of young men started to vote with their feet and head abroad to avoid the call-up, it was only a matter of time before somebody had to call it a day. The politicians would not (and probably could not) so a bunch of young recalcitrant officers did it for them.

It is interesting that exactly the same sort of thing happened in the Rhodesian War, though obviously on a much smaller scale. I knew former Prime Minister Ian Smith quite well and after hostilities ended, he confided that he became aware of his own military shortcomings when it was reported that he was losing a company of men *every month* to emigration. These were the same people who had been doing most of the fighting and they simply moved on: like young Portuguese who fled abroad, they felt that had to do the same because there was no future in fighting for a cause that was patently hopeless. In both countries (as well as with South Africa, incidentally) the consensus was that there was essentially no future in losing unnecessary lives in a succession of African wars.

DIAS: Was Portugal ready to fight on three fronts: Angola, Portuguese Guinea and Mozambique?

VENTER: Of all the wars in the post-Second World War epoch, Portugal was arguably the most unprepared nation to embark on a major conflict, never mind a succession of wars in three separate territories that lasted thirteen years.

One needs to take into account that the Portuguese had almost no experience or training for an insurgency-backed war even in *one* of the overseas provinces. The last time Portuguese troops had heard shots fired in anger was in the First World War, which also happened in Africa (against the Kaiser's army in both Angola and Mozambique, where both colonies bordered on German colonies).

That the Portuguese Army was able to haul itself out of what was clearly a soporific haze and rally to a cause that had suddenly become an urgent 'do or die' affair is enormously commendable. In the eyes of most European observers, it was also totally unexpected, especially since the French had recently been driven out of Algeria and if the powerful and seasoned French Army couldn't do it, ran the argument, how the hell could poor little Lisbon?

But then, to the surprise of all, it was not long before young Portuguese troops were able to give as good as they got and in record time they were able to recapture many of the gains made by the revolutionaries in northern Angola and got back onto the offensive.

The difficulties faced by Lisbon were almost insuperable, finance being a major part of it. Portugal had very little cash to spare and it stayed that way for decades.

Compared to today – with instant communications and jet travel – Angola might have been on the other side of the globe. Troops did not generally fly to Africa, like the Americans were able to do to Vietnam: they went by ship and that took time. It took almost a month, with stops along the way in Bissau and Luanda, to travel from Lisbon to Lourenço Marques in faraway Mozambique on the Indian Ocean.

More salient, the country had no real armaments industry, but it did not take long to get things going, first by acquiring the rights for the local manufacture of the G3 rifle (and several other weapons) and getting hold of the kind of heavy vehicles needed in a modern war and, of course, all the vital air components that went with fighting battles. Some of this stuff was in place, but it was part of Lisbon's commitment to NATO, and the Americans, though helpful at first, soon started restricting some of the assets for deployment to Africa.

John P. Cann phrased it well when he declared that the Portuguese Army was incredibly brave: its men 'had the ability to fight under conditions that would have been intolerable to other European troops … They could go for days on a bag of dried beans, some chickpeas and possibly a piece of dried codfish – all to be soaked in any water that could be found'. He added that they were able to cover on foot and through elephant grass and thick jungle vast distances over a three-day patrol period. They quickly learned how to fight well, and did so successfully for thirteen years across three fronts in regions that were almost half the size of Western Europe and that stretched across the African continent.

There are few countries that fared as well in any guerrilla conflict in the past two centuries. But in the end, it just became too much for the Portuguese nation and the self-elected leaders decided arbitrarily to move on and not without good reason.

DIAS: From all independents movements – PAIGC, FLING, MPLA, FRELIMO, FNLA, RENAMO etc. – who do you think was better, or improved over the years to face Portugal's military forces?

VENTER: There is no question that Amilcar Cabral's PAIGC was head and shoulders above any of the liberation groups, not only in the Portuguese territories but throughout Black Africa's efforts to be rid of what their leaders called 'the colonial shackles that have bound us for too long'.

Cabral's irregulars were brilliantly aggressive and fairly well disciplined, but then again they had geography on their side. Guiné is a tiny country, a sixth smaller than Holland, so Cabral and those who followed were faced with none of the logistical problems encountered by groups like FRELIMO or the MPLA. Both those movements had to haul their military hardware hundreds of kilometres into the target country, usually on the shoulders of porters, no easy task in tropical Africa.

Also, the PAIGC was solidly backed by Sékou Touré, the president of Guinea and himself an avowed Marxist. Following independence from France, he had totally alienated the French (Guinea's former colonial overlord) and was immediately embraced by the Soviets as a close ally. There was a good reason for this: Moscow needed a naval base in the eastern Atlantic and Conakry, the country's major deep water port, was strategically suited for this role.

At the same time, one cannot ignore the abilities the other two revolutionary groups because they fought hard for many years to unseat Lisbon's position in Angola and Mozambique.

The MPLA eventually won the day in Angola (with significant clandestine support from radical elements within the Portuguese armed forces) and has retained power since 1974. That guerrilla movement was also more disciplined, structured and motivated than the FNLA, as was FRELIMO, its guerrilla counterpart in Mozambique which also got the bulk of its succour from the Soviets or the Chinese.

Dr Jonas Savimbi, the Swiss-educated UNITA leader, was somewhere in between, with its leader an entrenched Maoist and still getting much of his military aid from the West. Prior to independence – and for a long time afterward UNITA went on to dominate 90 per cent of Angolan territorially, even if this guerrilla group was never able to hold onto a single Angolan city.

Speaking personally, I rate Savimbi as one of the great guerrilla leaders of the twentieth century because he led by example. Moreover, he faced formidable odds: the majority of his men were hardscrabble illiterate, badly equipped but they marched the length and breadth of Angola to achieve their gains. When the average UNITA grunt went into battle, his intention was to win: nothing less would do and very often they achieved exactly that. It helped that many UNITA Special Forces units were trained by South African military specialists. It was also his former allies from down south who ended his efforts to gain power in Angola.

While he remained active, however, UNITA irregulars remained a formidable adversary. Luanda was eventually forced to hire a bunch of South African mercenaries to hobble Savimbi's forces and force the man to the negotiating table. But then, as we have seen, the majority of MPLA leaders are a duplicitous lot – then and now – and that ceasefire did not last.

Finally the MPLA paid to have Jonas Savimbi assassinated; there is a lot of intrigue who did the deed because, as I know the man, he was extraordinarily cautious. He was lured to a meeting in the bush by 'friends' where he was ambushed and shot. Some say that the Israelis were responsible, others reckon it was South African veterans who had originally trained his forces and knew him well.

In the Mozambican theatre of unconventional warfare, I place Renamo in its own slot because this small rebel group sometimes produced outstanding gains in the field against a FRELIMO leadership that had become inordinately bloated and corrupt. Founded by the Rhodesians and supplied in large part by the old South African apartheid government, these bush recalcitrants fought a brilliant war against the original Portuguese adversary, to the extent that Afonso Dhlakama's people –

(he died in his bed in 2018) eventually ended up crippling Mozambique economically.

I visited Bazaruto Island in the Mozambique Channel not long ago and spoke to Louis Erasmus who built the first luxury tourist lodge on the island. He recalls watching the fireworks that resulted from nightly battles between RENAMO and FRELIMO across the water in and around Vilanculos. It was quite spectacular, he declared. Once the ceasefire had been signed, and he was able to travel overland to Maputo for the first time, he was amazed at the amount of destruction he encountered en route. Every few kilometres, for much of the distance while he headed south, he would see burned-out vehicles, trucks and quite often armour destroyed in ambushes. RENAMO, he ventured, had been 'an extremely competent insurgent force', all the more so since their fighters were relatively few in number in comparison to government forces who opposed them.

As for the guerrilla groups, Angola's FNLA or FLING – which operated out of Senegal – both were pro-West and received American backing. For various reasons, their efforts were lacklustre. Whenever push came to shove, the combatants of both guerrilla groups seemed to be unmotivated, in large part because whenever their forces encountered Soviet protégé guerrillas and there were shootouts, they fared second best. Essentially, neither FNLA nor FLING had the kind of competent leadership needed in a guerrilla struggle.

Also, Holden Roberto, the FNLA leader (and brother-in-law of Mobuto Sese Seko, the Zairean leader) was a devious drunk and as about as corrupt as they come. Why the Americans ever backed the man we will never know, but then that is how the CIA sometimes works. Bottom line: were the guerrillas able to match Portuguese forces in the field? Up to a point both in Portuguese Guinea and Mozambique, but not always in Angola and toward the end, hardly ever. I'll come back to reasons for this anomaly.

DIAS: What do you think about the Portuguese soldiers and their commitment?

VENTER: If you had to suggest today that any small nation would send its boys into a war for more than a dozen years, pay them a pittance and keep them isolated in remote regions like tropical Africa, you'd be ridiculed.

The sentiment then and now is that it is an impossible concept, not only in terms of money but also manpower, logistical limitations and of course the ultimate test: morale.

The truth is, the youth of yesterday was a very different kind of individual to the young of today. That applies as much to Portugal as it does to the average American, Israeli or British youngster. It is also a fact that decades ago, young people – in the majority of cases – would accept challenges as an essential part of life because, simply put, they had to. Also, in many instances, there was no alternative.

One example puts this into perspective. When the Israelis invaded Hezbollah strongholds in 2006, conscripts were ordered to leave all personal electronic gear like cellphones and computers behind. Many did not, with the result that when they called their families or their girlfriends from their bunkers well inside Lebanon, Hezbollah communications specialists were able to triangulate those positions and rain mortars down on them.

Also, can you imagine your son or your neighbour's son being sent to Africa for two years' military service without once being allowed home? And without any kind of instant communication? Forget it!

In the 1960s and into the '70s, while war raged in Africa, those who were called up tended to accept their lot. It was only at later stages that some of the men awaiting their call-up papers decided that Africa was not for them. Thousands of these youngsters slipped across the border and sought refuge in other countries. For the majority, the continent of Africa was as alien to the average kid who has just left school in Vila Real, Lisbon or Castelo Branco as landing on the moon, yet the majority did accept their lot because they and their families believed it to be in the national interest.

It was exactly the same when the youth of America, the British Isles, Australia, South Africa, Canada and others in the Commonwealth rose to the occasion once the world was threatened by Japan and Nazi Germany in the Second World War.

DIAS: And what about the enemy forces?

VENTER: Guerrilla forces varied between the three overseas provinces at war, as they did in Rhodesia and with the South Africans along the southern frontier of Angola during that country's twenty-three-year-long Border War.

In fact, as all these hostilities progressed, the guerrillas improved markedly. South African troops on the frontier with southern Angola often talked disparagingly about the enemy, but one must accept that it takes a specially committed type of combatant who is willing to go to war for a seemingly unending period. The Border War lasted so long that sons were often drafted into the same units in which their fathers served. Also, make no mistake, SWAPO boasted some good combatant who were often than extremely well-motivated. Those Owambo fighters learned a lot from the MPLA.

From personal observation, I would rate Amilcar Cabral's PAIGC at the top of the pile, with certain MPLA and FRELIMO units but certainly not all, a close second. Obviously, a lot depended on training, as well as the ability to be able to handle complicated weapons systems efficiently.

Quite a few insurgents were killed laying heavy anti-vehicle landmines that had been hauled hundreds of kilometres across country because they did not observe the basics that had been taught to them by their Soviet or Cuban instructors. Quite a few ignored the simple task of keeping the detonator clean so that when it is screwed into place in the landmine it did not jam. Some of those nitwits would use force to try to position the detonator, with an inappropriate result.

That said, the guerrillas overall were remarkably resilient. They could march for weeks across some of the most difficult parts of Africa and survive quite comfortably off the land. Few European troops – apart from Special Forces units – could do the same. The majority of insurgents came from the land and they operated very well in their own backyards.

Also, the guerrillas usually liked to keep almost all their needs close by, usually on their backs, which helps when you are mobile. Modern armies need enormous logistic back-up. And when wounded, I have seen black troops (both guerrillas as well as those serving in the Portuguese Army) with horrendous wounds. Such wounds would have killed most city boys, who would have been mentally ill-prepared for the rigours of bush warfare and the kind of primitive conditions which prevailed.

It was the same in Biafra where there were no drugs and most times no anaesthetics. I spent time with the French doctors (the forerunners of Médecins Sans Frontières) routinely cutting off limbs without chloroform. It must have been hell, but these victims accepted their pain and very few cried out.

DIAS: Back at the beginning of 1974, did you believe war was near the end?

VENTER: I was in and out of these wars quite a lot, especially Mozambique because it was close to my base in South Africa. In one or two visits to Angola around 1970, I was astonished at the progress made by the Portuguese forces. But then my old friend Colonel (later General) José Bettencourt Rodrigues was running the show in the east of the country, as he did from 1971 to 1973.

In fact, things were going so well in this southwestern region that many *Angolanas* believed – with good reason – that they had actually won their battles against the communist insurgency. There was even talk that if things all went wrong in the *metropole*, they would declare Angola independent in the same kind of UDI or unilateral declaration of independence that the Rhodesians had embarked upon a few years before, when that rebel state broke all ties with Britain and tried to go it alone.

In Portuguese Guinea, General Spínola had also started reaping rewards from taking the populace into his confidence and waging a more basic, unsophisticated war against the PAIGC (on both the military and political fronts). Spínola always said that Lisbon's African campaigns would eventually be settled not in the field, but around the negotiating table. Essentially then, things in Guiné were going reasonably well, which was when, in the final stages, Spínola handed over command to General Bettencourt Rodrigues.

Conditions in Mozambique were different. In fact, while hostilities never reached far south of the Zambezi River (neither Beira nor Lourenço Marques saw conflict), the war in the bush in this African territory was heading very much in favour of FRELIMO. My impressions were that Portuguese soldiers in the north – along the Rovuma and the Mueda Plateau – lacked the kind of motivation that produced dividends. Also, the command structure in Mozambique seemed to me, as an independent observer, as deficient.

As they say in any army, the rot always starts at the top and here I lay the blame squarely on the shoulders of General Kaulza de Arriaga. He might have been a brilliant administrator but many of his contemporaries felt that he was incompetent when it came to fighting a war. Others believed him to be out of his depth, which resulted in a lot of 'grandstanding' on his part. Unlike Spínola and Bettencourt Rodrigues, he enjoyed being in the public eye.

Cases in point: in any conflict, troops out on patrol try to become 'as one' with the environment in which they are operating. In Portuguese Guiné, while out on patrol with Bacar's *comandos africanos*, I never saw one of his troops light a cigarette. Patrols in Mozambique were doing that all the time. They would trundle through the bush, smoke and chat and once camp had been made, they made enough noise to ensure that the enemy was aware that they were there.

The Rhodesian Selous Scout commander Colonel Ron Reid-Daly went on patrol with the Portuguese Army many times and was appalled at the levels of indiscipline. It was almost as if the troops were giving strong warning of their presence so they would *not* be attacked.

I also found a distinct lack of communications between those members of the Portuguese Air Force and the men who were doing the fighting on the ground. Air Force personnel – with notable exceptions of course – often regarded themselves as superior to ground forces and there was little liaison in the day-to-day matters that affected the overall conduct of the war.

In both the Rhodesian and the South African guerrilla wars, in strong contrast, army and air force personnel would regularly get together and sort out problems. I would often observe them sharing tactics in order to prepare for the next day's action. That kind of liaison generated trust and invariably produced good results.

Additionally – and this is something I saw quite often in Mozambique, but not in Angola or Guiné – senior officers, generals included – would sometimes go into operational headquarters and watch the goings-on in the field, usually over the shoulders of the officers who were supposed to be running the show. These senior commanders would even ignore usual procedures and countermand instructions that had been laid down, in spite of the fact that details had invariably been planned beforehand. Of course, all this had an enormously debilitating effect on morale, all the way down the line. Troops talk, and as a consequence, things are likely to get out of hand.

On my last two visits to Mozambique in 1973 and early 1974, the writing was on the wall that things in the Portuguese territories could not go on as they were. I returned to Johannesburg in late 1973 and at an off-the-cuff backgrounder that involved Peter Younghusband of the London *Daily Mail*, John Monks of the *Daily Express* as well as John Edlin of Associated Press, I told them I was left with a distinct impression that FRELIMO was actually winning the war. Naturally, they did not believe me because hostilities had been going on for more than a decade. Then, months later, the crunch came and the Carnation Revolution happened.

DIAS: António de Spínola was a clever officer?

VENTER: There were many excellent officers fighting Portugal's wars in Africa, many of them brilliant. I rate General Antonio de Spínola as one of the best. Indeed, in one of my recent books, I put him way up there with the likes of Orde Wingate of Chindit fame, France's Roger Trinquier and North Vietnam's General Vo Nguyen Giap.

Overall, I had quite a bit to do with General de Spínola and found him to be a rather unusual man. He was both tough and direct, sometimes almost embarrassingly so and was also a stickler for discipline: orders were meant to be followed and he would not tolerate slacks, some of whom would be removed from positions of trust if he felt it necessary.

His most significant attribute was that he could sit down with people – ordinary people from villages and the bush – and listen to what they had to say. It was the same with his own junior officers and men. General Antonio de Spínola had decided very early on, following his arrival in this West African enclave, that in order to achieve results he had to get the general populace involved and he did so in a very positive way.

The man, as we have seen, had a solid military background and some of it is worth repeating.

It is not generally known that during the Second World War he spent time as an observer of Wehrmacht efforts on Hitler's Eastern Front during the encirclement of Leningrad. Portuguese volunteers were then fighting for the Nazis, having been incorporated into what was known as the Blue Division and from all reports, they apparently gave a pretty account of themselves.

What is also not known is that Spínola met clandestinely with Leopold Senghor, the much-esteemed President of Senegal. The two men shared a common interest in what the Leninist Sékou Touré – the Guinea president – would do next. Also, he was not afraid to take chances. When he was offered the opportunity to rescue a bunch of Portuguese soldiers being held in a high security prison in Conakry, he sent in his commandos to pull them out. It was an extremely risky venture listed in the record books in Lisbon as Operation Green Sea.

It is worth mentioning that he was happy to bend the rules occasionally. Scribes such as myself were well down the list of priorities in Portugal's African wars, but when my plane almost came down in the Atlantic and had to limp back to Bissau, I appealed to him (through my liaison officer who, interestingly, was Captain Otelo Saraiva de Carvalho) to help me out. I had an interview scheduled with the Ghanaian foreign minister in Accra a few days hence and unless he put me on the regular TAP flight back to Lisbon the next day, it would be forfeited. He arranged for me to leave Bissau the following morning.

DIAS: Did you witness any atrocities like those of Vietnam's Mai Lai massacre of innocents?

VENTER: This is a question often raised. And yes, at the start of hostilities in Angola in 1961 there was an incredible level of mindless and brutal violence on both sides.

That followed the invasion by UPA insurgents into northern Angola from the Congo, an undisciplined and violent group of revolutionaries, almost none with any military training who were determined to overrun Luanda in as short a time as possible. For all their shortcomings, because the authorities in Luanda were totally ill prepared (even though they had been warned beforehand by informers), the rebels actually came close to doing just that, penetrating southward to within a couple of days' march of the capital.

So while some sources like to make out they were bandits or rabble, that cannot be altogether true because they had their successes. They took the regional command centre at Nambunagongo from the Portuguese in their push southward with little resistance.

The rebel agenda was as clear as day: shock and intimidate the Portuguese nation into a state of terror and in effect, force them to leave Africa. Let us be blunt: thousands of people, both black and white Angolans died in the process because the attacks were so unforgivingly ferocious. It had been anticipated by Lisbon's intelligence agencies, but not on that scale.

UPA cadres killed everybody: men women and children. People's eyes were gouged out and pregnant woman had their bellies slashed open. In Leopoldville, capital of the Congo, UPA leaders afterward boasted quite openly about their deeds. One smilingly told a French journalist '*avec un large sourire*' about Portuguese logging families in the north that he and his men had slaughtered. His words were: 'We fed them lengthwise into the circular saws' (this is on record with Agence France-Presse).

It was to be expected that Portuguese security forces retaliated with equally brutal vigour. They spared no effort and in retaliation many thousands of local people were killed, whether they were attached to invading groups or not. It is all there, documented in the archives in Lisbon. A hallmark of this period was the number of heads cut off and put onto stakes to rot in the sun (something that both sides were guilty of).

Then, Lisbon's forces having stabilized the situation in the Dembos, that huge jungle area north of Luanda, a measure of sanity returned. The first thing the army did was to impose severe strictures on any kind of brutality or retaliation.

Obviously, there were still excesses when units came under fire or when troops were found mutilated, but the rule of law eventually prevailed. In fact, when I covered the war I discovered several units where the United Nations Declaration of Human Rights was pinned up in the mess hall.

Were there any massacres like Mai Lai in Portugal's overseas wars? I would say yes, in the very early days of Angola's war, but that was a period of totally senseless violent exchanges on both sides and lasted less than a year. Nothing like that happened in either Mozambique or Portuguese Guinea, though the massacre of fifty workers at Pijiguiti Docks in Bissau might be categorized as such. It was certainly a senseless slaughter on the part of the authorities and led directly to Amilcar Cabral preparing the PAIGC for a full-scale war.

Overall, Lisbon fought the rest of its colonial conflicts 'by the book' and this obviously did not please everybody. It certainly did not restrain PIDE and other secret security agencies from overstepping the mark.

DIAS: Have you followed other guerrilla wars, in Africa or Vietnam?

VENTER: I have been covering conflicts for most of my professional life, more often than not for Britain's Jane's Information Group and also for London's *Daily Express* and a variety of magazines, as well circulating my photos to Gamma Presse Images and Sipa, both originally in Paris. I also made about 100 television documentaries over a dozen years. That included producing and directing a TV film on the war in El Salvador as well as a one-hour TV documentary on the Soviet invasion of Afghanistan (1985). My film on the civil war in Rwanda – *Africa's Killing Fields* – was screened coast to coast in the United States by American Public Television (PBS) and a film I did on Aids, titled *Aids: The African Connection*, was shortlisted for the Pink Magnolia Award in China.

Apart from my work in Africa, I was in and out of the Lebanese civil war for a decade, covering everything going on largely from the Christian Arab side. I also accompanied units of the Israeli Army into Lebanon when they invaded Beirut in 1982 and was embedded with their navy on patrol in the eastern Mediterranean.

During the Balkan War, I was mainly with the United States Air Force and involved with landmine clearing afterward. Before that I covered numerous conflicts ranging from Biafra, through the Congo (where I was arrested on an espionage charge), Somalia (many times), the Rhodesian War (about a dozen operational visits) and, off and on for twenty years, South Africa's Border War along the Angolan frontier.

There was also Uganda, Sudan, the civil war in Sierra Leone as well as three times operational into Angola (against Savimbi's forces) and Sierra Leone with the South African mercenary group Executive Outcomes. The three Portuguese overseas territories were obviously very much a part of it. I never covered Vietnam because I was too busy elsewhere. From it all, I have written dozens of books. I have been wounded twice: once from a landmine blast in Angola.

DIAS: Why did you write this book?

VENTER: Let me start by saying that to my mind there was good reason for getting this modest work done. I'd written several previous books about Portugal's wars, including Angola (*The Terror Fighters: Guerrilla War in Angola*) which I wish had not because it was my first published title and, in retrospect, I consider it really quite awful.

The other book covered my time in Portuguese Guinea and was titled *Portugal's Guerrilla War*. It was published by the Munger Africana Library of the California Institute of Technology and in Cape Town in the 1980s. Until then, only Basil Davidson had ventured into the field, but always with the guerrillas because he was one of Moscow's favourite sons.

My initial motivation (after I'd returned to my base in South Africa from Angola) was that almost nobody in southern Africa was aware of the enormous challenges facing Lisbon in its struggles in Africa. These were big wars, people were getting killed – on both sides – but the average South African seemed not to care a hoot. So I needed to set the record straight and I started scribbling.

There was another factor which predominated and that was my perception that the Angolan and Guiné wars (as well as the conflict in Rhodesia) would eventually affect everybody living south of the Cunene and Rovuma rivers (the southern borders of Angola and Mozambique respectively). There was no question that the African community in South Africa had been politicized by apartheid and were only too aware of the 'liberation struggles' to the north. One and all, they were hoping for their own freedom.

It is notable that when I first published my book *The Terror Fighters* (about the Angolan war), I was ridiculed by several South Africa parliamentarians because I warned that the country should take notice of what was taking place immediately to the north of us. I was actually dubbed an alarmist: the consensus was that 'it can never happen here'. Well it did, not long afterward.

My warning on the cover of that book was explicit: I wrote, 'It is not generally realized that on its outcome [the war] – one way or the other – may depend the future of the whole southern African sub-continent.'

Shortly afterward, when it became clear that hostilities really were gathering strength and that South Africa would be sucked into a guerrilla conflict whether its leaders wanted it or not, I wrote another book, which was even more far reaching. This one was titled *Coloured: A Profile of Two Million South Africans*. It was an absolute castigation of apartheid and the race-orientated polices of the all-white government. I pulled no punches and again I was attacked by many of my fellow countrymen as a 'reactionary troublemaker'.

My reason for writing *Coloured* was elementary. The South African government needed to get its house in order or it would be faced with a race war, black against white. Though I focused largely on the 'coloured' or *mestico* community in that country, the laws and injustices I dealt with covered everybody.

It is fair comment that liberal people don't generally become war correspondents. Well I did, and some of the strongest support I eventually received was from the military establishment in South Africa. There were a lot of soldiers and aviators – many of them pragmatic, thinking people – who seemed to have taken the message to heart, or some of it, anyway. The South African Army was among the first of the country's institutions to become 'multiracial'.

That experience helped me a lot when I covered other wars in later years, especially in the Middle East where Jew fought Arab while Christians were ranged against Muslims.

I was not alone. One of the most liberal leaders I met during the course of my career was a fine, upstanding figure of a man by the name Antonio de Spínola. Always the maverick, he never tolerated racism in any form.

DIAS: Were your articles censored by the Portuguese authorities?

VENTER: It is of interest that the authorities in Lisbon (or any of the overseas colonies) never once asked to vet any of my material. In those days it simply wasn't done. I suppose they could have censored my writings because sometimes I was critical, a few times especially so, but they did not.

Nor did they ask to view the photos I took, though obviously there were some sensitive issues (like the deployment of helicopter gunships and F-84 bombing missions) from which I was discreetly steered clear of. Once in the field, I was usually on my own (without an escort officer). Obviously, there would have liaison officers appointed to coordinate my trip, but they never ventured into the field with me. We called them 'jam stealers' because few of them ever saw any real action.

Glossary

A luta continua!	The struggle continues! (a guerrilla mantra)
AAA	anti-aircraft artillery
AK/ AK-47	Avtomat Kalashnikova 7.62mm assault rifle
aldeamento	protected village
alferes	second lieutenant
ALO	air liaison officer
APC	armoured personnel carrier
assimilado	Africans overseas who had 'assimilated' sufficiently to earn full Portuguese citizenship rights
AU	African Union, formerly the Organization of African Unity (OAU)
BfSS	(South African) Bureau for State Security, generally referred to as 'BOSS'
BMP-2	*Boyevaya Mashina Pekhoty*, Soviet amphibious tracked infantry fighting vehicle
BRDM	*Boyevaya Razvedyvatelnaya Dozomaya Mashina*, 4x4 (converting to 8x8) amphibious combat reconnaissance patrol vehicle
BTR	*Bronetransportyor*, armoured transporter, 8x8 armoured personnel carrier
C4	plastic explosive
CAS	close air support
chefe do poste	local Portuguese administrator
CIA	Central Intelligence Agency (US)
COIN	counterinsurgency
comandos africanos	all-black Special Forces
ComOps	Combined Operations
Congo-Brazza	abbreviation for Congo-Brazzaville

CT	communist terrorist
DF	direction finding
DGS	Direcção-Geral de Segurança, Portuguese General Security Directorate
DRC	Democratic Republic of Congo, formerly Zaire, formerly Belgian Congo, also called Congo–Kinshasa
DShK	*Degtyaryova-Shpagina Krupnokaliberny,* Soviet 12.7mm heavy anti-aircraft machine gun
EO	Executive Outcomes
EW	electronic warfare
FAA	Forças Armadas de Angolanas, the Armed Forces of Angola
FAF	forward airfield
FAL	*Fusil Automatique Léger* (light automatic rifle), a self-loading, selective-fire battle rifle produced by the Belgian armaments manufacturer Fabrique Nationale de Herstal (FN).
FALA	UNITA's military wing
FAP	Força Aerea Portuguesa, Portuguese Air Force *also* PAF
FAPLA	Forças Armadas Populares de Libertação de Angola, People's Armed Forces for the Liberation of Angola, or today Forças Armadas de Angolanas
FLEC	Cabinda Liberation Movement
FLING	Frente de Luta pela Independência Nacional de Guiné-Bissau/ Front de Lutte de l'Indépendence Nationale de Guinée, Struggle Front for the Liberation of Portuguese Guinea
FNLA	Frente Nacional de Libertação de Angola, National Front for the Liberation of Angola
FPLN	Frente Patriótica de Libertação Nacional
FRELIMO	Frente de Libertação de Moçambique, Front for the Liberation of Mozambique
G3	7.62mm battle rifle developed in the 1950s by the German armament manufacturer Heckler & Koch GmbH (H&K) in collaboration with

	the Spanish. Adapted by the Portuguese armed forces
GPMG	general-purpose machine gun
GRAE	Govêrno Revolucionário de Angola no Exílo, Revolutionary Government of Angola in Exile
GRU	Main Directorate of the General Staff of the Armed Forces of the Russia Federation and Soviet intelligence organization
Grupos Especiais	Portuguese Army Special Forces units
Grupos Especiais de Pisteiros de Combate	combat-tracker groups
Grupos Especiais Paraquedistas	Special Forces paratroopers
HK21	Heckler & Koch 7.62 mm general-purpose machine gun
HVAR	122 mm rockets
IFV	infantry fighting vehicle
JOC	joint operational centre
Katyusha	Soviet 122mm multiple rocket launcher
KGB	Komitet gosudarstevennoy bezopasnosti, (Soviet) Committee for State Security
KIA	killed in action
LZ	landing zone
MAG	*Mitrailleuse d'Appui Général*, Belgian FN 7.62mm general-purpose machine gun
MANPAD	man-portable air defence system (like the Soviet Strela)
MASH	Mobile Army Surgical Hospital (US)
metropole	Metropolis, generic reference to Portugal
metrópole-províncias ultramarinas	overseas provinces, euphemism for Portugal's colonies
MG 42	*Maschinengewehr* 42, a general-purpose machine gun, originally German and much favoured by Portuguese ground troops in all three African theatres of war

MG 51	7.5mm *Maschinengewehr* 1951, general–purpose machine gun manufactured by W+F of Switzerland
MPLA	Movimento Popular de Libertàcao de Angola, Popular Movement for the Liberation of Angola
NATO	North Atlantic Treaty Organization
OAU	Organization of African Unity, today African Union
OP	observation post
OZM-4	metallic bounding fragmentation mine
PAF	Portuguese Air Force *also* FAP
PAIGC	Partido Africano para a Independência da Guiné e Cabo Verde, Portuguese Guinea liberation movement headed by Amilcar Cabral
Panhard AML	*Automitrailleuse légère*, light 4x4 armoured car, developed by South Africa into the Eland
Panhard EBR	*Engin Blindé de Reconnaissance*, French-built, light 8x8 armoured vehicle
PCA	Angolan Communist Party
PIDE	Polícia Internacional e de Defesa do Estado, International Police for the Defence of the State (Lisbon's equivalent of the secret police)
PLAN	People's Liberation Army of Namibia, the military wing of SWAPO
PMD-6	anti-personnel mine
POM-Z	Soviet anti-personnel stake-mounted fragmentation mine, much used in Africa
PPSh-41	Soviet submachine gun of World War II vintage
províncias ultramarinas	overseas provinces, euphemism for Portugal's colonies
PSYOPs	psychological warfare operations
RAF	Royal Air Force
RPD	Soviet-made 7.62mm light machine gun
RPG	rocket-propelled grenade, either RPG-2 (used by guerrillas in African conflicts), or latterly, RPG-7 with Portuguese additional variations

RPK	Soviet-made 7.62mm light machine gun
SAAF	South African Air Force
SADF	South African Defence Force
SAM	surface-to-air missile, SA-6, SA-8 et al
SAP	South African Police
SAS	Special Air Service
SDU	self-defence unit
SF	Special Forces
SG-43 Goryunov	Soviet medium machine gun introduced during World War II and issued to liberation forces in Africa
SIS	Secret Intelligence Service (MI6)
STOL	short takeoff and landing
SWA	South West Africa, now Namibia
SWAPO	South West Africa People's Organization
T-34 and T-55/ T-54	Soviet tanks supplied to Angola and Mozambique
tabanca	village, town
TAP	Transportes Aéreos Portugueses
TM-46/ TM-57	Soviet anti-tank mines used by liberation groups
TNT	trinitrotoluene, an explosive chemical compound
Tropas Especiais	Special Troops, commonly known by the acronym TEs, which came into effect when a UPA/ FNLA guerrilla defected to the Portuguese with 1,200 of his men
UDI	unilateral declaration of independence (Rhodesia)
Unimog	2.5l multi-purpose all-wheel-drive medium truck produced by Daimler and produced under licence in Portugal for the army
UNITA	União Nacional Para a Independência Total de Angola, National Union for the Total Liberation of Angola
UPA	Unià̀o dos Populacèes de Angola, Patriotic Union of Angola
USAF	United States Air Force
WMD	weapons of mass destruction

Bibliography

Abshire, David and Michael Samuels (Eds), *Portuguese Africa: A Handbook*, Pall Mall Press, London, 1969.

Beckett, Ian and John Pimlott (Eds), *Armed Forces and Modern Counter Insurgency*, Croom Helm, London, 1985.

Borges Coelho, João Paulo: *African Troops in the Portuguese Colonial Army, 1961–1974: Angola, Guinea-Bissau and Mozambique*, Eduardo Mondlane University, Maputo.

Caetano, Marcello, *Depoimento*, Distribuidora Record, Rio de Janeiro, 1974.

Cann, John P., *Brown Waters of Africa: Portuguese Riverine Warfare 1961–1974*, Helion, Solihill 2014.

——, *Counterinsurgency in Africa: The Portuguese Way of War 1961–1974*, Helion, Solihill 2012.

——, *Flight Plan Africa: Portuguese Airpower in Counterinsurgency, 1961–1974*, Helion, Solihill 2015.

——, *The Fuzileiros: Portuguese Marines in Africa, 1961–1974*, Helion, Solihill 2016.

Chilcote, Ronald H., *Portuguese Africa*, Prentice-Hall, Upper Saddle River NJ, 1967.

Clark, Desmond J., Roland Anthony Oliver, J. D. Fage, A. D. Roberts, *The Cambridge History of Africa*, by Cambridge University Press, Cambridge, 1986.

Cooper, Tom and José Matos, '*Ginas über Afrika*' in *Fliegerrevue Extra*, Vol. 24.

Cornwall, Barbara *The Bush Rebels*, André Deutsch, London, 1973.

Cunha, J. da Luz et al, *Africa, a Vitoria Traida: Intervenqao*, Lisbon, 1977.

Cunha, Silva, *O Ultramar, A Naoo e o "25 de April"*, Atlantida Editora, Coimbra, 1977.

Davidson, Basil, *In the Eye of the Storm: Angola's People*, Penguin, London, 1975.

——, *No Fist Is Big Enough to Hide the Sky: The Liberation of Guinea-Bissau and Cape Verde, 1963–74*, Kindle edition.

Duffy J., *Portuguese Africa*, Harvard University Press, Cambridge MA, 1959.

Duignan, Peter and L. H. Gann (Eds), *Colonialism in Africa 1870–1960* (5-volume set) Cambridge University Press, Cambridge, 1969.

Fontanellaz, Adrien and Tom Cooper, *War of Intervention in Angola: Angolan and Cuban Forces, 1975–1976*, Helion, Solihull, 2016.

Gibson, Richard, *African Liberation Movements*, Oxford University Press, Oxford, 1972.

Gleijeses, Piero, 'First Ambassadors: Cuba's Role in Guinea-Bissau's War of Independence' in *Journal of Latin American Studies*, Vol. 29, No. 1, February 1977.

Greene, T. N., *The Guerrilla and How to Fight Him: Selections from the Marine Corps Gazette*, Praeger, New York NY, 1967

Grundy, Kenneth, *Guerrilla Struggle in Africa*, Grossman Publishers, New York NY, 1971

Johnson, Robert Craig, 'COIN: The Portuguese in Africa 1959–75' at www.worldatwar/chandelle/v3/v3n2portcoin.html.

Minter, William: *Portuguese Africa and the West*, Penguin, London, 1972.

Nguyen van Tien, *Notre Strategie de la Guerrilla*; Partisans, Paris, 1968.

Paret, Peter and John W. Shy, *Guerrillas in the 1960's*, Praeger, New York NY, 1965.

Pélissier, René, 'Angola, Guinées, Mozambique, Sahara, Timor, etc.: Une bibliographie internationale critique' (1990-2005)

Porch, Douglas, *The Portuguese Armed Forces and the Revolution*, Croom Helm, London and Stanford CA, 1977

Spinola, Antonio de, *Portugal and the Future*, Perskor, Cape Town, 1974; originally published in Lisbon as *Portugal y el Futuro*, 1974.

Stockwell, John, *In Search of Enemies: A CIA Story*; W. W. Norton & Co., New York NY, 1984.

Sykes John, *Portugal and Africa*, Hutchinson, London, 1971.

Taber, Robert *War of the Flea: The Classic Study of Guerrilla Warfare*, Potomac Books, Omaha NE, 2004.

Thompson, Robert: *Defeating Communist Insurgency: The Lessons of Malaya and Vietnam*, Chatto & Windus, London, 1966.

Trinquier, Roger, *Modern Warfare: A French View of Counterinsurgency*, Praeger, New York NY, 1962.

van der Waals, Willem S., *Portugal's War in Angola, 1961–1974*, Ashanti Publishing, Johannesburg, 1993.

Venter, Al J., *Africa at War*, Devin-Adair, Old Greenwich, 1974.

——, *Barrel of a Gun: Misspent Moments in Combat*, Casemate, Philadelphia PA and Oxford UK 2010

——, *Battle for Angola: The End of the Cold War in Africa*, Helion, Solihull 2017.

——, *Coloured: A Profile of Two Million South Africans*, Human and Rousseau, Cape Town, 1973.

——, *Portugal's Guerrilla Wars in Africa: Lisbon's Three Wars in Angola, Mozambique and Portuguese Guinea*, Helion, Solihull 2013; in Portugal the book is published as *Portugal e as Guerrilhas de A'frica*, Clube do Autor, Lisboa 2014.

——, *Portugal's War in Guiné-Bissau*, Munger Africana Library, California Institute of Technology, Pasadena 1973; also published as *Portugal's Guerrilla War*, John Malherbe, Cape Town 1973.

——, *The Chopper Boys: Helicopter Warfare in Africa*: Helion, Solihull 2016.

——, *The Terror Fighters: A Profile of Guerrilla Warfare in Southern Africa*, Purnell, Cape Town 1971.

——, *War Stories by Al Venter and Friends*, Protea Books, Pretoria 2012.

Index